# Netizenship, Activism and Online Community Transformation in Indonesia

Ario Seto

# Netizenship, Activism and Online Community Transformation in Indonesia

palgrave
macmillan

Ario Seto
Goethe University Frankfurt
Frankfurt, Germany

ISBN 978-981-10-5396-2 ISBN 978-981-10-5397-9 (eBook)
DOI 10.1007/978-981-10-5397-9

Library of Congress Control Number: 2017950087



Cover illustration: Ario Seto

Printed on acid-free paper

This Palgrave Macmillan imprint is published by Springer Nature
The registered company is Springer Nature Singapore Pte Ltd.
The registered company address is: 152 Beach Road, #21-01/04 Gateway East, Singapore 189721, Singapore

# Preface

One night in September 2009 in Surakarta, popularly known by its shorter name 'Solo', I was taking a public microbus on my return to Indonesia after two years in field research. It was shortly after 10 p.m., about the time when shops around the city were closing and workers were rushing home. A few minutes later, I realized that, very much in contrast to my experience a few years back while taking the microbus in Solo, the bus was silent even though it was full. These passengers, who are co-workers, were not talking with each other. That experience was both different and memorable, as, a few years back, taking a ride together in such cramped space in this small city of Solo would have unavoidably required small talk—at the very least—in the interest of being polite. That night, instead of chatting with each other, the passengers were engaging with their mobile phones. Indeed, while everybody said goodbye to the other passengers, and sometimes even exchanged hugs and handshakes, during the trip they were absorbed with their phones.

Some weeks later, I met with some old friends at a small reunion in Jakarta and there was a moment when they took a break from our cozy chat in order to quickly check their phones so they could reply to their messages before returning to our conversation. Although texting or online short message communication has been popular on the archipelago since the late 1990s, such avid use of digital communication was relatively new for me even though I had only been away from Indonesia for two years. These encounters also reminded me of a while back when I asked one of my German friends about his vacation in Borneo in 2008. He quickly recounted his fascination with the use of smart technology in Indonesia, declaring: 'Everybody has a Blackberry in Borneo!'

Besides these visible usages of smartphones, I also encountered the gathering of a bicycle club while campaigning for bike-to-work. These bicyclists had matching T-shirts with 'Kaskus online community' written on it. I was intrigued at that moment. A few years earlier, Kaskus members would not have gone offline publicly and called themselves a 'community' since, being famous for its circulation of illegal material circulation, the forum was an underground online medium.

These relatively random experiences motivated me some years later, to conduct research on the subject of digital (new) media engagement in Indonesia. The basic question at that time was simply: What do Indonesians like to do when they go online? One of the initial answers that I received from my interlocutors is that they like to go to online forums to have steady online chatting partners.

There are some issues that I would like to share in this introduction. First, is the main challenge of undertaking a new media study, namely the actuality of the research. As digital media rapidly changes, the study evolves immensely as well. In 2015, Google Trends indicated that global searches on 'computers' have been rapidly declining since April 2007 while inquiries about 'smartphones' were steadily increasing. The same comparison shows an even sharper result if the recorded search is limited to Indonesia, as 'smartphone' has been more popular than 'computer' since August 2013.

Google Trends shows that after September 2007, the then three-year-old 'Facebook' was already more popular than 'E-Mail' and 'Internet Relay Chat', which had been a popular entry in the early 2000s.[1] Such data however does not guarantee that Facebook will always reign as a digital medium. Studies show that with the exception of Twitter, there will be a general decline of social media platforms including Facebook in the years to come (Bauckhage and Kersting 2014; Miller 2013). Global public interest in 'digital networks' has been declining since 2004, while the 'online community' has remained relatively stable despite fluctuations.[2] Google Books' Ngram data from 1998 to 2016 show that there was a shift in 2002 when 'social media' became more popular as a subject than 'virtual media'.[3]

During my research period from 2010 to 2015, several online threads in the online discussion forum where I dwelled were archived, and some even deleted; other online spaces like Politikana.com and Salingsilang.com—which were famous in Indonesia during this research—have dissolved and their websites have met their end. As a programming platform, technology, user interest, and inventors change; current research is required to comprehend the rich texture of user-technology interaction. Accordingly, this research is an attempt to determine what will outlast 'smartphones', 'computers', 'Facebook', 'social media', or maybe 'digitality' itself. I started this research with a primary focus on mobile telecommunication and Internet connection. At its end, I have written my ethnographic research based on my interlocutors' experience, which shows the pertinence of 'online community' more than anything proposed earlier.

The second concern is what I refer to as the 'particularity-universality discussion'. Studies on digital and online media have presented that although media engagement creates shared practices across cultures, classes, genders, and political constraints (e.g. Wellman and Haythornthwaite 2002; Katz 2008; Jones 2002; Boellstorff 2008), they also show that each engagement is particular and bound to the contextuality of the users, the gadget, the platform, and sometimes their offline world (e.g. Castells et al. 2009; Smith and Kollock 1999; Wellman and Haythornthwaite 2002; Gerbaudo 2012; Danet 2001; Barendregt 2005; Wellman and Gulia 1999).

This research is no exception. Therefore, in presenting the life of an online community in Indonesia's Java, I always kept the particularity of my interlocutors—Indonesian, Javanese, Solonese, online dwellers, online forum members—and their universal digital and online media engagement—online dwelling, forum making, cyberculture, online chatting, shielded identity chat, and communication organization—as two sides of a single coin. For this reason, other media studies drawn from other parts of the world are included in the discussion to seek out enriching comparative insights. For example, Tom Boellstorff (2008) and Celia Pearce's (2009) approaches have been pivotal in underscoring the creativity and reproduction of online communities, while the classic works of Howard Rheingold ([1993] 2000) and Brenda Danet (2001) are reminders of the online-offline reciprocity in digital media engagement.

On the subject of community and digital media-based social movements or citizenship in Indonesia, Merlyna Lim (2003a, b, 2005, and 2013) and David Hill and Khrisna Sen (2005) are fundamental authorities. Their findings have provided entries into observing the contours of Indonesian online and civic participation, especially while capturing the media engagement dynamic after the fall of the authoritarian government of President Suharto in 1998.

Since digital media engagements are closely related to communication and the subject of perception, the work of Tim Ingold (2000, 2010, 2011), Maurice Merleau-Ponty (2002), and George Herbert Mead (1938) offer a helpful frame for the discussions on the procedural course of intersubjective communication and individuals' relation to their environments both online and offline. Taken together, their studies enrich the effort to understand the unique online and gadgetry experience of my interlocutors.

It is also worth noting that I differentiate 'digital', 'online', and the prefix 'cyber-'. While 'digital' underscores the technical terms of a multimedia technology which is not analog, 'online' signifies the existence of an Internet connection and connectivity. Taking a picture with a smartphone is a digital practice as the visual scene is captured, stored, and manipulated with a digital gadget, but it only becomes an online practice when the picture is uploaded to the online space. Digital practice could be conducted offline, while online practice refers to the existing flow of data bytes. When a particular case, event, practice, or act involves both states of digital and online or when it is to be approached as an entirety, I use the prefix 'cyber-'.

This book contains seven chapters. The first chapter delivers my doubt about today's fascination with social media and online-based digital protests, arguing that it is misleading to be optimistic about digital citizenship simply by looking at the large number of protests, because netizens' struggle to establish civic participation that goes beyond the time of the event. In this chapter, I also discuss how Tim Ingold's (2000, 2010, 2011) approach on wayfaring by reflecting on the dynamics of environments could help in understanding the struggle of netizens. I will do this by advocating approaches to the online community by looking at members' experience of 'being-in-the-online world' (e.g. Rheingold 2000; Jones 1995; Pearce 2009). Chapter 1 also illustrates the history of Kaskus, the online community in which I dwelled, and its surrounding environments, in an effort to make sense of the cultural resources of my subjects, the Solo Kaskusers.

Chapter 2 explores the online forum as a place of dwelling where cyberspace and cyberculture intersect to simultaneously guide both the merriness of chatting and the discipline required for online dwelling. It purports that for Kaskus members, or Kaskusers, the experience of being online is as meaningful as face-to-face interactions as it signifies the community's presence tied to five modalities that shape Kaskus: colloquial language, norms of equality, continuous participation, databanking, and online reputation in fighting against hoaxes and fake news or simply bad information.

The members' discipline in establishing digital footprints acted as an early filter to identify who could become a netizen and deserves to dwell in the online community.

As the community expanded their activities, the borders between online dwelling and the offline worlds became obscured. It is this intersection that Chapter 3 explores as part of online community activity transformation. It explains how going offline became a rite of passage that allowed users to pursue a deeper relationship in both worlds with their fellow online community members, while also acting as a medium by which online norms could be advocated in offline practices. The reflective detachment between the two worlds allowed the online community's role in the society to take shape, influenced by the Javanese approach to body and sense, and of the world and self.

Chapter 4 further explores Kaskusers' efforts to make sense of the parallel online and offline realities by looking at their struggle to establish a normative order. As Kaskus members began to realize that their chat community was becoming more involved in various social movements while taking their leisure time away, they determined that a narrative of justification, such as the notion of prudence, was urgently needed. This production of ethic for netizenship was a contingency to keep the community alive at the risk of losing those members who refused to participate in such engagements. Accordingly, the chapter also describes how the shift from the online to the offline marked how 'social activism' becomes a tangible realization of digital power.

Chapter 5 describes the effort of members of the Kaskus online community to become active netizens in everyday life through monitoring sanctions, and civil correction. Chapter 6 summarizes the problems they are facing because of their 'organic community' model. Chapter 7 offers the reasons why the current practice of digital citizenship remains unsettling. Accordingly, it discusses how the approach on the organic community is methodologically influential since Kaskus, the community of netizens, was not shaped overnight; instead, it evolved through procedural consequences.

Frankfurt, Germany Ario Seto

## Notes

1. Each word and keyword was entered on https://trends.google.com/trends/
2. Ibid.
3. Ngram data analysis on October 2016: https://books.google.com/ngrams

## References

Barendregt, Bart. "The Ghost in the Phone and Other Tales of Indonesian Modernity." In *Mobile Communication and Asian Modernities*, edited by S. Barnes and S. Huff, 47–70. Hong Kong: Hong Kong University, 2005.

Bauckhage, Christian and Kristian Kersting. "Strong Regularities in Growth and Decline of Popularity of Social Media Services." *arXiv.org* (2014): 1–11. Retrieved from Cornell University Library, eprint arXiv:1406.6529. Accessed July 30, 2014.

Boellstorff, Tom. *Coming of Age in Second Life*. New Jersey: Princeton University Press, 2008.

Castells, Manuel, Mireia Fernández-Ardèvol, Jack Linchuan Qiu, and Araba Sey. *Mobile Communication and Society: A Global Perspective*. Massachusetts: MIT Press, 2009.

Danet, Brenda. *Cyberpl@y: Communicating Online*. Oxford: Berg, 2001.

Gerbaudo, Paolo. *Tweets and the Streets: Social Media and Contemporary Activism*. London: Pluto Press, 2012.

Hill, David T. and Krishna Sen. *The Internet in Indonesia's New Democracy*. Oxon: Routledge, 2005.

Ingold, Tim. *The Perception of the Environment: Essays on Livelihood, Dwelling & Skill*. London: Routledge, 2000.

Ingold. Tim. "The Textility of Making." *Cambridge Journal of Economics* 2010/34 (1) (2010): 91–102. Accessed March 1, 2014. doi:10.1093/cje/bep042.

Ingold, Tim. *Being Alive Essays on Movement, Knowledge and Description*. Oxon: Routledge, 2011.

Jones, Steven G. *Cybersociety: Computer-Mediated Communication and Community*. Thousand Oaks: Sage, 1995.

Jones, Steven G. "The Internet and Its Social Landscape". In *Virtual Culture: Identity and Communication in Cybersociety*, edited by Steven G. Jones, 7–35. First publication in 1997. London: Sage, 2002.

Katz, James E. "Mainstreamed Mobiles in Daily Life: Perspectives and Prospects." *Handbook of Mobile Communication Studies*, edited by James E. Katz, 433–446. Massachusetts: Massachusetts Institute of Technology Press, 2008.

Lim, Merlyna. "The Internet, Social Networks, and Reform in Indonesia." In *Contesting Media Power: Alternative Media in a Networked World*, edited by Nick Couldry and James Curran, 273–88. Maryland: Rowman & Littlefield, 2003a.

Lim, Merlyna. "From Real to Virtual (and Back again): Civil Society, Public Sphere, and Internet in Indonesia." In *Asia.com: Asia encounters the Internet*, edited by Kong-Chong Ho, Randy Kluver and Kenneth C. C. Yang, 113–128. London: Routledge, 2003b.

Lim, Merlyna. *Archipelago Online: The Internet and Political Activism in Indonesia*. Dissertation. Twente: Universiteit Twente, 2005.

Lim, Merlyna. "Many Clicks but Little Sticks: Social Media Activism in Indonesia." *Journal of Contemporary Asia* Volume 43 Issue 4 (2013): 636–657.

Mead, Herbert. *The Philosophy of the Act*. Chicago: University of Chicago Press, 1938.

Merleau-Ponty, Maurice. *Phenomenology of Perception*. London: Routledge, 2002.

Pearce, Celia, and Artemesia. *Communities of Play. Emergent Cultures in Multiplayer Games and Virtual Worlds*. Massachusetts: MIT Press, 2009.

Rheingold, Howard. *Virtual Community*. Originally published by Addison Wesley, 1993. Massachusetts: MIT Press, 2000.

Wellman, Barry and Milena Gulia. "Virtual Communities as Communities: Net Surfers Don't Ride Alone". In *Communities in Cyberspace*, edited by Marc A. Smith and Peter Kollock, 167–194. London: Routledge, 1999.

Wellman, Barry, and Caroline Haythornthwaite. *The Internet in Everyday Life*. Malden: Blackwell Publishers, 2002.

## News and Online Source

Miller, Daniel. "Facebook's So Uncool, but It's Morphing into a Different Beast." *The Conversation* December 20, 2013. Accessed on December 20, 2013. http://the conversation.com/facebooks-so-uncool-but-its-morphing-into-a-different-beast-21548

# Acknowledgments

This book could not have materialized without the help of a large number of friends. I deeply thank Mas Aryo for providing the access to dwell in the online community and its off-screen reality. It is heartbreaking that one of my gatekeepers, the late Ananta Harya, to whom I also owe much gratitude, passed away at such a young age without having read the final product of this book. To my beloved Solo Kaskusers, who welcomed me as their trusted neighbor in their online forum, Mas Armin, Mas Prima, Mas Wahyu, Mas Sodron, Mbak Dyah, Mas Erick, Mbah Sur, Mas Chris, Mas Adhy, Mas Heru, Mas Bayu, Mas William, and other dwellers of f=160, thank you.

I sincerely thank Susanne Schröter, my supportive guru, without whom this scholarly journey would not have materialized. I am deeply grateful to Yarsi and Suka Hardjana, my discussion partners and agents of socialization in Jakarta/Solo. My sincere gratitude goes to Janine Murphy, who has become my reliable critic and editor in investigating the subject of citizenship.

This work also would not have been possible without the support and insights about mobile culture from Hans Peter Hahn and my dearest anthropologist sisters/brothers: Amporn Madern, Dominik Müller, Gunnar Stange, and Veratrina Suprabasari. They have shared their time and were an enormous help, offering source recommendations, enriching my point of view, and commenting on my work. My gratitude also goes to Svenja and Matthias Heilmann, Ida Ruwaida Noor, and Hari Nugroho for their support. I would thank Ivan Bárbaric, Heinrich Geiger, and Karin Bialas from KAAD (*Katholischer Akademischer Ausländer-Dienst*) for making this study possible with their enormous financial assistance. I deeply thank Sara Crowley-Vigneau and Connie Li of Palgrave Macmillan for publishing this book and for their detailed works.

To those who have provided insights and supported my research but would not let me reveal their names, I cannot thank you enough.

# Contents

1 **Clicked Participation** 1
*1.1 The Over-Optimistic View on Digital Protests* 4
*1.2 Four Problems of Digital Citizenship* 6
*1.3 The Unsettling Online Wayfaring* 10
*1.4 Locating Kaskus and Some Contexts* 15
*1.4.1 Digital Communication in Indonesia* 17
*1.4.2 Solo and Javanese Cultural Settings* 23
*References* 29

2 **The Structure of an Online Community** 37
*2.1 The Merriness of Being in Kaskus* 38
*2.1.1 Choosing a Location* 39
*2.1.2 Casual Communication* 42
*2.1.3 Voces Paginarum* 48
*2.1.4 Home and Dwelling in Forum* 49
*2.2 Reputation and Online Militancy* 52
*2.2.1 Crafting Reputation and Visually Ordered Regime* 53
*2.2.2 Online Militancy, Hoax, and Cybersense* 56
*2.2.3 Rich Communication* 60
*2.2.4 Exchange: Friends as Repository* 64
*2.3 What Makes an Online Community?* 68
*2.3.1 The Itch and Belonging* 71
*2.3.2 Modalities of Online Community* 74
*References* 76

**3 Going Offline, Order and the Environment** 79
*3.1 The Procedures of Going Offline* 82
*3.1.1 'Messy Online, Messy Offline'* 83
*3.1.2 Organizing the Text* 90
*3.1.3 Going Offline and Moral Vocabulary* 95
*3.2 The Context of Cultural and Political Geographies* 103
*3.2.1 The Gathering and the City* 107
*3.2.2 The Problematic Interpretation of Gathering* 115
*3.2.3 Against Alienation: The Practical Function of a Gathering* 120
*3.2.4 The 'Early Base of Citizenship'* 123
*References* 128

**4 Netizenship: Between Ignorance and Prudence** 131
*4.1 The Production of Ethic in the Time of Crisis* 132
*4.1.1 Prudence and the Consequences of Being Online* 134
*4.1.2 Digital Power and Being Alert* 138
*4.1.3 The Feasibility of Social Activism* 141
*4.1.4 The Institutionalization of Guilt* 145
*4.2 Militancy in an Ever-Changing Community* 147
*4.2.1 Community on the Move* 148
*4.2.2 Reliance within Networks* 151
*4.2.3 Responsiveness to Change and Militancy* 153
*References* 157

**5 Bricked and Buried: Sanctions Against Fake News** 161
*5.1 Civil Correctness* 162
*5.1.1 Fight Club Legacy: Bravery* 163
*5.1.2 Support and Bullying Mechanism* 165
*5.1.3 Collective Validation* 168
*5.2 Speedy Feedback and Intimacy* 172
*5.2.1 Speed and Digital Intimacy* 175
*5.2.2 Fandom* 179
*References* 184

**6 The Unsettled Online Community** 187
*6.1 Tempering Certainty and Being Organic* 188
*6.1.1 Organic Community* 189
*6.2 Personal Communication and Intimate Mobilization* 196
*6.2.1 Personal Communication and Senior Kaskusers* 197
*6.2.2 Mobilization and Intimacy* 204
*6.3 The Ghost of Play: The Myth of Real and 'Real'* 207
*6.3.1 Can Leisure Be Real?* 207
*6.3.2 The Four Perplexities* 213
*6.4 The Stock of Wonder and the Remnants of the Past* 220
*6.4.1 Moral Vocabularies and Practice* 220
*6.4.2 The Gadget of the 'Future'* 223
*References* 226

**7 Conclusion: We Need More Red Bricks** 229
*References* 236

**Bibliography** 239

**Index** 253

# Author Bio

*Ario Seto* is a researcher at Collaborative Research Centre 'Discourses of Weakness and Resource Regimes' Goethe University Frankfurt, Frankfurt am Main, Germany. He is a member of the International Sociology Association Global Dialogue Indonesian editorial team and was a lecturer at the Department of Sociology, Universitas Indonesia. His research interests include media studies, popular culture, citizenship, urban studies, science, technology and society (STS) and post-colonial studies.

# List of Abbreviations and Terms

| | |
|---|---|
| 3G | Third generation of mobile telecommunication |
| AFK | Away from keyboard |
| ASEAN | Association of Southeast Asian Nations |
| Bappeda | Badan Pembangunan Daerah (Provincial Development Planning Agency) |
| Bata Merah | Red brick; sanction given to other Kaskuser |
| BB17 | Buka-bukaan 17 (pornographic online forum, literally: Stripped 17) |
| BBM | BlackBerry Messenger |
| BPS | Badan Pusat Statistika (Central Bureau of Statistics) |
| BTS | Base transceiver station |
| Bukber | Buka Puasa Bersama, *Iftar* or breaking the fast |
| CB | Community band |
| CCPB | Cara Curang dan Program Pembajakan (Tricks and Pirated Software) |
| CDMA | Code division multiple access |
| Cendol | Green badge; credit given to other Kaskuser as a token of appreciation |
| CNN | Cable News Network |
| GSM | Global system for mobile communications |
| CSO | Civil Society Organization |
| Emoticon | Emotion icon; visual graphic presentation to represent a certain human emotion |
| F=160 | Online web page address designated for Kaskus Regional Solo |

| | |
|---|---|
| FC | Fight Club |
| FoS | Freedom of Speech, a term in Kaskus for 'free speech' |
| FR | Field report |
| FPI | Front Pembela Islam (Islamic Defender Front) |
| Guyub | Togetherness |
| ID | Identity |
| IDR | Indonesian Rupiah |
| IM | Instant messaging |
| IP | Internet Protocol |
| IRC | Internet Relay Chats |
| ISO | International Standard Organization |
| ITB | Institut Teknologi Bandung (Bandung Institute of Technology) |
| Kaskuser | Member of Kaskus |
| Kaskus Gathering | Annual forum gathering of Kaskus |
| KaskusStatistics | Chat archives |
| KRS | Kaskus Regional Solo |
| KTP | Kartu Tanda Penduduk (Indonesian identity card, literally: Resident Identity Card) |
| Manga | Japanese cartoon |
| MMOG | Massively multiplayer online adventure game |
| NGO | Non-governmental organization |
| OOT | Out-of-topic |
| PAD | Pendapatan Asli Daerah (Original Local Government Revenue) |
| Pencak silat | Indonesian martial arts |
| PD | Police Department |
| Ping | A signal test for computer network to check whether the destination host is currently active and reachable |
| PM | Private Message |
| RL | Regional Leader; forum coordinator in Kaskus, responsible for online and offline activities of the forum |
| RRI | Radio Republik Indonesia, state national radio network |
| SARA | Suku, Agama, Ras atau Antar golongan (ethnic, religious, race or inter-group) |
| SEO | Search engine optimization |
| Sembada | Javanese term for prudence, fairness |

| | |
|---|---|
| SMS | Short message service |
| Solo Kaskuser | Member of Regional Solo forum in Kaskus |
| TGPF | Tim Gabungan Pencari Fakta (National Fact Finder Join Team) |
| Thread | Organization or classification of online conversation through which messages are compiled under a web link or a location, based on a particular subject |
| TS | Thread starter |
| Warnet | Warung Internet (Internet shop/Café) |
| Wartel | Warung Telekomunikasi (Call shop) |
| Wayang | Shadow puppet |
| Wedhangan | Javanese social practice for small meet-up for coffee or tea |

# List of Figures


| | | |
|---|---|---|
| Fig. 5.1 | Network analysis of references to Mayor in Kaskus Regional Solo, 2011 | 177 |
| Fig. 6.1 | Kaskus regional solo network | 199 |
| Fig. 6.2 | Priority given as semantic comparison between importance and *Real* according to Solo Kaskusers | 211 |

# List of Tables


| | | |
|---|---|---|
| Table 2.1 | Emotion and threads | 63 |
| Table 3.1 | Comparison of Kaskus Regional Solo gathering statistics | 112 |

CHAPTER 1

# Clicked Participation

This book is about digital citizenship in the making and the struggle of ordinary citizens to justify and expand their order. Each of its chapters underscore that any investigation into digital participation should go beyond the screen to understand the complexity and experiences that the actors are facing in producing and establishing an online community's ethical cyberpractice. These experiences are intersubjective; they expose the bottom-up digital citizenship to its main risk: the unsettling nature of online participation. The making of sustainable digital citizenship, therefore, should be crafted through disciplining the community building and cannot be instantaneous.

Digital citizenship, according to my observation on Kaskus—the largest Indonesian netizen forum, is trained through expanded experiences and the sophistication of rules in online wayfaring, reflective gatherings, and reproducing new norms. As such, in explaining why many forms of current digital citizenship are failing, I argue that instead of being fascinated with social media's timelines, we should go back to look at the online forums to focus on how members of organic communities are struggling in their everyday life to become netizen while refining their online participation and stabilizing their new online practices. This book, thus, explores how Kaskus transformed itself from an underground online forum into a



A. Seto, *Netizenship, Activism and Online Community Transformation in Indonesia*, DOI 10.1007/978-981-10-5397-9_1

community for digital citizens, active in civic monitoring and social activism. It assesses two key problems in this transformation: first, the notion of ethical community and, second, the notion of netizenship.

Digital citizenship, in Kaskus members' experience, is materialized only after a series of normative experiences in community building as part of personal online wayfaring that has to be recognized by other fellow community members as a mode of online dwelling. Throughout their trajectory as online dwellers, online community members exploit the closest normative resources while reflexively transforming their activities from the online to the offline. Exposing these stages of experience of online dwellers, I observe that sustainable digital citizenship should not simply be engineered, but ought to rely on the online community's exposure to its reconnection to the offline world and its recognition by the exterior, such as the state, the city and the people in the offline world.

Such an approach in understanding the effort to stabilize civic participation is crucial against the background of a world that has recently witnessed the emergence of global digitally mediated politics. From the Arab Spring between 2010 and 2012, to the 2014 Umbrella Movement in Hong Kong and recent elections in the United States, mediated politics have highlighted how digital communications influence civic participation and negotiations. Twenty years after the proliferation of the Internet, digital and social media have become hype words and the means through which citizens are interconnecting and organizing themselves.

The online sphere is filled with interconnected actors, which presumably enlarge both civic agency and networks of citizens (e.g. Fuchs 2008; Howard and Hussain 2013; El-Nawawy and Khamis 2013). In an unstable political constellation, digital communication has expanded protests, such as in the recent civil uprisings in Tunisia, Egypt, Libya, Yemen, and neighboring countries. The movement, dubbed the Arab Spring, brought down Zine El Abidine Ben Ali in Tunisia, Hosni Mubarak in Egypt, Ali Abdullah Saleh in Yemen, and Muammar Gaddafi in Libya (see Castells 2012; Nordhausen and Schmid 2012; Howard and Hussain 2013; El-Nawawy and Khamis 2013).

Digital communication has not only made it possible to accumulate a massive amount of interest and supporters, as in the case of the uprising in Egypt and the Arab Spring, it has also to some degree helped activists streamline the language of the movement and organize previously scattered activists through communicative consolidation (Lim 2012). In the Western hemisphere, citizens marched on the streets of New York, Frankfurt am Main, Madrid, and in almost every strategic city under the organization of the Occupy Movement to protest global capitalism (Castells 2012; Gerbaudo 2012; Cammaerts et al. 2013).

In Southeast Asia, where states were hardly contested in the 1980s and 1990s, countries like Malaysia, Thailand, and Indonesia have witnessed the emergence of citizens who have organized themselves in various online movements to monitor the state, bureaucrats, and fellow citizens, forming an omnipresent public sphere (Lim 2003a, b; Chin 2003; Wayansari 2011). In Indonesia, the popularity of digital protest was marked by one of the first national-scale digital movements in 2009 during the Coin for Prita campaign.

Prita Mulyasari, a housewife and a mother of two, was a misdiagnosed patient at a private hospital in 2008. Coming out of the hospital, she shared her experience on an electronic mailing list for young families. The email went viral and she was sued by the hospital. The State Court later found her guilty of defamation against both the hospital and the doctor. In addition to the fine, she was also sentenced to jail. The court decision triggered widespread outrage and the public depicted it as an injustice, especially in the context of suspicions about corruption in the state legal system, as cases pursued by influential individuals and companies hardly lose in the court of law.

In response to the perceived injustice, those in support of Prita decided to raise funds to pay the fine. For the fundraiser, one requirement was imperative: the donation had to be submitted in the smallest Indonesian denomination, the 100-Rupiah coin, the symbol of the have-nots. Eventually, the fundraiser needed five dump trucks to deliver the coins to the bank.[1] The hospital later dropped the civil lawsuit and in June 2012 the Indonesian Supreme Court overturned the conviction and jail sentence.

On January 29, 2010, the prominent Jakarta-based newspaper, The Jakarta Post, released an editorial titled 'Goodbye, People Power' underlining how protests have moved from the street to digital avenues. As these protests could amount to enduring social pressure rather than rallies, the editorial concludes that digital protests are no longer virtual 'but real'.[2] What the article misses, however, is that protest is only a condensed arena of democracy that does not necessarily lead to the certainty of democratic ideals and the realization of a better life. For example, despite the 'Coin for Prita' hype, the movement did not result in a stronger policy to protect patients from malpractice.

Being stuck in the moment is not only an Indonesian problem. Reflecting on the Arab Spring in Egypt, Mona Abaza emphasized in a 2017 interview that people should further consider how little power has shifted since the heyday of the protests, as the spirit of democracy echoed by the protesters has yet to be delivered.[3] The Umbrella Movement in Hong Kong and the Occupy Movements across the globe are two further examples of how massive protests were unable to negotiate with power structures and eventually passed their own peaks. The United States' elections indicate that even when social media engagement could move voters to support the first African-American presidential candidate Barack Obama in 2008 (Cogburn and Espinoza-Vasquez 2011), the same method could not sustain the would-be first female president in the 2016 election.

These examples were indeed successful in terms of mobilization and forming social pressure, but on the other hand they are also examples of how mass protests and movements are sporadic, leaving the grassroots formation in question. It is misleading to view the development of democracy and citizenship simply through the quantity of protests, the augmented political episode, and what people write on social media.

## 1.1 The Over-Optimistic View on Digital Protests

From the legacy of the enlightenment, media is viewed in the hope of a better life manifested through literacy sustained by information circulation and communication. The same hope continues to be traced in the reign of online media and the proliferation of digital gadgets. Take the famous Nicholas Negroponte's *One Laptop per Child* campaign as an example.[4] The program's website states: 'children in developing nations need laptops' because '[Laptops] are a wonderful way for all children to learn through independent interaction and exploration'.[5] This program purports that digital gadgets like laptops are not only able to sustain 'learning' and 'exploration,' but are also a medium of interaction through which ideas are spread.

Such information and communicative interaction are also two prominent foundations of the Habermasian public sphere. Jürgen Habermas' (1991, 1992) work on the transformation of the public sphere has catalyzed a significant consideration of the relationship between everyday life 'communicative action' and democracy or democratic consciousness. Building his approach on Herbert Mead's intersubjectivity and utopian sociality, such exchanges fulfill the potential of communication resulting in consensus and social coordination (1992).[6] It is only through the ability to understand others and 'strong communicative action' (Habermas 1998) that communication as a dialog will advance to social organization, as each realizes that they need to formulate a common ground to achieve their goals (Habermas 1992, 1998). He (1991), however, expresses his fear that as capital power appropriates media production and media companies, public debates and the public sphere in which such communication is circulated will merely become a staged performance through which no actual intersubjective process takes place.

Today, Web 2.0's social media is the hope to offer the answer to such fear as users have direct access to alter the content of what is presented on the digital screen and interconnecting actors can use this access to keep the public sphere afloat. Examining the role of Twitter and Facebook in the Arab Spring and Spain's Occupy Movements, however, Paolo Gerbaudo (2012) argues that while social media interactivity has helped to widen interconnectivity between actors and has made it possible to open spaces, it also increases the complexity and heterogeneity of the messages. He argues that to some degree, each social media platform plays a different role for the public to shape and appropriate the public sphere and reorganize citizens (Gerbaudo 2012). He notes, therefore, that the main importance of social media communication is the availability of space to train netizens in democratic practices (ibid.: 145).

The notion of training becomes important since it provides, at the same time, an 'omnipresent' public sphere (Wayansari 2011: 31). Taking an example of the now-obsolete politics-dedicated online forum Politikana.com, Wayansari (2011) argues that online discussions have brought political matters, which was an exclusive subject for the elites, closer to citizen's everyday life. With such possibilities for digital-based discourse mainstreaming, Erwin Alampay and colleagues (Alampay 2009) argue that the complexity of the digital gadget's chip is perceived as modernity, not simply for its technological invention, but mostly for what it represents: access to communication in pursuing social equality, social justice, and justifiable norms.

Habermas' public sphere for social justice, which is constructed through communicative action, however, requires more than interconnectivity, dissemination of information, and organized social pressure. It also relies on the discipline of intersubjective reflectivity between actors (Habermas 1992).[7] While arguing against the Cartesian regime of meaning, Habermas' (1992, 1998) pragmatic communication is intended to form an ethical procedure, which stipulates that common understanding is needed as human beings possess the ability to become reflective. Such attitude, which is systematically habitualized in everyday communication, is required to collectively measure plural intersubjective experiences as an antecedent of a valid justification of the common good. Castells (2000) and colleagues (2009) critically responding to such an approach, argue that new digital media could become a resource for a network society only when exchange-capable actors or a knowledge society has been established first. Here, in such a line of reasoning, political and social changes require more than social pressure; they ought to be part of discursive communication.

The public sphere's discursive direction leading to cooperation is the highest human virtue according to Christian Fuchs (2008). He argues that cyberculture is confined within the dilemma of cooperation and competition; while the first leads to socialization, the latter leads to alienation (2008: 300). He argues that since digital media technologies empower agency and are intuitively social, communities could capitulate to social activities and eventually realize that cooperation requires less risk than competition or seclusion (ibid.: 349).

These approaches, while relying on collectivity and giving the object or the world its own dynamic of justification, seem rather confident that complex unstable everyday life experiences will lead to a functional common understanding as a sensible choice in overcoming plural realities. Such paths of understanding undermine the risk of unsettling the formation of digital citizenship. In reality, netizens are struggling to achieve common understanding, which is actually a continual power contestation of everyday life politics that influences the discourse of digital interaction within civil society and the public sphere.

Accordingly, 'common terms', 'network', or 'cooperation' ought to be viewed as unsound dynamics or temporary states. Furthermore, the greater role of civic exchange should not merely be about cohesion or networking, but should emphasize the capacity of organization to cope with citizens' struggle to maintain continuous participation. It is therefore necessary to consider whether civic participation as an achievement could form an articulate sequence of actions rather than sporadic collective uprisings.

## 1.2 Four Problems of Digital Citizenship

There are four problems with current digitally mediated citizen participation. *First*, there is a discrepancy between the spirit to deliver democratic ideas through citizen participation and its dependence on various supporting agents. Taking an example from the United Kingdom's shrinking development of public library service and experts, Frank Webster (2006) argues that there is a great dependency on the public budgeting, and its related bureaucracy, in creating a public sphere for the 'knowledge repository' (ibid.: 179–180). As such, when support for these repositories declines, there will also be a decline in the democratic sphere (ibid.: 170–179). To add to such complications in the context of digital communication, the relationship between the use of digital media and the pursuit of a better life through education and the formation of the public sphere is also correlated to offline institutions as the authority to make changes. Tait (2006) presents the case of Internet Protocol censorships against YouTube, Twitter and Facebook in the Middle East during the Arab Spring and argues that although such censorship could be technically bypassed, the location and the policy of streaming were still controlled by the state and not the activists.[8] This infrastructure capital sets digital civic participation at the mercy of the state-approved existence of the Internet and on other digital properties of the communication.

*Second*, when the knowledge resource and media are working flawlessly, these digital media spaces—regardless of whether they are offline forum threads, Facebook pages, or Twitter hashtags—are also not solitary spaces and are dependent on their social-political environments which sometimes limit the transformation of democratic ideas. They are nodes within networks, both online and offline, where other institutions produce discourses that might influence the content of the space.

Gary Bunt's (2003) study on Islam and digital democracy, as an example, shows that online discussions about democracy among Muslims are hardly making any democratic impact without further offline communication. Although online media in Islamic societies offers a medium for the possibility to challenge religious institutions and political authority at large, the challenged religious institutions are still located and organized in the offline. These organizations could strategically counter the developing discourse that is catered to in the online sphere with offline communication. To effect change in religious discourse, therefore, online discussants' involvement in the offline community is equally as important (Bunt 2003).

In terms of the making of the Indonesian public sphere and social movements in the years prior to the fall of Suharto, David Hill and Khrisna Sen (2005) argue that new digital media is not an independent variable but was greatly controlled by political agency and agendas, especially by a social leader as the locomotive of the movement apart from digitalities itself (ibid.: 54–55). They also underline that the route between information to modern democracy is not straightforward. While acknowledging the productive online discussion and the dissemination of social-political material among students and activists, Hill and Sen (2005) question the discursiveness of the phenomenon, criticizing that online democratization practice is far from convincing, as actors will hardly take the path of the European enlightenment. Discussion and debate alone could not be considered as an accountable public sphere (Hill and Sen 2005).

Furthermore, the Internet and social media are not a neutral space that could simply bring 'civility,' as digital media has also become a location for anti-social activities. During the troubled times of communal conflict in Indonesia, for example, digital space and communication have been proven to fuel conflicts, provocation, and the dissemination of misleading facts (Bräuchler 2003; Van Klinken 2007). The first web address or information to be clicked would be a site within the subject of interest that is already implanted with a motive and therefore, those who are anti-social would also try to find their related space in the online sphere.

It is therefore essential to understand how a digital movement is correlated with other discourses and realities that are taking place in the offline or other events that take place elsewhere in the online world. Since the digital media communicator is also subjected to other realms, regardless of whether that is the offline world or other mediation, digital activism exists and congruently is related to other actors and institutions outside the mediation practice. Working on the case of Egypt, Elizabeth Iskander (2011) asserts that social media like Facebook and its inhabitants could indeed become relevant to the ongoing political change, but only if it conjoins with other existing traditional media and civil society organizations to endure, or mainstream, a longer process of social transformation.

Digital actors' involvement in online activities is therefore subjective and dependent on other socializing agents. Jan Van Dijk asserts that people go online while 'always carrying their personal "baggage" at the same time' (2006: 168). Eli Pariser (2011), an Internet activist, warns of the risk of a 'filter bubble', whereby a digital algorithm has the ability to keep our Internet-search interest within the track of our data retrieval history. Such a filter will therefore keep netizens segmented and confined within their own interest while pushing other realities, that the Internet actually has to offer, into the realm of the irrelevant. These social-political environments are the bubbles that limit the circulation and production of universal moral vocabularies. Communication and interconnectivity alone do not guarantee social cohesion or even further discursive common understanding. The complexity of discursive exchange is, as Axel Honneth (1995) reminds us, that there is a great dependency on the common understanding of virtue and actors and the motives for developing it as a form of mental organization that could motivate an intersubjective operation.

Within a certain exchange or circulation itself, instead of unifying, social media communication has facilitated the polarization of the political movement and democratic transition rather than forming a linear cooperation, as Lisa Goldman (2013) reported on Egypt's Arab Spring. Online communication has empowered citizens both politically and socially by its 'many-to-many' or 'person-to-person' connectivity, facilitating indifferent groups to rapidly form its own masses. As a result, there is increased contestation instead of a streamlined direction.

Nowadays, everybody talks. She even tones down the role of social media in the Arab Spring by expressing the concern that because of these complexities, activists are burned out and social media might actually have harmed the movement itself with the circulation of false reports and political polarization.

Digital citizens are also further polarized by their dependency to the mainstreaming agents of discourse and their exposure against the buzzers of the elites. Already a decade earlier, Merlyna Lim (2003a) had warned that despite digitally tangible information dissemination and a greater wave of democratization among various actors and institutions, the circulation of information and civic organization was continuing to face elitism. She points out that 'layers of disseminators', and their own agendas, decisively play a role in disseminating information, thus intersecting the interconnection between actors and the public (ibid.: 282). This brings us to the *third* problem of today's digital: the problem of mobilization, which is dependent on the actors behind the screen.

It is misleading to assess digital participation simply as a normative moral call because each movement is made popular by buzzers. Paolo Gerbaudo (2012), assessing digital movements operating on Twitter and Facebook during the Arab Spring and Occupy Movements, sees 'core activists'—those 'layers of disseminators', to borrow Lim's term (2003a)—as moving and capable organization. It is not the form of 'elite' activist that concerns him, but the 'choreography' of the social movements that denies the spirit of the Internet's *horizontalidad* (Gerbaudo 2012).

On the other hand, however, sometimes such elitism of the action is unavoidable. In order to avoid state monitoring, much of the communication traffic corresponding to the Middle East activism took place on the deep web and in private messages, excluding the general public from deep engagement (Goldman 2013).

Digital participation in open public online spaces also does not secure deeper engagement. The study from Kevin Lewis et al. (2014) which examined the 'Save Darfur Cause' on Facebook shows that, from the 1.2 million Facebook-Cause members, only a very limited number of members actually had deep engagement by recruiting other members or donating to the cause. Recruitment and donation rates showed a significant drop after only two months, and a further drop after the seventh month, with fluctuation graphic rate dropped nearly to zero. Furthermore, they found that civic activism and the sense of belonging to the cause are only effective in the first seven months. These reports tone down or invite scholars to revisit the excitement stemming from several studies that argue the contrary (e.g. Quan-Haase et al. 2002), relating the Internet to civic engagement and the ability of the digital world's self-reproduction.

The *fourth* problem of digital citizenship is, therefore, about the assessment of civic participation. Digital media-based civic participation relies on friendship-based recruitment and because of its informal form of organization it has no discipline mechanism to maintain its sustainability. Lewis et al. (2014) conclude that Facebook membership in a cause does not signify any deep commitment to the movement, and that such a movement is simply an event and state: 'Facebook is less useful a mobilizing tool than a marketing tool' they conclude (ibid.: 7).

Reporting from Tunisia and Egypt, Peter Beaumont (2011) delivers a grim picture that the actual process of transforming online engagement to the offline during the Arab Spring was more complicated than what has been organized digitally. He fears that quantitative measurement of the massive digital participation could not even represent the complexity of the event, especially in relation to the offline complexity. The ghost of social media and the hype of an online movement is that its liquid association is able to transcend any traditional boundaries such as geographical location, identity, and the body, but also requires a new formula for disciplining the members. Thus, online movements will always be shadowed by the mechanism of its organization to ensure the online-offline transformation.

These studies are a great reminder that between vigorous online participation and the streets, there is an operational online-offline discrepancy or a performance gap that has to be resolved to care for the sense of belonging and solidarity. While Gerbaudo (2012) warns of digital movements' operational reliance on core activists and narrative enlargement as a space for recruitment, it seems that 'movements' and 'reflective communication' are two different projects. The first concentrates on the rapid operation, while the latter stresses the process of continual training or citizenship in the making. All these four problems of digital movements warn that assessing mediated politics simply as a visual phenomenon and its representations is a reification of digital citizenship, democratic improvement, and the complexities that are actually taking place.

## 1.3 The Unsettling Online Wayfaring

These underlying problems of digital civic participation call for the practice of digital communication to be revisited in the context of citizenship from a grassroots level or the participants' view. While digital avenues are filled with socio-political discussion and streets may be taken by protesters, antagonists defined by the public may be bullied in the online sphere, and public pressure arises through popular decision, central questions remain unanswered: What makes digital citizenship relatively sustainable, and through which procedures? Kaskus online dwellers' experience could provide some answers to these questions as it shows that digital citizenship is a set of processual circumstances, unsettling and always in the making.

Kaskus, a short for *Kasak-kusuk* (lit. hush-hush, secretive, lobbying), is an Indonesian-based discussion forum founded in 1999 by Andrew Darwis (@adarwis) as a college project when he studied in Seattle, United States. Started as an online bulletin forum, Kaskus at that time could only be accessed through the website interface; today, it has three social media applications making it possible for users to access the Kaskus world from a mobile smartphone.

With around 650 forums and around 8.5 million users dubbed as 'Kaskusers',[9] Kaskus is the largest online forum in Southeast Asia. Similar to the United States-based Reddit, Kaskus hosts various forums and sub-forums with subjects ranging from agricultural skills, sports, gossip, politics, citizen journalism, to comic fans, daily chat, and humor corners, to name a few. In 2017, it boasts 10,960,000 visits/day, 54,799,644 page views/day and is ranked the eleventh busiest website in Indonesia and 319th in the world. The website's value has been estimated at US $775,000,000.[10] In 2012, its classified advertisements alone generated US $50,390,667/month in circulation.[11]

Darwis explained that he had started the web forum to serve as a space for news exchange and citizen journalism for Indonesian students abroad regarding current updates from their homeland. It was still around the time of uncertainty, only a year after the 1998 riots and Suharto's resignation after a three-decade-long authoritarian regime, during which the gloomy political situation was still tangible and the economy, as well as national security, was shaky. After the website was launched, he did not pay much attention to the growth of his creation. Occupied by server maintenance and his own studies, he was unable to monitor the forum's content and growth. Four years later, he returned to Indonesia for a vacation and while visiting one of his family members, he was told that there was a website trending in the Indonesian digital sphere, which was 'a website to search for pornographic and pirated materials', he recalled. When he was shown the site, he was very surprised to learn that the website was in fact, his own.

Apparently because of its censor-free environment, Kaskus had, at that time, gained massive popularity as a space to exchange and deposit-and-search both legal and illegal digital materials, such as pirated software, harsh political debate, pornographic material, and to advertise black market items. After shutting down its piracy and pornographic forums in 2008, Kaskus refocused its growth as a host for online communities, such as various hobbyist forums and subject-related discussion forums. Although Darwis himself was not a political activist when he launched the online forum, Kaskus stated in 2015 that online-based social activism generated by its members has played a great role in shaping its model of activies.[12]

With its large number of inhabitants and dynamics, Kaskus' 'online forum' offered a model for 'community' for Indonesian 'early adopters', to use Roger's term (1962), during which they established new cyberculture, such as *kopi darat* (offline meet-up), *bahasa Kaskus* (Kaskus language), chat regulations, and offline gatherings. These inventions of cybercultures have since been imitated by members of other online communities and Kaskus has thus become trendsetter for Indonesian cyberculture in general.

Over a decade ago, Kaskus was an underground online forum used to avoid the norms in the offline world; today, Kaskus offline meet-ups are regularities of community rituals and participating in them is socially expected. Codes and norms of digital practice have been accordingly and continually transformed in forums, or what Kaskusers call *komunitas* (community), to organize the communication, system of exchange, and personal and social relations.

The first decade of Kaskus history, which will be described in Chap. 2, shows that digital practices have changed over time. Each sequence of practice is contextual to its online and offline historical context and resource. The subject of change and transformation has attracted digital media researchers since it provides an approach to observe the swift evolving media engagement in society and media. As technology develops, how people construct social relations also eventually changes. Sherry Turkle's (2005) seminal work, *The Second Self*, substantiates such claims that change is certain for the Internet and digital gadgets are 'objects-to-think with' (ibid.: 6).

Furthermore, the object, or the gadget, is not only about technology but also a matter of what it delivers and how it is perceived by users. In the context of Kaskus, the web page and forums are larger than ubiquitous digital interconnection; it is the presence of community and social affairs. Thus, to access Kaskus is to think with the community. Wellman (1999) argues that throughout history, social change has not ruined the notion of communities, although how communication happens and its media practice has changed. Instead, it is suggested that online communication transforms the community to 'networks of personal relationships' rather than as simply a stationary 'place' (see Bruhn 2011: 24).

Tim Ingold's anthropological approach on the environment as an active agent could help shed some light on this discussion of change, transformation, influencing objects, and unceasingly changing the online environment. As such, Ingold (2000, 2011) proposes an approach that considers the matters that influence human course. From his ethnographic research among hunters in Finland and northern circumpolar regions, he (ibid.) formulates that, historically, life is not a designated form, but a process of skillful reflective becoming or 'wayfaring' along the path on which one is navigating.

Pointing at the historical construction of 'lines' (Ingold 2007) and 'way of walking' (Ingold and Vergunst 2008), he argues that the modern standardization of making things straight has decreased the possible experiences that life could encounter (see also Ingold 2000, 2011). The risk of this designated life system and provision marks decreasing human skill in the face of the unknown. The notion of becoming is pivotal in his work, as he argues that it is the basis of understanding the world, our environment, which is a series of appropriation of skills and knowledge against the encountered world. As he states:

> Learning to see, then, is a matter not of acquiring schemata for mentally constructing the environment but of acquiring the skills for direct perceptual engagement with its constituents [...]. (Ingold 2000: 55)

According to Ingold, therefore, each experience is perceptual as objects exist as a reference to the perceiving individual. The meaning of objects survives in the relation between the perceiving individual, the environment, and the social.

Following this approach, it is appropriate to consider the online environment and digital media as a space with its own activities and dynamics as an environment that offers us the possibility to reveal new worlds and new skills. Thus, social activism, civic engagement, or any outcome from digital practices cannot be assessed as end-product as that would neglect the detailed growing perceptual experience of the netizens.

Ingold's approach to the perceived objects and environments provides access to answer the four problems of digital citizenship described earlier. Because each digital engagement is perceptual, it is this perspective of wayfaring that could describe the dynamic of digital engagement while making clear the importance of the particularities of a specific form of online sphere, gadget, and time. Understanding the transformation of skillset provides a way to observe the detailed struggles that netizens are facing while explaining the common outcomes. This approach echoes Faye Ginsburg, who, while observing mass media engagement, suggests that an important anthropological contribution to media studies is to 'break up the "massness" of the media [...] by recognizing the complex ways in which people are engaged in processes of making and interpreting media works in relation to their cultural, social, and historical circumstances' (Ginsburg 1994: 8).

The subject of perception is crucial in mediated civic participation because it is a decisive element in deciding whether a user will continue to be digitally engaged. Such engagement is embedded in the form of the gadget and online space. No user is going to buy a strange gadget or dwell in a foreign forum. Steinbock (2005) investigates how a mobile phone, its operating system, its form, size, and software features are strongly related to the local offline contextuality for the latter provides some degree of familiarity. He also adds, while investigating the production of mobile devices from one of his interviews with a digital product designer, that the main character of digital media technology production is driven by humans' sensory perception (Steinbock 2005: 61); that is, not simply by digital interaction in the virtual sphere.

The virtual world therefore could be perceptually significant since our gadget is also sensory interactive. In short, any online act is conscious or unconsciously part of its intersubjective experience with the offline world. These studies, which I will describe in more detail throughout the chapters, illustrate that in everyday digital engagement, the early intention of going online might only be a start and hardly becomes a direct, end-product of engagement because each change has the agency to alter how Kaskusers perceptually experience the gadget, the digital sphere, the social connection, and the meaning of being in Kaskus. This approach underlines that the proper approach to digital engagement is not to see how the digital sphere affects the offline, or the reverse, but rather how these actors could experience their activities, practices and environments, and how the digitalities of online media continually reveal themselves to new subjects—or to citizenship in the context of this book.

As previously mentioned, Kaskus started as a bulletin board for Indonesians exchanging news and a space for online chats. Along the way of these leisurely activities, the website eventually gained its fame as a notorious underground website for circulating and promoting illegal materials and activities. Today, however, it is home to various online forums, endorses citizen journalism, and works closely with offline grassroots civil society organizations while establishing networks with prominent industrial companies. To reconstruct Kaskusers' digital-based activism, consequently, requires consideration of their perceptual experience of online dwelling, which has also changed over time: from dwelling in an underground space to the location for grassroots movements. The Kaskus experience is not simply a 'success story' of digital citizenship in the making, but above all, it is a narrative of procedural perceptual experiences of how they choose the path they have chosen. Such fortitude is reflected in their narrative of becoming; in explaining their notion of citizenship, Kaskusers always recount their story of how they revealed new social activism through evolving online practices.

## 1.4 Locating Kaskus and Some Contexts

To 'experience Kaskus', I have particularly dwelt in *Kaskus Regional Solo* (KRS), a forum, or a chapter, dedicated for Kaskusers who live or have an interest in the central Javanese court-city, Solo, formally Surakarta, Indonesia. As it is with the general Kaskus realm, KRS was initially established as a thread for chatting. While in the beginning KRS was a location to chat about random subjects without an administrator, today it is managed by numerous online administrators and thread hosts.

KRS is also currently active both as an online forum under Kaskus and as an offline community that engages with various local social movements and works closely as a civil society organization (CSO) with other CSOs and the city government. Although actively participating and generating various social activism, KRS members, or *Solo Kaskusers*, never consider themselves as activists; instead, they always underline their identity as the 'commons' (Ind. *orang biasa*) or simply 'Kaskuser'. This self-positioning is an appealing contrast to the elite activist layer as a common aspect of digital citizenship (see Gerbaudo 2012; Lim 2003a; Nugroho and Syarief 2012).

I would generally describe my fellow Kaskusers as young, urban-traditional, 'semi-secular', and educated Solonese. Although there are members who are in their 40s or 60s, most members are in their 20s or 30s. Most are males and Muslim. While most Solo Kaskusers I have encountered pray regularly, religion never became a subject of discussion, and they only organized religious activity once a year during Ramadan. The diversity among members can be seen in a quick portrait: @Fleew_meneer was a start-up manager and an Islamic preacher; @areMean went to Islamic boarding schools and was a santri (Muslim scholar); @Mbah_Sur is a Christian deacon; @primapunya; @amakuzalek; and @Whyyy are Christians. @sweet_mochi, @dolphin.88, @Becomingmoon, and @novi are female Solo Kaskusers who wear the hijab.

Class distinctions are quite vague in the community. Harya, whose mother is a respectable state official and comes from a middle-upper class family, was comfortable wearing old worn-out T-shirts. @Amakuzalek comes from a noble family and has a noble title, rode a motorcycle and did not have a car. @areMean, an IT manager, lived simply in a server room in an Internet shop. Most Solo Kaskusers I encountered between 2011 and 2014 used middle or entry-level smartphones. Conspicuous consumption was rather absent in the community.

At that time, the prominent Solo Kaskusers' educational background was also varied as most members have or were still pursuing their higher education. @Superpekok is a university lecturer, @primapunya and @sweet_mochi were in the final year of their bachelor's degrees. @Mbah_Sur, an entrepreneur with various establishment, had not attended any higher education institution. @amakuzalek has a diploma in Chinese literature, had worked as a translator at an international company, and currently works as a political publicist. @Sodronezz and his wife @Becomingmoon both have a university degree in economics and currently work as civil servants.

With the exception of @Plerdisk and @areMean, most members are urban dwellers, born and raised in Solo. Some Solo Kaskusers I encountered, @Amakuzalek, @Whyyy, @Sodronezz, @Becomingmoon, @Icesusujahe, @Linux, and @novi, live in Jakarta. The rest live in Solo.

Solo Kaskusers dwell in www.kaskus.co.id/forum/160/solo. This webpage is what I consider the '*main screen*' where the public communication takes place. Additionally, secondary pages, like KRS's Facebook group and statuses, or KRS's Twitter handle and hashtags could also be considered the main screen as long as the message is located in the public accessible by any Kaskuser. The second location of Kaskusers' online sphere is the '*off-page*' spaces. This refers to online locations that do not involve the Kaskus public, that is, the private or direct messages and mediated platforms such as SMS (Short Message Service), Facebook, Twitter, and Path. The third location is the '*off-screen*' communication, which includes the offline interactions.

### *1.4.1 Digital Communication in Indonesia*

At the early peak of digital communication a decade ago, Indonesia was hardly mentioned as a case study. In 2016, the country is home to the third largest Twitter user base and the fourth largest number of Facebook users in the world.[13] CNN dubbed the country the 'Twitter Nation'.[14] As the densest city of Facebook users, Jakarta has been referred to as the 'capital city of Facebook' by Socialbaker.[15]

Internet penetration growth in the archipelago has been increasing rapidly from approximately 30% in 2004 to almost 42% in 2016.[16,17] Indonesia has the tenth largest number of main line holders in the world, but, as the Indonesian landlines cable service is slow, 47.6% of Internet access in 2016 occurs via mobile telephones, while 31.1% of users have a 2GB monthly data package.[18,19]

Studies on media in Indonesia illustrate that media usage has a longstanding influence on the nation's political and social history (Anderson 2006; Mrázek 2002b). In this Southeast Asian archipelago, media technology is a recognized medium that not only delivers practical communication affecting social and political relations, but also signifies modernity and class status (Mrázek 2002b; Barendregt 2008). In the late era of the Dutch East Indies Period, Rudolf Mrázek reveals that besides playing a role not only in circulating the notion of nationalism in the colonial Dutch East Indies, radio also became the 'shiny thing,' or *fantasie meubelje* (Dutch, trans. little furniture of fantasy), which was perceived as the presence of modernity and the future (Mrázek 2002b: 166–169).

During the struggle for independence and the Indonesian National Revolution, radio became a machine to transmit the virtual imagination of the hardship of battles, evoking emotional solidarity. Such early virtualities were sonic. The voices of charismatic leaders like Sukarno and Sutomo, popularly called by his radio personality name Bung Tomo, were both effective in mobilizing the masses but were also picturesque as well. Posters and images of their poses illustrated the sonic national speeches (see Anderson 2006: 156–157). In this sense, the voice became the visual and the visual presents an imaginative voice in iconic photographs.

Bung Tomo's picture taken during a speech, for example, which was taken on February 14, 1947 by a journalist from the *Nanyang Post*, became an icon of the Surabaya Battle in November 1945 and a visual symbol of the struggle for independence and nationalism in Indonesia's post-colonial era. Until today, the picture is popular in Indonesian schoolbooks and during the National Hero Day on 10th of November and his voice is played on mass media.

In the post-colonial era, Sukarno's radio programs between 1945 and 1967 and Suharto's television programs between 1966 and 1998 were significantly manufactured by the state to raise the sense of nationalism, belonging, boundaries, and loyalty. Benedict Anderson (1991) in his seminal work, *Imagined Communities,* highlights that through such practices with the then-new media of radio and television, people were brought together by the same 'imagination' of belonging to a nation. During these eras, media regularly covered national state ceremonies (*upacara*) or the biweekly cabinet meeting to become 'media events', to use Katz and Dayan's (1994) term.

Furthermore, the state's fascination toward media advancement is also believed to be a leap-frogging strategy. The state strongly views that keeping up with new technology infrastructure, gadgets, and usage will deliver the resources necessary in shaping an industrial society (*masyarakat industri*), which would therefore give Indonesia the chance to become a developed nation. In addition to being a military and bureaucratic stronghold, therefore, Suharto's New Order also comprised technocrats. To facilitate the modernization process, Suharto initiated the Palapa Satellite program in February 1975 in order to transmit state radio and television programs across the entire archipelago. Suharto appointed the German-educated B. J. Habibie to lead the national technological development. He chaired the national aerospace company Industri Pesawat Terbang Nusantara (abv. IPTN) from 1976 to 2000, and at the same time became Minister of Research and Technology from 1978 to 1998. Habibie's navigation of the nation's technology created a generation referred to as 'Habibie's Kids' (*anak-anak* Habibie), who were among the first to use the first generation of Internet in Indonesia (Hill and Sen 2005).

At the same time, the state's friendly new technology market policy made it possible for radio electronic and computer hobbyists to set up digital technology businesses in the 1980s and 1990s. This increased public access to the technology. In the early 1990s, Indonesians could already buy locally assembled no-brand computers (*komputer rakitan*). In the same era, facilitated by government programs, Indonesian pupils and students witnessed computer utilization in schools, referred to as the 'computerization' (*komputerisasi*).

Didik, a school computer teacher, recalls that his public school in Jakarta started to add 'computer courses' as extracurricular courses that all students were required to take in 1992. An air-conditioned room, the 'computer lab', characterized by rows of local-brand desktops, began to appear as additional facilities in schools in major cities.

In these spaces, students could learn how to draw with computer programs, create their own fonts, along with other basic programming drills. Exams were no longer conducted using a paper copy, but were instead printed on computer readable paper, and students were required to use a special computer-dedicated 2B pencil. The *komputerisasi* program also marked the second installment of Suharto's modernization Long-Term Development (*Pembangunan Jangka Panjang*, abv. PJP) project, which was referred to as the Take Off Era (*Era Tinggal Landas*) started in 1993.[20]

Simultaneously in the early 1990s, cellular telecommunication technology was introduced to urban markets. With a market price of around 10 million Rupiah, however, it was rare and had a very limited market. Wireless telecommunication became accessible after the proliferation of GSM (Global System for Mobile Communications) technology from the state-owned PT Telkom Indonesia in 1993. Furthermore, Nokia's low-cost products and its market penetration in the late 1990s and early 2000s polarized the market creating a large entry user segment. Its iconic 3310 and 5110 series were popular among students and urban middle class consumers. It was so popular that it was dubbed the cell phone of a million *ummah* ('*handphone sejuta umat*').[21]

During the early 1990s, satellite dishes made it possible for PT Telkom Indonesia to create telecommunication corner shop as a new franchise business model: the *Warung Telekomunikasi* (abv. Wartel). While establishing wired cables for landline phones across the 922 inhabited islands was a great challenge for the company and an expensive proposition for customers, the Wartel provided a much cheaper and stable telephone service. It soon became popular across the archipelago, connecting family members and social networks.

Later in the 1990s, the Wartel telecommunication shop business model was adopted for Internet shops called *Warung Internet* (Internet shop, abv. Warnet). In 1997, PT Pos Indonesia, the state-owned postal service, launched its own Internet infrastructure franchise, Wasantara.net, which gained a stronghold throughout the archipelago and brought the service price down. By 1998, it was common for Wartels to add Warnet to their businesses.[22]

At that time, still using radio transmission technology, Internet connection was slow and unstable. While waiting for webpages to load, users chatted with each other making the Warnet into a community hub (Lim 2003b). Such early findings quickly dismissed the premise that offline and online interaction domains are mutually exclusive.

Online communication and mobile telephony rapidly also became popular among students as a means to escape the oppressive Suharto regime's government censorship. Along with its use for interpersonal telecommunication and escaping government monitoring, the access it provided to underground information on democracy and government misconduct was celebrated as the new entry to democracy and the public sphere. Around the uncertain time of the 1998 student protest, the Internet and mobile telephony were considered assets for student consolidation especially in avoiding the watchful monitoring of the government and generating widespread political discussion (see Tjakraatmadja et al. 2011; O'Rourke 2002; Hill and Sen 2005).

Civil society in the Indonesian online sphere, however, does not always feature a civic attitude. For example, during the troubled times of the sectarian Moluccan conflict from 1999 to 2002, the online sphere became a catalyst for fake news and hatred and was therefore far from the ideal of a peace medium (Bräuchler 2003; Van Klinken 2007).

Besides becoming a nest for political discussions, Bell (2006) observes that with the development of interactive web 2.0, story sharing and personal communication started to emerge as new digital practices. In addition to Warnet, she also finds that those using digital media at home started to chat online, knitting family networks and interpersonal relationships. She illustrates that those social networks started not in the foreign digital land of anonymous masses, but rather with family connections at the utmost starting point, the home. With a population scattered across 922 inhabited islands, digital media has been seen as an effective medium to reconnect social ties (Bell 2006).

In 2015, Warnet as a chatting center lost its charm, losing the competition against the proliferation of mobile gadgets. When I conducted my offline field research between 2010 and 2015 in Solo, most Warnets had turned into online gaming centers. Unlike the descriptions that Lim (2003b) and Bell (2006) presented a decade ago, today there are no university students gathering in Warnets to discuss political activism or leisurely surf the online world. Instead, these Warnets have become spaces for school age children to play multiplayer online games or compete against each other. Older students play games using universities' hotspots or at home.

In 2016, while the Indonesian Association for Internet Service Providers (Asosiasi Jasa Penyelenggara Jasa Internet Indonesia) recorded that 47,6% Internet users were accessing the online space through their mobile phone, the Singaporean-based Wearesocial.org reported that the number had actually reached 70%.[23] I also encountered many people who did not have phone credit to make a call but would have mobile Internet data access. Smartphone penetration among mobile phone users also grew to 53% by 2017, with a total of 103.6 million users.[24] This phenomenon, however, is still largely an urban phenomenon with 56.4 million urban users out of the total of 61.1 million Internet users, as MarkPlus Insight reported in the same year.[25]

During this time of proliferation, mobile media gadgets were domesticated according to local needs and practices. At first, besides its practical functional value, mobile phones were perceived by Indonesians to have symbolic economic status as the material appropriation of success, wealth and lifestyle (Barendregt 2008). Nonetheless, this conspicuous consumption utilization and the perceived purchase value are changing as the gadget's price goes down and more users appropriate the device.

Texting is a major feature of the gadget, which changed how mobile phones are experienced in Indonesia (Ericsson Mobility Report 2014). As texting is much cheaper than making calls and has been depicted as a direct personal medium for messages, SMS, together with IM (Instant Messaging) chats, became more popular than mobile telephone calls (Asosiasi Jasa Penyelenggara Internet Indonesia 2016, Purwanto 2012). Texting has influenced social practices. Several studies find that, for example, Indonesian women now have a greater possibility to navigate their way through courtship (*pacaran*) through intimate online chatting while bypassing the shyness associated with domestic women's culture, a traditional limitation on women's mobility and public intimacy (e.g. Nilan 2006; Slama 2010).

In the hands of traditional Indonesians, modern mobile devices are not necessarily utilized in 'modern' ways. Bart Barendregt (2008) found that Indonesians also exploit the digital gadget to sustain traditional supernatural practices, particularly to communicate with the spirits of dead ancestors. In the hands of politicians, texting has become a primary medium for managing daily politics (Hill and Sen 2005). As such, in contrast to the long-standing middleman's circuit of asymmetric feudal political strata, direct political lobbying has created the possibility for the polarization of lobbying and has created an increased risk of greater opacity to veil political deals (ibid.).

The platforms Indonesians use have also changed over time. In the early 2000s, Warnet users were familiar with ICQ, mIRC, or Yahoo!Messenger IM service accessed through computers—both PCs and laptops. In 2016, the four most popular services were BBM, Facebook

Messenger, WhatsApp, and Line (Balea 2016). While the location of access, the gadget and platforms might change over time, the most popular Indonesian digital activities in 2016 remain similar to those in the heyday of the Warnet a decade earlier: information updates (25.3%), working-related activity (20.8%), browsing (13.5%), and social connection (10.3%).[26]

These descriptions of the variations of Indonesian digital users' behaviors and activities from 1984 show that human digital activities are related to the given political dynamics, the development of technology, location of access, market, price, and offline cultural setting. Around a decade after the popularization of Internet and digital gadgets, digital technology in Indonesia has many faces. Like any part of the world (e.g. Wellman and Haythornthwaite 2002; Castells et al. 2009), Indonesian digital engagement cannot be confined to a single trend.

This is where Ingold's explanation comes in handy. Using his thesis that dwelling is a meaning-making experience of skillful wayfaring (Ingold 2011), the online sphere and the development of its properties could be viewed as an impacting environment on modes of communications and the importance of digital engagement. He argues that the human skill set is not predefined and should 'continually emerge as developmental outcomes within matrices comprised of mutually conditioning relations' (Ingold 2011: 9).

In the context of citizenship and the formation of democracy in Indonesia, then, it is necessary to pose questions about how these changes could impact the notion of citizenship. Does technological change also change the forms of civic engagement of the same participants? Answering this question in an Indonesian context is crucial because studies have also found that the presence of new media does not necessarily replace the role of 'old media'. Instead, rather than the online circulation, radio in Indonesia still has a strategic and significant influence on organizing communities and civil society, and has been able to reach out to a greater scope of society members, especially in rural areas (Sen 2003; Birowo 2011; Jurriëns 2011).

If digital media only works to mobilize the masses to join protests on the street or to become a medium of public political discussions, radio already did this job pretty well around the fall of Suharto's regime (Birowo 2011; Jurriëns 2007). In times of emergency too during the 2004 tsunami disaster in West Sumatra and Aceh, the radio community became a pioneer and established the groundwork for setting up radio communication, acting as a medium for social coordination (Afrizal and Prakoso 2009).

In contrast to the Habibie-kids' global urban Internet approach, Sen (2011) shows that radio is more effective as a medium for the rural and regional areas not only because of its coverage, but because New Order's policies have positioned radio as the repository of local cultural politics, which has influenced the creation of content that is often more local and psychologically and culturally closer to the people. Edwin Jurriëns indicates that radio works as a public sphere since it serves as a meeting point for both parties of citizen and state, which he believes 'address[es] the issue of the accessibility and representativeness of the mass media—as a main constituent of the public sphere—as well as the accessibility and representativeness of the public sphere itself' (2007: 116). These findings therefore call for an investigation of the newness of digital media, especially when compared with the old media.[27]

### *1.4.2 Solo and Javanese Cultural Settings*

Since my fellow dwellers mostly live and have their offline meet-ups in Solo, it is necessary to account for the city's cultural environment as part of Kaskusers' their cultural and normative resources. Solo is a prominent court-city in Java. Many scholars working in Indonesia come to Solo to conduct research on the performing arts, language and literature, religion, politics, or agriculture. Together with the neighboring court-city of Yogyakarta, from which it split in 1755, Solo is the heir to the larger Mataram Sultanate—the last major Kingdom in Java, which governed two-thirds of Java island.[28] Throughout this almost one and a half millennium history, religions—animism, Hinduism, Buddhism, and Islam—have influenced power and culture (Ricklefs 2001).

The Solonese and those living closer to the center of the court realm, have been characterized by their aristocratic, traditional, and eloquent mannerisms (see Pemberton 1994; Siegel 1993) along with a hierarchical system in Javanese society which, in general, is found in everyday Javanese language. Benedict Anderson (1996) argues that there is, however, a clear distinction between 'hierarchy' and 'class', underscoring that the former acts as a form of ordering and not the latter, a concept based on the distinct segregation of the classes that characterizes Javanese society.

Solo, although surrounded by agricultural villages, is an urban-centric city. The 44.04 square kilometer city was home to 512,226 inhabitants in 2015, an increase of 10,576 from 2011 (Badan Pusat Statistika 2014). Sixty-five per cent of the land under its administration is occupied by residential areas, followed by 16.5% occupied for economic activities. The city has 271,199 residents that are economically active in the workforce, with a 4.53% unemployment rate among the work-age population. Most educated working adults are vocational senior high school graduates (65,514) and higher education graduates (49,096). At 80.14, the Urban Human Development Index is relatively high by Indonesian standards.[29]

Most workers are employed in trades (108,207) and industry (62,226). The textile industry and printing business are two major industries in the city. The number of those living below the poverty line has decreased from 13.96% in 2010 to 10.89% in 2015. In general, the city's economy is thriving; numbers on Actual Revenues of Surakarta Municipality (*Pendapatan Asli Daerah Pemerintah Kota Surakarta*) quadrupled from IDR 45,112,371,235 (around US$3,4 million) in 2002 to IDR 181,096,816,152 (around US$13,6 million) in 2011 and IDR 291,862,178,678 (around US$21,8 million) in 2015.[30]

Such promising economic growth is however haunted by the struggle to establish security and political stability. Solonese always remember that their hometown has been vulnerable to riots in the past. In 1965, during the emergence of military power, military forces swept the city's communists (Siegel 1993). Fifteen years later in November–December 1980, violence against the Chinese broke out, triggered by a fight between two local high school students, one of whom was of Chinese descent (Siswoyo 1981). The fight between these two individuals grew into a brawl in November, but became riots as people used this moment to protest the cronyism between the government and the Chinese community. The riot later grew even larger and spread to two other cities: Semarang and Kudus.

Similar riots erupted again during another regime change in 1998. Following the May 1998 riots in Jakarta which had been motivated by political dissatisfaction resulting from inflation, rioters in Solo looted and burned Chinese houses, shops, factories, and warehouses as well as government properties and the public market. The National Fact Finder Join Team (*Tim Gabungan Pencari Fakta*) also found that two women had been raped following the civil unrest.[31] The most recent riot occurred in May 2012 when the Islamic Defender Front (*Front Pembela Islam*, abv. FPI) attacked and clashed with residents of Gandekan, Solo. The fights between the two marked an outburst in a long antagonism between the FPI and local gangsters.[32]

Solo is currently of heightened interest as the city was formerly governed by then-mayor Joko Widodo, popularly called Jokowi, who is now the President of Indonesia. Active on Twitter since he was mayor, Jokowi is a Kaskuser himself. He told me that he has been dwelling in Kaskus since the mid-2000s all the while keeping his ID secret. During my interviews with him, he was indeed keeping himself up-to-date with the various discussions developing in Kaskus, even some details that I had overlooked.[33] One of his children is also an active member of the forum.

As mayor, Jokowi established the Solo Techno Park complex area as a digital and technical center for students and digital start-ups in 2009. He eagerly promoted online services to simplify the city's bureaucracy and reduce red tape. In addition to private scattered free hotspots, Solo is home to the largest public hotspot in Indonesia comprising a two-kilometer square area provided by the city government.[34] In terms of digitality, Solo itself is a host for various 'digital festivals' and 'online community festivals', such as the Solo Online Community Festival, Solo Cyber Day,[35] and the 2013 ASEAN Blogger Festival. The Solonese are not new to media-based events as the city's local Radio Republik Indonesia also regularly hosts cultural festivals and traditional Wayang performances.

While the Javanese practice of correlating everyday life with, for example, the philosophy of Wayang stories may not be as present as it was in the past as many young Javanese are influenced by various other competing norms and cultures (e.g. Kam 1987), its normative terminologies or concepts, as this book illustrates in the following chapters, are still commonly used in conversations.

Besides being the stock for Javanese normative vocabulary, Wayang stories and performances also bear a form of virtuality. Wayang characters are animated behind the screen, with stories that are morally and politically entangled as a metaphor of events in everyday life. The stories are myths that are rewritten based on the local actualities where the theater performs, discussed off-stage. It transforms from a virtual world into everyday life as the Javanese diligently associate the stories with their own life experiences and events. People associated, or associate themselves, with a certain character from a Wayang story (see Jan Mrázek 2002a). Such a social relationship preference provides the first inference that Javanese communication is intersubjective.

Intersubjectivity also transpires in 'feeling-meaning' (*rasa*) communication (Geertz 1976: 238). *Rasa* as a Javanese art of communication for political communication—the goal of which is to achieve order based on predicting the other's reactionary feelings—exposes several dimensions. First, it is a mechanism of social order and collective control (Geertz 1976; Magnis-Suseno 1988: 197–199). Second, Yumarma understands such communication exchange as 'the capacity to gather up the scattered pieces of self' (1996: 3) in order to understand the external as the practice of belief in the amalgamation of the microcosm and macrocosm.

This classic approach to Javanese communication, however, seems rather focused on agreement and the idealistic. Unlike the two harmonious interpretations, Stange (1984) proposes that the Javanese communication style has its flux and limitations, as it relates to the temporality of the environment. In contrast, therefore, he considers *rasa* as constant training of social connections as part of the temporality of intersubjective responses. Recent studies on Javanese communication and particularly political communication have strongly criticized the bloated interpretation of *rasa*, arguing that its elements have been engineered for politically strategic ends, particularly during the Dutch Colonial and Suharto eras to avoid formal and transparent social order, rather than to produce a moral code (e.g. Sears 1996; Pemberton 1994).

It is against this background that the complexity of being a Kaskuser in Solo emerges, as Solo Kaskusers never confine themselves to simply being Javanese, but also have multiple identities: Indonesian, Solonese, Kaskuser, youth, and so on. This makes the dynamics of attempting to develop an online community and an online community's ethical life all the more complicated. This is the stock of wonder and the normative vocabularies that influence the perceptual online wayfaring in KRS. Now, let's go online.

## Notes

1. MSH, "Koin Untuk Prita Bisa Diangkut 5 Truk," *Kompas*, December 19, 2009. Accessed December 19, 2009. http://nasional.kompas.com/read/2009/12/19/10215466/koin.untuk.prita.bisa.diangkut.5.truk
2. "Editorial: Goodbye, People Power," *The Jakarta Post*, January 29, 2010. Accessed January 29, 2010. http://www.thejakartapost.com/news/2010/01/29/editorial-goodbye-people-power.html
3. Michael Burawoy, "The Fate of Post-Revolutionary Egypt: An Interview with Mona Abaza," *Global Dialogue*, Volume 7, Issue 1 (March 2017), 4–9.
4. http://one.laptop.org/about/mission
5. "Why do children in developing nations need laptops?" *OneLaptop.org*. Accessed October 10th, 2013. http://one.laptop.org/about/faq
6. Herbert Mead emphasizes that intersubjectivity is 'the meeting of minds' which occurs in conversation, learning, and reflecting (1938: 52–53). The goal for this is an agreement for social norms, shared meanings, and systems of morality. Individuals take part in symbolically mediated interactions as socialization to train the capacity to understand others.
7. Habermas (1998) relates intersubjectivity with a kernel of communication to pursue common terms, as he explains: '[…] the term "intersubjective" no longer refers to the result of an observed convergence of thoughts or

representations of various persons, but to the prior commonality of a linguistic pre-understanding or horizon of the lifeworld—which, from the perspective of the participants themselves, is presupposed—within which the members of a communication community find themselves before they reach an understanding with one another about something in the world' (1998: 355–356). Such understanding has to be operational as he formulates, '[T]he aim of reaching understanding (*Verstädigung*) is to bring about an agreement (*Einverständnis*) that terminates in the intersubjective mutuality of reciprocal comprehension, shared knowledge, mutual trust, and accord with one another' (1998: 23).

8. Robert Tait, "Censorship Fears Rise as Iran Blocks Access to Top Websites," *The Guardian*, December 4, 2006. Accessed December 9, 2006. http://www.theguardian.com/technology/2006/dec/04/news.iran
9. Official record in 2017 with subforums included.
10. Assessed by Worthofweb.com. Data retrieved on February 14, 2017, http://www.worthofweb.com/website-value/kaskus.co.id
11. Oik Yusuf, "Transaksi FJB Kaskus Rp 575 Miliar Per Bulan," *Kompas*, November 25, 2012. Accessed December 3, 2012. http://tekno.kompas.com/read/2012/11/25/13233388/Transaksi.FJB.Kaskus.Rp.575.Miliar.Per.Bulan.
12. Siti Alia Sarifah and Mitra Angelia, "Kaskus Klaim Punya 8,6 Juta Pengunjung Aktif, Siap Meramaikan Ulang Tahun Melalui Gerakan Sosial," *VivaNews*, November 6, 2015. Accessed November 6, 2015. http://teknologi.news.viva.co.id/news/read/696512-kaskus-klaim-punya-8-6-juta-pengunjung-aktif
13. https://www.statista.com/statistics/242606/number-of-active-twitter-users-in-selected-countries/ and https://www.statista.com/statistics/268136/top-15-countries-based-on-number-of-facebook-users/
14. Sara Sidner, "Indonesia: Twitter Nation," *CNN*, November 23, 2010. Accessed November 15, 2012. http://articles.cnn.com/2010-11-23/tech/indonesia.twitter_1_twitter-nation-social-media-social-networking?_s=PM:TECH
15. Socialbaker.com is an online statistic and online data counter. Data retrieved on November 19, 2012. See also: Jon Russell, "Jakarta Named World's Facebook<!--Facebook--> Capital," *Asian Correspondent*, March 18, 2011. Accessed Nov. 15, 2012. http://asiancorrespondent.com/50592/jakarta-recognised-as-the-worlds-facebook-capital/
16. RezaWahyudi, "Naik 13 Juta, Pengguna Internet Indonesia 55 Juta Orang," *Kompas*, October 28, 2011. Accessed October 30, 2011. http://tekno.kompas.com/read/2011/10/28/16534635/Naik.13.Juta.Pengguna.Internet.Indonesia.55.Juta.Orang
17. Asosiasi Jasa Penyelenggara Internet Indonesia, *Penetrasi dan Perilaku Pengguna Jasa Internet Indonesia 2016*. Jakarta: Asosiasi Jasa Penyelenggara Internet Indonesia, 2016.
18. Ibid.

19. Afrilia Suryanis, "Bisnis Internet Mobile Makin Cerah," Tempo, March 18, 2012. Accessed November 15, 2012. http://www.tempo.co/read/news/2012/03/19/090391182/Bisnis-Internet-Mobile-Makin-Cerah
20. The terminology, 'take off' was also a word play on Habibie's aeronautical industry project, which at the time was a popular exemplar of Indonesia's advanced industry.
21. The title was a language play on '*da'i sejuta umat*' (preacher of a million *ummah*), a self-claimed term popularized by the late Zainuddin MZ, a Jakarta-based Islamic preacher.
22. At a rate of approximately Rp 9,000 per dollar. Data and date are compiled from the collective Wiki from computer-related actors in Indonesia: http://opensource.telkomspeedy.com/wiki/index.php/WARNET. See also: David T. Hill and Krishna Sen, *The Internet in Indonesia's New Democracy*. (Oxon: Routledge, 2005), 116–119; Merlyna Lim, "From Real to Virtual (and Back again): Civil Society, Public Sphere, and Internet in Indonesia." In *Asia.com: Asia encounters the Internet*, edited by Kong-Chong Ho, Randy Kluver and Kenneth C. C. Yang, 113–128. (London: Routledge, 2003b), 113–128.
23. Asosiasi Jasa Penyelenggara Internet Indonesia, Penetrasi dan Perilaku Pengguna Jasa Internet Indonesia 2016. Jakarta: Asosiasi Jasa Penyelenggara Internet Indonesia, 2016. See alsoJudith Balea, "The latest stats in web and mobile in Indonesia". TechnInAsia, January 28, 2016. Accessed January 28th, 2016. https://www.techinasia.com/indonesia-web-mobile-statistics-we-are-social
24. "In Indonesia, a New Digital Class Emerges," *Emarketer.com Report*. Accessed March 12th, 2013. http://www.emarketer.com/Article/Indonesia-New-Digital-Class-Emerges/1009723#bqTGyZxJGZ8MDkOV.99
25. Ibid.
26. Asosiasi Jasa Penyelenggara Internet Indonesia, *Penetrasi dan Perilaku Pengguna Jasa Internet Indonesia 2016*. Jakarta: Asosiasi Jasa Penyelenggara Internet Indonesia, 2016.
27. At the turn of the millennium, Liebes and Curran (2002) argued that television remains the most important medium as democracy relates strongly to the nation-state model. They identify the following reasons: (i) most national television programs are still produced nationally and therefore mediate local representation; (ii) the state still holds the power of authorization before the television program is aired; (iii) different nations have different cultures, political systems, economies, etc., crystallized through each program representation. Ginsburg (2008) describes that cultural activists still use 'traditional media', such as documentary films, through which they are 'talking back' to the state and supply the public sphere with adequate material for debate.
28. The history of Javanese Mataram itself could be traced as far as back as the Kutai Kingdom in Borneo around 300 A.D, with the rise and fall of 11

kingdoms: Kutai, Tarumanagara, Kalingga, Srivijaya, Sailendra, Sunda, Medang, Kahuripan, Kediri, Singhasari, Majapahit (see De Graaf 1987; Ricklefs (2001).

29. Badan Pusat Statistika, *Surakarta dalam Angka 2011*. Surakarta: Badan Pusat Statistika, 2011; Badan Pusat Statistika, *Surakarta dalam Angka 2015*. Surakarta: Badan Pusat Statistika, 2015; Badan Pusat Statistika, *Ekonomi Kota Surakarta 2014*. Surakarta: Badan Pusat Statistika, 2015.
30. Badan Pusat Statistika, *Surakarta dalam Angka 2011*. Surakarta: Badan Pusat Statistika 2011, p.232; Badan Pusat Statistika, *Surakarta dalam Angka 2016*. Surakarta: Badan Pusat Statistika 2016, p.157.
31. Tim Gabungan Pencari Fakta (TGPF). *Fact Finder Join Team Report*. http://semanggipeduli.com/tgpf/laporan.html on June 2011.
32. "Konflik di Solo Bernuansa SARA." *Berita Satu*, May 20, 2012. Accessed May 20, 2012. http://www.beritasatu.com/nasional/46268-konflik-di-solo-bernuansa-sara.html
33. Three years later during his presidential campaign it is also evident that he still dwells in Kaskus, and has adopted the currently popular Kaskus meme slogan "Rapopo" ("I am fine"; Jav.) to his campaign. The slogan was generated by members to support his campaign as a strategy facing smear campaigns from other candidates. See: http://megapolitan.kompas.com/read/2014/03/25/1704217/Alasan.Jokowi.Gunakan.Istilah.Aku.Rapopo.
34. HAW, "Solo bakal miliki jalur akses Internet terpanjang di Indonesia," *Solopos*, October 11, 2011. Accessed October 11, 2011. http://www.solopos.com/2011/10/11/solo-bakal-miliki-jalur-akses-internet-terpanjang-di-indonesia-119241
35. http://www.solocyberday.com/

## References


Afrizal, R., and Prakoso I. "Berbagi Kisah dari Seantero Negeri: Upaya-upaya Penanggulangan Bencana oleh Radio Komunitas." In *Mengudara Menjawab Tantangan*, edited by A. Nasir, P. Wijoyono and A. Tanesia, 19–47. Yogyakarta: Combine Resource Institute, 2009.

Alampay, Erwin. *Living the Information Society in Asia*. Singapore: ISEAS, 2009.

Anderson, Benedict R.O'G. *Imagined Communities: Reflections on the Origin and Spread of Nationalism*. First published in 1983. Revised edition. London: Verso, 1991.

Anderson, Benedict R.O'G. *Java in a Time of Revolution: Occupation and Resistance, 1944–1946*. Jakarta: Equinox Publishing, 2006.

Anderson, Benedict R.O'G. *Mythology and the Tolerance of the Javanese*. Ithaca: Cornell University, 1996.

Asosiasi Jasa Penyelenggara Internet Indonesia. *Penetrasi dan Perilaku Pengguna Jasa Internet Indonesia 2016.* Jakarta: Asosiasi Jasa Penyelenggara Internet Indonesia, 2016.

Badan Pusat Statistika. *Surakarta dalam Angka 2011.* Surakarta: Badan Pusat Statistika, 2011.

Badan Pusat Statistika. *Ekonomi Kota Surakarta 2014.* Surakarta: Badan Pusat Statistika, 2015a.

Badan Pusat Statistika. *Surakarta Dalam Angka 2014.* Surakarta: Badan Pusat Statistika, 2014.

Badan Pusat Statistika. *Surakarta dalam Angka 2015.* Surakarta: Badan Pusat Statistika, 2015b.

Barendregt, Bart. "Sex, Cannibals, and the Language of Cool: Indonesian Tales of the Phone and Modernity". *The Information Society: An International Journal* Volume 24 Issue 3 (May 2008): 160–170.

Bell, Genevieve. "Satu Keluarga, Satu Komputer [One Home, One Computer]: Cultural Accounts of ICTs in South and Southeast Asia." *Design Issues* Volume 22 Number 2 (2006): 35–55.

Birowo, Mario Antonius. "Community Radio and the Empowerment of Local Culture." In *Politics and the Media in Twenty-First Century Indonesia: Decade of Democracy,* edited by Krishna Sen and David Hill, 49–66. Oxon: Routledge, 2011.

Bräuchler, Birgit. "Cyberidentities at War: Religion, Identity, and the Internet in the Moluccan Conflict." *Indonesia* 75 (April 2003): 123–51.

Bruhn, John G. *The Sociology of Community Connections.* Second Edition. Dordrecht: Springer, 2011.

Bunt, Gary R. *Islam in the Digital Age: E-Jihad, Online Fatwas and Cyber Islamic Environments.* London: Pluto Press, 2003.

Burawoy, Michael. "The Fate of Post-Revolutionary Egypt: An Interview with Mona Abaza." *Global Dialogue*, International Sociology Association Volume 7, Issue 1 (March 2017): 4–8.

Cammaerts, Bart, Alice Mattoni, Patrick McCurdy. *Mediation and Protest Movements.* Bristol: Intellect Books, 2013.

Castells, Manuel, Mireia Fernández-Ardèvol, Jack Linchuan Qiu, and Araba Sey. *Mobile Communication and Society: A Global Perspective.* Massachusetts: MIT Press, 2009.

Castells, Manuel. *Networks of Outrage and Hope: Social Movements in the Internet Age.* Cambridge: Polity Press, 2012.

Castells, Manuel. *The Rise of the Network Society.* West Sussex: Wiley-Blackwell, 2000.

Chin, James. "Malaysiakini.com and Its Impact on Journalism and Politics in Malaysia." In *Asia.com. Asia Encounters the Internet*, edited by K.C. Ho, Randolph Kluver and Kenneth C.C. Yang, 129–142. London: RoutledgeCurzon, 2003.

Cogburn, Derrick L. and Fatima K. Espinoza-Vasquez. "From Networked Nominee to Networked Nation: Examining the Impact of Web 2.0 and Social

Media on Political Participation and Civic Engagement in the 2008 Obama Campaign," *Journal of Political Marketing* 10 (1-2) (2011): 189–213. Doi: 10.1080/15377857.2011.540224

De Graaf, Hermanus Johannes. *Runtuhnya Istana Mataram*. Jakarta: Pustaka Utama Grafiti, 1987.

El-Nawawy, Mohammed, and Sahar Khamis. *Egyptian Revolution 2.0: Political Blogging, Civic Engagement, and Citizen Journalism*. New York: Palgrave Macmillan, 2013.

Fuchs, Christian. *Internet and Society: Social Theory in the Information Age*. New York: Routledge, 2008.

Geertz, Clifford. *The Religion of Java*. Chicago: University of Chicago Press, 1976.

Gerbaudo, Paolo. *Tweets and the Streets: Social Media and Contemporary Activism*. London: Pluto Press, 2012.

Ginsburg, Faye. "Culture/Media: A (Mild) Polemic". *Anthropology Today* 10(2) (1994): 5–15.

Ginsburg, Faye. "Rethinking the Digital Age". In *The Media and Social Theory*, edited by David Hesmondhalgh and Joan Toynbee, 127–144. New York: Routledge, 2008.

Habermas, Jürgen. *On the Pragmatics of Communication*. Cambridge: MIT Press, 1998.

Habermas, Jürgen. *Postmetaphysical Thinking*. Translated by William Mark Hohengarten. Massachusetts: MIT Press, 1992.

Habermas, Jürgen. *The Structural Transformation of the Public Sphere*. Translated by Thomas Burger. First publication in 1989. Massachusetts: MIT Press, 1991.

Hill, David T. and Krishna Sen. *The Internet in Indonesia's New Democracy*. Oxon: Routledge, 2005.

Honneth, Axel. *The Struggle for Recognition: The Moral Grammar of Social Conflicts*. Translated by Joel Anderson. Cambridge: MIT Press, 1995.

Howard, Philip N. and Muzammil M. Hussain. *Democracy's Fourth Wave? Digital Media and the Arab Spring*. Oxford: Oxford University Press, 2013.

Ingold, Tim and Jo Lee Vergunst. *Ways of Walking*. Surrey: Ashgate, 2008.

Ingold, Tim. *Being Alive Essays on Movement, Knowledge and Description*. Oxon: Routledge, 2011.

Ingold, Tim. *The Perception of the Environment: Essays on Livelihood, Dwelling & Skill*. London: Routledge, 2000.

Ingold, Tim. *Lines: A Brief History*. Oxon: Routledge, 2007.

Iskander, Elizabeth. "Connecting the National and the Virtual: Can Facebook Activism Remain Relevant After Egypt's January 25 Uprising?" *International Journal of Communication* 5 (2011): 13–15.

Jurriëns, Edwin. "The Cosmopolitanism of Indonesian Radio Active and Public Sphere." In *Cosmopatriots: On Distant Belongings and Close Encounters*, edited by Edwin Jurrlëns, Jeroen De Kloet, 105–132. Amsterdam: Rodopi, 2007.

Jurriëns, Edwin. "'Radio Active': The creation of media literate audiences in post-Suharto Indonesia". In *Politics and the Media in Twenty-First Century Indonesia: Decade of Democracy*, edited by Krishna Sen and David Hill, 141–158. Oxon: Routledge, 2011.

Kam, Garrett. "Wayang Wong in the Court of Yogyakarta: The Enduring Significance of Javanese Dance Drama," *Asian Theatre Journal* Vol. 4 No. 1 (Spring, 1987), 29–51. DOI: 10.2307/1124435

Katz, Elihu, and Daniel Dayan. *Media Events*. First publication in 1992. Second edition. Cambridge: Harvard University Press, 1994.

Lewis, Kevin, Kurt Gray and Jens Meierhenrich. "The Structure of Online Activism". *Sociological Science* Vol.1 (February 2014): 1–9. Accessed March 1, 2014. DOI 10.15195/v1.a1

Liebes, Tamar, and James Curran. *Media, Ritual and Identity*. London: Routledge, 2002.

Lim, Merlyna. "Clicks, Cabs, and Coffee Houses: Social Media and Oppositional Movements in Egypt, 2004–2011". *Journal of Communication* 62 (2012): 231–248.

Lim, Merlyna. "From Real to Virtual (and Back again): Civil Society, Public Sphere, and Internet in Indonesia." In *Asia.com: Asia encounters the Internet*, edited by Kong-Chong Ho, Randy Kluver and Kenneth C. C. Yang, 113–128. London: Routledge, 2003b.

Lim, Merlyna. "The Internet, Social Networks, and Reform in Indonesia." In *Contesting Media Power: Alternative Media in a Networked World*, edited by Nick Couldry and James Curran, 273–88.Maryland: Rowman & Littlefield, 2003a.

Magnis-Suseno, Franz. *Etika Jawa: Sebuah Analisa Falsafi Tentang Kebijaksanaan Hidup Jawa*. Jakarta : Gramedia, 1988.

Mead, Herbert. *The Philosophy of the Act*. Chicago: University of Chicago Press, 1938.

Mrázek, Jan. *Puppet Theater in Contemporary Indonesia: New Approaches to Performance Events*. Michigan: University of Michigan, Centers for South and Southeast Asian Studies, 2002a.

Mrázek, Rudolf. *Engineers of Happy Land: Technology and Nationalism in a Colony*. Princeton: Princeton University Press, 2002b.

Nilan, Pam. "Mediating the Entrepreneurial Self: Romance Texts and Young Indonesian Women." In M*edi@sia: Global media/tion In and Out of Context*, edited by Todd Joseph Miles Holden and Timothy J. Scrase, 62–81. Oxon: Routledge 2006.

Nordhausen, Frank, und Thomas Schmid. *Die Arabische Revolution: Demokratischer Aufbruch von Tunesien bis zum Golf*. Berlin: Ch. Links Verlag, 2012.

Nugroho, Yanuar, and Sofie Shinta Syarief. *Beyond Click-Activism? New Media and Political Processes in Contemporary Indonesia*. Berlin: FES-MediaAsia, 2012.

O'Rourke, Kevin. *Reformasi: The Struggle for Power in Post-Soeharto Indonesia.* New South Wales: Allen & Unwin, 2002.

Pariser, Eli. *The Filter Bubble: What the Internet Is Hiding From You.* London: Penguin UK, 2011.

Pemberton, John. *On the Subject Of "Java".* Ithaca: Cornell University Press, 1994.

Purwanto, Didik. "Ponsel Pintar di Indonesia Cuma untuk SMS dan Media Sosial." *Kompas,* June 6, 2012. Accessed June 6, 2012. http://tekno.kompas.com/read/2012/06/06/18403922/ponsel.pintar.di.indonesia.cuma.untuk.sms.dan.media.sosial

Quan-Haase, Anabel, Barry Wellman, James C. Witte, and Keith Hampton. "Capitalizing on the Net: Social Contact, Civic Engagement and Sense of Community." In *The Internet in Everyday Life,* edited by Barry Wellman and Caroline Haythornthwaite, 291–324. Malden: Blackwell Publishers, 2002.

Ricklefs, Merle Calvin. *A History of Modern Indonesia Since C. 1200.* Stanford: Stanford University Press, 2001.

Rogers, Everett M. *Diffusion of innovations* (1st ed.). New York: Free Press of Glencoe, 1962.

Russell, Jon. "Jakarta Named World's Facebook Capital." *Asian Correspondent,* March 18, 2011. Accessed Nov. 15, 2012. http://asiancorrespondent.com/50592/jakarta-recognised-as-the-worlds-facebook-capital/

Sears, Laurie Jo. *Shadows of Empire: Colonial Discourse and Javanese Tales.* Durham: Duke University Press, 1996.

Sen, Krishna. "Radio Days: Media-Politics in Indonesia." *The Pacific Review* Vol. 16 No.4 (2003): 573–589.

Sen, Krishna. "Introduction: Re-forming media in Indonesia's transition to democracy." In *Politics and the Media in Twenty-First Century Indonesia: Decade of Democracy,* edited by Krishna Sen and David Hill, 1–12. Oxon: Routledge, 2011.

Sidner, Sara. "Indonesia: Twitter Nation." *CNN,* November 23, 2010. Accessed November 15, 2012. http://articles.cnn.com/2010-11-23/tech/indonesia.twitter_1_twitter-nation-social-media-social-networking?_s=PM:TECH

Siegel, James T. *Solo in the New Order: Language and Hierarchy in an Indonesian City.* New Jersey: Princeton University Press, 1993.

Siswoyo, Bambang. *Huru Hara Solo Semarang: Suatu Reportase.* Jakarta: Bhakti Pertiwi, 1981.

Slama, Martin. "The Agency of the Heart: Internet Chatting as Youth Culture in Indonesia." *Social Anthropology/Anthropologie Sociale* European Association of Social Anthropologists. Vol.18/3(2010): 316–330. Accessed February 15, 2012. doi:10.1111/j.1469-8676.2010.00110.x

Stange, Paul. "The Logic of Rasa in Java". *Indonesia* No. 38 (Oct., 1984): 113–134. DOI: 10.2307/3350848

Steinbock, Dan. *The Mobile Revolution: The Making of Mobile Services Worldwide.* London: Kogan Page, 2005.

Tim Gabungan Pencari Fakta (TGPF). *Fact Finder Join Team Report*. Accessed November 1, 2013. http://semanggipeduli.com/tgpf/laporan.html on June 2011.

Tim Gabungan Pencari Fakta (TGPF). *Fact Finder Join Team Report*. Retrieved from: http://semanggipeduli.com/tgpf/laporan.html on June 2011.

Tjakraatmadja, Jann H., A. Wicaksono and L. Martini. "Knowledge Sharing in the Indonesian Context: Institut Teknologi Bandung (ITB) as Potential Knowledge Hub to Create Value from Academia, Business and Government Linkages." In *Beyond the Knowledge Trap: Developing Asia's Knowledge-Based Economies*, edited by Thomas Menkhoff, Hans-Dieter Evers, Yue Wah Chay, Eng Fong Pang, 269–298. Singapore: World Scientific, 2011.

Turkle, Sherry. *The Second Self: Computers and the Human Spirit*. Massachusetts: MIT Press, 2005.

Van Dijk, Jan A.G.M. *The Network Society: Social Aspects of New Media*. First publication in English in 1999. Second edition. London: SAGE Publications, 2006.

Van Klinken, Gerry. *Communal Violence and Democratization in Indonesia*. Oxon: Routledge, 2007.

Wayansari, Agustina. "The Internet and the Public Sphere in Indonesia's New Democracy: a Study of Politikana.com." In *Internetworking Indonesia Journal* Vol. 3/No. 2 (2011): 23–33. Jakarta, 2011.

Webster, Frank. *Theories of the Information Society*. Third Edition. Oxon: Routledge, 2006.

Wellman, Barry, and Caroline Haythornthwaite. *The Internet in Everyday Life*. Malden: Blackwell Publishers, 2002.

Wellman, Barry. *Networks in the Global Village: Life in Contemporary Communities*. New York: Westview Press, 1999.

Yumarma, Andreas. *Unity in Diversity: A Philosophical and Ethical Study of the Javanese Concept of 'Keselarasan'*. Roma: Editrice Pontificia Universita Gregoriana, 1996.

Yusuf, Oik. "Transaksi FJB Kaskus Rp 575 Miliar Per Bulan." *Kompas*,November 25, 2012. Accessed December 3, 2012. http://tekno.kompas.com/read/2012/11/25/13233388/Transaksi.FJB.Kaskus.Rp.575.Miliar.Per.Bulan

## News and Internet Sources

"Alasan.Jokowi.Gunakan.Istilah.Aku.Rapopo," *Kompas*, March 25, 2014. Accessed March 25, 2014. http://megapolitan.kompas.com/read/2014/03/25/1704217/Alasan.Jokowi.Gunakan.Istilah.Aku.Rapopo

"Editorial: Goodbye, People Power." *The Jakarta Post*, January 29, 2010. Accessed January 29, 2010. http://www.thejakartapost.com/news/2010/01/29/editorial-goodbye-people-power.html.on

"Ericsson Mobility Report: South East Asia And Oceania". *Ericsson Mobility Report*, November 2014. Accessed December 15, 2014. https://www.ericsson.com/res/docs/2014/emr-november2014-regional-appendices-raso.pdf

"In Indonesia, a New Digital Class Emerges." In *Emarketer Report*. Accessed March 12, 2013. http://www.emarketer.com/Article/Indonesia-New-Digital-Class-Emerges/1009723#bqTGyZxJGZ8MDkOV.99

"Konflik di Solo Bernuansa SARA." *Berita Satu*, May 20, 2012. Accessed May 20, 2012. http://www.beritasatu.com/nasional/46268-konflik-di-solo-bernuansa-sara.html

Balea, Judith. "The Latest Stats in Web and Mobile in Indonesia". *TechninAsia*, January 28, 2016. Accessed January 28th 2016. https://www.techinasia.com/indonesia-web-mobile-statistics-we-are-social, on January 28th, 2016.

Beaumont, Peter. "The Truth About Twitter, Facebook and The Uprisings in the Arab World." *The Guardian*, February 25, 2011. Accessed on February 25, 2011. http://www.theguardian.com/world/2011/feb/25/twitter-facebook-uprisings-arab-libya

Goldman, Lisa. "Social Media Has Been a Mixed Blessing for the Arab Spring." *Techpresident*, February 15, 2013. Accessed February 15, 2013.http://techpresident.com/news/wegov/23510/social-media-harming-arab-uprising

HAW. "Solo Bakal Miliki Jalur Akses Internet Terpanjang di Indonesia." *Solopos*, October 11, 2011. Accessed October 11, 2011. http://www.solopos.com/2011/10/11/solo-bakal-miliki-jalur-akses-internet-terpanjang-di-indonesia-119241

MSH. "Koin Untuk Prita Bisa Diangkut 5 Truk." *Kompas*, December 19, 2009. Accessed March 1, 2012. http://nasional.kompas.com/read/2009/12/19/10215466/koin.untuk.prita.bisa.diangkut.5.truk

Sarifah, Siti Alia and Mitra Angelia. "Kaskus Klaim Punya 8,6 Juta Pengunjung Aktif, Siap meramaikan ulang tahun melalui gerakan sosial." *VivaNews*, November 6, 2015. Accessed November 6, 2015. http://teknologi.news.viva.co.id/news/read/696512-kaskus-klaim-punya-8-6-juta-pengunjung-aktif

Suryanis, Afrilia. "Bisnis Internet Mobile Makin Cerah." *Tempo*, March 18, 2012. Accessed November 15, 2012. http://www.tempo.co/read/news/2012/03/19/090391182/Bisnis-Internet-Mobile-Makin-Cerah

Tait, Robert. "Censorship Fears Rise as Iran Blocks Access To Top Websites." *The Guardian*, December 4, 2006. Accessed December 9, 2006. http://www.theguardian.com/technology/2006/dec/04/news.iran

Wahyudi, Reza. "Naik 13 Juta, Pengguna Internet Indonesia 55 Juta Orang." *Kompas*, October 28, 2011. Accessed October 30, 2011. http://tekno.kompas.com/read/2011/10/28/16534635/Naik.13.Juta..Pengguna.Internet.Indonesia.55.Juta.Orang

CHAPTER 2

# The Structure of an Online Community

This chapter argues that in the era of episodic social media-based civic participation, becoming a digital citizen is not straightforward. It requires an alliance of peers and takes more than a click. To become a netizen, it is important to first become an online dweller and experience community-building as Kaskusers did in Kaskus.

Kaskus is an online chatting forum comprised of subforums, in which conversations are organized under subject-related threads. Kaskus offers various forums: Buy and Sell, Groupee, Kaskus Online Radio, General Lounge, News & Politics, Computers, Humor, Movies, Supernatural, Sports, Games, Automotive, Music, Hot Threads, and Regional Forums. In general, Kaskus' index page offers a traditional web layout of a message board Internet forum, such those used on the US-based Reddit,[1] or the gadget-enthusiast forum XDA Developers.[2] Online chatting is considered public communication that is open to everybody and intended to reach a general and wider audience. As an online forum primarily characterized by public chats, Kaskus provides a vast number of forums and subforums where members can chat and discuss various subjects. The constant sequence of public chats via message posts and replies can take place at an intense rate during a specified period or over several peaks and stretch into an open-ended and continual conversation. In Kaskus, for example, General Lounge threads last more than a year.



A. Seto, *Netizenship, Activism and Online Community Transformation in Indonesia*, DOI 10.1007/978-981-10-5397-9_2

For a Kaskuser, the online forum is, however, not merely a digital page or a space to chat, but is also a social environment for new practices. 'Cyberspace and Cyberculture' comprise the theme of this chapter as this describes how the merriness of chatting requires codes of digital practice: colloquial language, norms of equality, continuous chat participation, and online reputation. Members have a sentimental attachment to the chats and enjoy their solidarity existence of having a space to live where they meet their friends, create, and strengthen social bonds crafted through, as this chapter illustrates, consistent modes of online dwelling, or what they call 'militancy'.

## 2.1 The Merriness of Being in Kaskus

As is the case for any online forum, entering Kaskus is a text-based visual experience. A visitor should first navigate through text-labeled categories to opt which forum to read. Afterwards, going deeper into the web page after entering a forum, a visitor arrives at the subforum index list. Here, the visitor can browse around until s/he finds an attractive subforum and then a thread to read. The visitor then has a choice, to either join or start a conversation and is faced with two possibilities: 'dwelling' or 'leaving'.

To lurk or to browse around, visitors are not required to register. They are called 'silent readers', as they do not leave comments or voice their opinion on the subject. To leave a comment, start a thread, or post a question or message, an individual will need to register as a user. Leaving the website will end the online experience in Kaskus. Conversely, registering with a certain online name and posting something provides a sign to other Kaskusers that a new person, a newbie, has arrived. If the post deviates from the subforum's general subject, the newbie's post will be deleted. This is the first discipline that a Kaskuser should learn as part of the baby steps to becoming a Kaskuser.

A Kaskuser becomes a Thread Starter (abv. TS), when s/he posts the first message in a thread with a certain content—that may be news, jokes, protests against something, gossip, articles, how-to's, stories, pictures, questions, or advertisements, to name just a fraction of possibilities. Readers can then respond with (a) posted comment(s) as feedback(s). Whether it is a chat, conversation, or debate between the TS and readers or between readers, such exchanges signify the communication among those in the thread. Each post will update the thread's live register of the forum; a new post will 'bump' (*sundul*) the thread to the top of the forum's index. A thread which is not getting any new message will slide down to the lower index list.

The thread with most visitors and replies will be named a 'Hot Thread' and linked to the shortlisted Hot Thread Index on Kaskus' homepage. In a thread, it is the TS' responsibility to monitor the chat or discussions. Therefore, it is a matter of great pride and prestige if a TS is able to initiate a subject of chat—analysis of a current issue or controversial news, for example—that gains many comments and makes it to the Hot Thread Index. This practice of posting comments, starting a new discussion, and/or reacting to one in a forum thread is what Kaskusers dub 'chatting-in-forum' or 'discussion'.

### *2.1.1 Choosing a Location*

There is no general pattern for how a member comes to and registers with Kaskus. Some users like William and Armin registered with the online forum out of boredom so were looking for a place to chat. Others, like Prima and Surandy, joined the web forum because they were searching for computer-related materials, while Harya and Erick initially visited the web forum in the early 2000s to access the underground pornography circulation. Another user, Mochi, came to Kaskus after a friend told her it might be a good place to look for online materials for her research paper. The stories continue to vary: Amakuzalek and Wahyu came to Kaskus to find new friends as they had just moved to a new city; Sodron decided to register because he was interested in the Anime and Comics forum; and Via went to Kaskus because she likes to see gore and deviant art pictures.

As of 2017, there are over 650 subforums in Kaskus organized under 'forums' and 'community' and the numbers are continuously increasing. Because of this vast selection of forums and subforums along with the diversity of chatting subjects, some members dub Kaskus a 'miniature Indonesia'. Almost all of Indonesia's provinces and major cities are represented in Kaskus. One of Kaskus' largest forums is the Regional Forums Discussion Groups, which caters to those who live in a common geographical area and/or those who have an interest in a certain geographical area. These forums are used by its inhabitants to exchange local news regarding the specific region in which they are interested. In these forums, Kaskusers organize themselves under subforums such as 'West Java,' 'Solo,' 'Bali,' 'Japan,' 'Germany,' and so on.

For this research, I specifically dwelled in an online neighborhood called the Kaskus Regional Solo (KRS) forum. Assigned the web page number 160, it is a subforum that serves as a chat forum for Kaskusers from the city of Solo and the surrounding regencies in Java. As a locale, f=160 was unintentionally founded in June 2006. It was Prima who had the initiative out of curiosity to list Kaskusers who were currently live in Solo and nearby areas. As it is a thread dedicated for Kaskusers from Solo, the language used inadvertently turned to Javanese, as an addition to the national language, Bahasa Indonesia. Apparently, according to Prima, this feature of the thread attracts many Kaskusers who do not live in the area but want to chat in Javanese.

For Solo Kaskusers, being an inhabitant in the regional Solo forum or returning to the forum, provides the image of being part of the city or the region. Adhy, one of the forum members who joined Kaskus in its early years, explained at an offline charity event while introducing KRS to the public:

> We call it 'page 160', or as we write it, 'f=160' (read: 'f one sixty'), as 160 is the address of the web page provided by Kaskus, and 'f' is the abbreviation for 'forum'. Page 160 is Solo, the city itself in the online world.

As an online city, the forum hosts threads with various random subjects, such as daily event news, citizen journalism, restaurant reviews, regional political discussions, barber shop reviews, academic writing clinics, photographer enthusiast corners, fishing clubs, Parkour training clubs, chat lounges, Javanese proverbs, and regional soccer clubs, among others. When I began to dwell in f=160 in 2010, there were 182 active threads; in 2017, there are 257. The forum has accordingly become a visual and textual representation of the city's actualities. 'In the end, we know who lives where, approximately how old they are, who does what, and so on; who would report a traffic jam or when a new restaurant opens,' as Prima stated.

While the Kaskus' regional forum section, which is defined geographically, is one of the largest subforums in Kaskus, its inhabitants, however, do not see regionalism as a matter of communality or geographical boundaries. Instead, they consider it a component of pragmatic registration and identification—identifying which friends or fellow Kaskusers are physically nearby while assuming that they will have some knowledge of local subjects. This common point of reference makes it easier to select a subject about which to chat. Harya's decision to dwell in KRS is an example. For him, choosing his hometown Solo's online forum was an impulsive, quick decision to end his status as a digital refugee as his previous forum was closed. At that time, it was the only destination he could think of, and a destination with subjects of conversation that he already 'could imagine', he told me. Armin recounted a similar story:

> I was working at a shop. When I had no customers, I would browse around and end up in Kaskus. Suddenly, I had to decide to which forum I wanted to go. As I live in Solo, I just went directly to f=160. That was just about it.

Unlike Armin, some Solo Kaskusers did not directly dwell in f=160. For instance, even though Sodron and Amakuzalek are native Solonese, they were not 'digitally born' in f=160. They both began dwelling in other forums before they joined KRS. While Sodron first inhabited the Anime and Comics forum, Amakuzalek went to the Workers and Professionals Forum. Both Sodron and Amakuzalek continue to be natives in their original forums until today. This again highlights the importance of choice and fluidity for Kaskusers: attachment to subject(s) is not singular and they can dwell in more than one forum with the same intensity and attention.

Indeed, some Kaskusers joined f=160 for more 'ethnic' reasons like language affiliation, as Prima experienced. However, it should also be noted that this language is their mother tongue, and as such, it could be seen as a limitation to their horizon of possibilities. Geographical attachment becomes an obvious reference for an initial online dwelling because it is related to Kaskusers' antecedent offline realities, making it a rather immediate search. As Armin, Harya and Prima's experience show, their reference to Solo is the simple result of being physically located in the city. My experience was the same. As I moved to Germany in 2007, I went to Kaskus-Germany Regional Forum instead of Kaskus-France Regional Forum or Kaskus-UK Regional Forum, just like I read the *Frankfurter Rundschau* and not the *Berliner Zeitung* online, because I lived in Frankfurt.

Merleau-Ponty (2002) argues that we first perceive what we face by reflecting instantaneously on the properties of our body and its sensory capability (Merleau-Ponty 2002). The properties of our body, to echo Merleau-Ponty, however, are not limited to its physical attributes, but also the properties of the whole environment where the body is located and confined. Such phenomena can also be seen not only in the subject of online attachment, but in other pairings, for example, soccer fandom where fans immediately support their home team more than any other team, even if they are not necessarily the best players (Ben-Porat 2013). Physical location influences an individual's reference system. Accordingly, since Solo Kaskusers' body or experience is related to, or located in Solo, it was a common answer to encounter, that they would recall 'Solo' as the subject of significance. Online experience is far from geographically neutral.

Choosing a forum is, therefore, a perceptual experience, that requires an understanding of the contextual form of the forum, which is created by the forum's content, Kaskus' indexing, and an individual's subject interests, subjective backgrounds, and physical proximity. The significance of the forum's contextual form suggests that each forum as a dwelling location pertains to the mental history and reference of the operator. Approaching Solo Kaskusers and their association to Solo should be considered a glimpse into their everyday life realities.

Such connection to the everyday encourages Kaskusers' decision to stay in a forum. Wahyu, a Kaskus thread administrator, explained that coming back to a thread reflects that the thread is a location of people, where message traffic represents a space consisting of reciprocal activities. 'It is thrilling' (*asyik*), he said. It is the interactive conversation among conversants that creates the excitement. The possibility of having an online chat and discussions about various subjects that cover mundane everyday life has shaped Kaskusers' imagination of being in a social environment or what Sodron, also a thread administrator, dubbed as the 'merriness' (*seru*). He explains,

> Say you like photography, you've learned everything from the Photography Forum, you've shared pictures and experiences, and, in the end, you would master the techniques. [Then] you are going to ask yourself, 'What's next?' You are done with photography, but on the other hand it has become a habit to go to Kaskus. [This is when] you realize, that you have begun to recognize who is posting what message and what kind of people are there in the forum, how they share their lives, and you miss them. So, it is not just photography. It is the social interaction [that matters]!

A forum is then, for Kaskusers, an assembly of digital interactivity with social experience. There are three layers of merriness supporting such experience: the colloquial language which conveys a warm connection, the text which signifies community presence, and the forum which provides a home.

### 2.1.2 Casual Communication

Kaskus' merriness is made possible because of the casual communication Kaskusers expect. Like a newborn baby, the first social action required for online forums is to learn the local language's communication code. Kaskus and its forums like f=160 attract many visitors because of its playful, informal and simple linguistic standard of communication. As Harya explained:

> It is the language of the common (*orang biasa*), simple and understandable. Look at the bloggers, they could be considered smart and knowledgeable, but many told me that the bloggers' writing style is too formal, not so cheerful. They are considered elites (*ngelite*), and now they feel that way too. This, I think, becomes a barrier for them to blend with the 'common' (Ind. '*merakyat*').

Harya's assessment of the simplicity of the language used in Kaskus could be understood by recollecting that the Internet in Indonesia was introduced as an educational media and as part of the state's technocratic modernization agenda. As the previous chapter described, computers and the Internet were parts of the *Komputerisasi* (computerization) national development program encouraged by both educational institutions and the state, with the Internet commonly occupied by university students and technocrats (Lim 2003a, b; Hill and Sen 2005). As such, digital technology use was rapidly perceived to be, to use Judith Irvine's (1979) term, 'formal'.

As a linguistic anthropologist, Irvine (1979) finds that in communicative events, such formality does not simply appear from the language but also from other possible codes during message delivery that may include the communicant's body gestures, message, location, associated institutions, or other properties. Such association with formality eventually will result in, as Irvine reflects, exclusivity, limitation of freedom, and power for the communicant, whereby identities and situations can be managed through behavioral alteration by competent actors (ibid.: 785).

When Kaskus was launched as an online chat forum, its informal speech form was soon perceived to be an alternative to the formalities of the Internet as an educational medium. With this unique entry point, Kaskus rapidly gained popularity as a space for the non-elites, or using Kaskusers' term, an online space for the 'commons' (*rakyat*). To retain this attachment to the commons, maintaining the colloquial tone and style of conversation becomes a crucial unwritten norm.

For the KRS subforum and its preponderance of the Javanese language, the removal of formality should, presumably, be difficult. Javanese is an honorific language that contains three degrees of politeness, from the lowest to the highest: *ngoko*, *kromo madya*, and *krama inggil*. In Javanese culture, where being refined (*halus*) is an imperative conduct for politeness, to speak in the proper manner is to imagine an entire hierarchy of kingship and aristocratic society (see Siegel 1993). Each level of spoken Javanese signifies the hierarchical relation between communicants, a manifestation of social status and roles through which power is exercised. Communicants have to carefully select with which level of the language to speak depending on the communication partner (Siegel 1993; Irvine 1992).

Each level reserves its own specific expressions to convey emotions. James Siegel (1993: 15–44) describes how the least sophisticated language, *ngoko*, is the most intimate language and it is the first level of language that a child learns. Formality in this intimate language is, however, not simply dismissed as there is a social order among speakers of when, with whom, and how to use the language within the play of formality as well as within colloquial communication (ibid.: 25). Speakers are expected to convey a demand without dismissing intimacy (ibid.: 19–20). This practice is what the Javanese call being '*luwes*' (flexible). It is this flexibility that allows intimacy to be preserved.

Inhabitants of f=160 communicate mainly in the level that they considered most suitable for a playful chat, which is *ngoko*. The higher levels of politeness, *krama madya* and *krama inggil*, are seldom written, only on occasions where jokes and interruptions are not at all to be expected, such as in expressing condolence. The preference for *ngoko* to keep the merriness alive, eventually led to the dissolution of the Javanese aristocratic and social stratification in KRS. In everyday conversation when Solo Kaskusers exercise the *ngoko*, the offline world's social stratification is suspended. As such, the absence of an imaged hierarchy projects a sense of equality among Kaskusers and among Solo Kaskusers. Furthermore, the playful casual language of *ngoko* is perceived to be an instrument for establishing bonds and solidarity; by contrast, a formal Javanese assertion would be considered cold, suppressive, and unfriendly.

Kaskusers also converse using slang and euphemisms. The words, which at first signify the locality of Kaskus, are now widely used by Indonesians on other websites and digital spheres. Furthermore, Kaskus words, like '*juragan*' (boss), '*sundul*' (bump-up), '*cendol*' (green jelly), '*pertamaX*' (read: first comment), and '*meluncur*' (slide) are even used by non-Kaskusers in both the online and offline spheres. A cardinal term that emerged from Kaskusers' conversations is '*juragan*,' which means boss and is used to refer to the singular second and third person. In Indonesian, the third person is addressed by their gender role and hierarchy, like '*bapak*' (sir, father) or '*ibu*' (madam, mother), '*bang*,' '*kak*' or '*mas*' (older brother), and '*kak*,' or '*mbak*' (older sister). Such titles are further complicated as they need to be adjusted to reflect language conventions in the local ethnic language and the conception of respect within age as a hierarchy. *Mas* and *mbak*, for example, are only applicable in Java, while '*bli*' (older brother) is only spoken in Bali, and '*uni*' (older sister) is spoken only in West Sumatra. A person who uses the Javanese '*mas*' to address a Batak from Sumatra, for example, could be considered culturally ignorant and insensitive because in the Batak language, the term '*bang*' should be used. In Kaskus, employing 'juragan' is a method to avoid these hierarchical and culturally sensitive designations. The word *juragan* itself is commonly used in the marketplace to address an owner of a shop. In the realm of Kaskus, age seniority and ethnic cordiality are not only dismissed, but everyone is also a 'boss'.

Furthermore, the informal and casual language presentation style has made it possible for emotional expressions to be conveyed through a comical graphical display, such as emoticons and memes. The simple emoticon facial expression or meme character is, however, a complex code as it signals a complex imagination of an event. Both serve as an imaginative lever for Kaskusers to raise their sensory activity. They not only represent a comical graphic representation of a body language gesture, but are also a narration of imaginative events and communication happenings.

Some emoticons used in Kaskus are internationally common, while others have been developed locally. Local emoticons are created collectively by Kaskusers to represent local humor and the collective imagination of a typical Indonesian event. These emoticons, which remind us of George Condo's pop art, are called 'Kaskus-Only Smiley'.

'*Ngacir*', which means 'running away' in Jakarta's Betawi language, is an example of a completely locally-developed emoticon. The name of the emoticon '*ngacir*' is indeed local, but the running-away emoticon works not only as the imposition of an expression but mostly it works as a collective memory of an imaginative speedy motion that is understood by Kaskusers. In the forum, the emoticon is usually used by a post messenger to 'run' away from/to a thread after posting an aggravating or ridiculous comment, or to tour to a redirect link, or to provoke other Kaskusers' fast response to an action. Besides representing the 'quick' motion, the emoticon also ridicules the circumstance. These emoticons represent an imaginative scene of 'running away', or 'rushing to somewhere or something'.

The expression is animated and represented through three different animated emoticons: a running Linux-mascot penguin, an emoticon of a male and a female Kaskus mascot riding a speedy scooter, and a speedy Bajaj—the three-wheeled micro taxi in Jakarta. The *emoticons* are visualized with.gif (Graphics Interchange Format), which makes the emoticon both graphic and comical; as animation, it is not only read but also seen. Each emoticon represents a certain imagination of an event. The speeding-away couple emoticon, for example, is associated with scenes from comedy movies. Erick describes that he imagined the scene to be rather absurd. He explained, 'running away, but you could not go that fast with a Vespa [scooter]!' Erick himself never had such an experience with a scooter, but he understands the meaning of the emoticon: a comical depiction of a slow runner. It raises a sense of excitement, comedy, and, importantly, a lack of formality.

When such images are included at the end of a harsh post, the animated emoticons presented as a silly graphic are expected to tone down the chat's emotion and avoid debates or quarrels. They imply an action of 'hit and run', the idea that the writers do not want any further response and they are 'currently' running away from the conversation.

By recalling this imagination, or even a true memory, a shared experience is transmitted as a mutual understanding regardless of the true existence of the subject the icon is representing. One could simply employ an emoticon to underline a dramatic expression, shorter than any detailed textual description as readers have the cognitive ability to interpret it. Like Chinese characters and Japanese kanji, emoticon language is a logogram.

The language has become common and has permeated the online world. During a conversation in an offline gathering, for example, Wahyu once mimed the animated *ngacir* emoticon. He raised his hands, reaching for the imagined scooter handle to ride his 'air' scooter. All of that was enacted in 2 seconds, at the end of a humorous story he had told. Such emoticon miming has become common among Kaskusers and has become part of their everyday life gestures.

The use of emoticons and memes is therefore a mental process as it recollects a connection and an actual face-to-face communication with other Kaskusers. Employing an emoticon has to be exact, otherwise the intended message will not be conveyed and the installment of the emoticon would be a waste of presentation. Employing graphical display in text messages is a form of language skill.

The subject of technological innovation and development has been part of the debates investigating the reproduction of human skill. In his book, *A Brief History of Lines*, Tim Ingold notes as an example that the ability to draw and write are not natural talents but are instead skills acquired through learning (2007: 147–148), by functioning as part of our complex sensory experience and engagement. He argues that unlike reading simplified alphabets, reading calligraphy is adventurous, imaginative, interpretative, and challenging, criticizing the typewriter as it 'bears no trace of human sensibility' (2007: 143) and that 'modern electronic keyboards have removed even this possibility of expression.' (2007: 144). Contrary to Ingold's concern, the modern keyboard has made it possible for Kaskusers to present complex messages. Emoticons as logograms can be understood as the new calligraphy; they deliver complex sensibility for the readers and attachment among them.

While the medium might differ, whether it is a face-to-face communication, calligraphy, or emoticon, the intention is the same: to convey a certain emotion that is expected to create the same result among communicants. Each Kaskuser is expected to master such emoticon grammar and its emotional meaning so as to seize the most from the chat in its entirety.

Preece and Ghozati (2001) suggest that one of the strongest powers of virtual graphics, such as the emoticon and its contribution to online conversation, is that they provide a means to express empathy. A virtual hug, the example they pose, does indeed give the awareness of and evoke an emotional scene in the reader's imagination. It eventually communicates emotion among the distant communicants, as it is a product of both effort and creativity to overcome limitations (Preece and Ghozati 2001).

The emoticon is part of a collective code of an imaginary state of emotion. It makes the effect of the emoticon durable, through which the emotion perceived becomes real to the Kaskuser. In Kaskus, emoticons are part of a rich and informal perceptual experience that is no less than what is offered by other mediums. The information presented through an emoticon is condensed and it is as magical as descriptive text. Most importantly, it delivers a nuance of the informality of playful and warm communication; symbolic gestures from communicants that are sometimes even larger than the text itself.

### 2.1.3 *Voces Paginarum*

For Kaskusers, the presence of text is, therefore, not a silent world; instead, it presents the existence of actors who post messages. It denies a solitary digital experience. A text is placed within the possibility of readership and comments. Thus, a thread is not simply a register of messages, but a register of actors. Accordingly, the greeting, 'who's there?' is common when one returns to a thread.

Kaskusers' experience of how reading conversation can bring up certain emotion echoes scholars who argue that imaginatively, when people read text, they actually listen to it. Ingold (2007), citing Olson (1994), reminds us further that the more a reader reads, the 'more their heads would be filled with a chorus of such voices' (Ingold 2007: 14). This is what Olson coined as *voces paginarum* or 'voices of the pages' (Olson 1994: 183–5).

This example of a 'morning chat' in Kaskus exemplifies the voices of merriness:

| | | |
|---|---|---|
| Digital Location | : | Lounge Regional Solo |
| Source page | : | http://archive.kaskus.co.id/thread/16750389/100 |
| Date stamp | : | October 5th, 2012 |

*Post # 113 at 06*:57 AM// @andypitung: Good morning all.

*Post # 114 at 07*:17 AM// @okkirush: [quoting Andy's post] brother Andy. Early in the morning and you are online already.

*Post # 115 at 08*:24 AM// @super.pekok: @denmase_ari: [he wrote a song lyric from a local folk music group to tease @denmase_ari who is longing for his wife] not to wonder who would not miss, my dear husband. Hard to close my eyes. Not to wonder, who wouldn't be touched, being apart for some time, who wouldn't miss.

*Post # 116 at 09*:23 AM// @p0ng6ky: [quoting @super.pekok] wow, so early in the morning and you are singing already. I wonder, are you dancing as well?

*Post # 117 at 09*:26 AM// @asmoroaji: morning all

*Post # 118 at 09*:31 AM// @amakuzalek: [note: @amakuzalek is @denmase_ari, he has two Kaskus IDs] I am going to see my wife tonight!

*Post # 119 at 09*:41 AM// @laserferguson: It has been exactly a week that Prima could not log in. he is not with us.

*Post # 120 at 09*:49 AM// @amakuzalek: poor him.

The chat excerpt imitates that of a morning gathering among neighbors, where each neighbor knows the other's actuality: @super.pekok knew that @denmase_ari's wife was away and teased him; @laserferguson knew that Prima could not join them that morning because of technical difficulties; @okkirush was surprised to see @andypitung since he knows that the latter hardly joins a morning conversation. The conversation has no designated subject and was light, comprised of short posts. It was sequenced at a slow pace; the first post appeared a few minutes before 7 am and a post written at nearly 10 am marked the end of the page.

Andre, a Solo Kaskuser turned blogger, admitted that there was a significant chance of sensing a space's sociality between having a conversation in Kaskus and blogging. In contrast to the merriness of being in Kaskus, for him, staying on a blog page could become a solitary experience. Andre shared his experience of having a 'plain (*hambar*) feeling' when he left Kaskus and moved on to develop his blog:

> It feels quite plain, to be all alone (*sendirian*), when transitioning from Kaskus to blogs. [In] Kaskus it feels instant that there are things on going, [...] people could see what's there directly. It is not like that with blogs. We would get the appreciation [for the shared article] from readers only when they pass by (*lewat*), unlike the direct chats in Kaskus where we will get appreciation through discussion.

### *2.1.4 Home and Dwelling in Forum*

In a deeper experience, reading text conveys the sense of being home. This is the third layer of merriness. For Kaskusers, home is a specific subforum where they have steady chatting partners. It is where online dwelling takes place. Having a home in Kaskus establishes roots in the platform and serves as the foundation for identity, social recognition and warm connection, thus raising the sense of being part of a self-selected community(ies).

The idea of being-in-home sparks the next challenge: to establish recognition by other inhabitants. Unlike placing the avatar in the virtual environment like Second Life (Boellstorff 2008) or in online games (Pearce 2009), to hang out in spaces where text is the main visual representation such as Kaskus, existence is represented through chat messages not a digital body. Without posting a message, a forum member's existence will not be realized by others. Without a forum or a certain thread, a Kaskuser could not have a space and friends.

Kaskuser Harya imparted his experience of being an 'online refugee' after the forum for sharing pornographic materials, in which he used to stay, was closed in March 2008. 'I was like a motherless child (*'anak ayam kehilangan induknya'*). I signed in to Kaskus and did not know where to go. It was confusing. I had nobody to talk to,' he recalled. A user without a home, he then sought refuge in the KRS forum. His move to the regional forum was a strategy to avoid 'being lost in the digital world,' Harya said. For him, having a home provided a clear framework for the subject about which he was to post and chat.

This experience of being 'motherless' is emotionally disturbing for Kaskusers like Harya. It brings with it a state of emergency that makes finding a new destination—home—urgent. Unlike a newbie looking for a place and taking the time to choose a forum, such urgency drove Harya to quickly migrate to a new forum. After all, he could not remain a refugee forever.

Similarly, Sodron compares being a lurker, or an online surfer without a certain location to dwell, to being a 'ghost'. A digital ghost does not have a steady chatting partner and 'does not belong to any world', he said. Here, Sodron's classification of a homeless Kaskuser parallels Javanese popular myths in which the spirit form—ghost—is not accepted in the afterlife and remains in limbo and has no real goal of existence. While such spirits are not necessarily evil, the myth has it that they will always bother the living. 'Like the trollers and lurkers, they [Ghosts] only interrupt our flow of conversations' Sodron says.

The comparison between 'online dweller' and 'ghost' is a direct comparison between 'being social' and 'being uncertain.' Both Harya's experience and Sodron's explanations underscore the importance of a steady existence of digital friends and steady community connection confined to a certain online location. As such, continuous and routine presence and participation in conversations is needed.

Hence it is necessary to become a local by visiting regularly and participating in conversations to make other chatters aware that our digital persona exists. Such online textual manifestation to gain recognition in the crowd is what Indonesians and Kaskusers called '*ngeksis*' (existing). In sum, Kaskusers require two fundamental needs to exist: regular visits to a certain location and constant participation. This is the second discipline that one needs to learn to become a Kaskuser.

Space is therefore governed by a dynamic of 'I post therefore I am' and its inverse: 'I am therefore I post'. Consequently, the location(s) where the user joins the conversation indicates his/her interest, that is, his/her identity.

As a remark from a fellow Kaskuser indicates, digital presence is important: 'Say again, where do you normally stay?' This question was posed to me during my first conversation with Laserferguson when we met for the first time at KRS's weekly offline gathering. He was trying to remember if he ever heard, or read, my name on the web forum. I explained that I was actually new to KRS subforum, as I had been primarily active in other forums. Laserferguson continued to wonder about my strong point for a certain subject, as my name alone was not enough to introduce myself,

> Ah, but it seems you know the '*sesepuh*' [lit. the elderly; read: senior members] well, and I heard you were the Master Ceremony at the *buka puasa bersama* [Ramadhan's fast break, an event held by Solo Regional Kaskus]. So, I think you must have been in the regional forum for quite some time, one of the senior members maybe? But again, forgive me that I am so uninformed, in which forum do you usually stay? What topic?

Eventually, for Laserferguson and Kaskusers, the subforum represents not only a location of people with common interest, but also the pattern of a Kaskuser's online activity in Kaskus, which represents their subject of interest. Therefore, to them, a subforum is an identity. Mentioning the name of the subforum we frequently visit during an introduction is a way to let the other counterpart grasp our identity. Eventually, the composition of a text as identity presentation is rather complex. It is the sum of a Kaskuser's digital existence comprising the role play dynamic, subject of interest and chat location, and a strategy of how to form a circle of friends.

At the same time, the search for a group of online friends with common interests should not be considered a binary mode of selection. Having a home does not mean that once an individual decides to stay in Kaskus, s/he will no longer maintain her Facebook, Twitter, or other accounts. It is just a matter of selective temporal necessity.

Mailing lists and chat groups like BBM and WhatsApp groups, which also act as a medium for exchange and discussion, are considered closed groups by Kaskusers, as they limit the possibility to meet new inhabitants. At the same time, Twitter is considered too open to the public, which makes it difficult to identify who 'stays' in a conversation. Not to mention that for Kaskusers, Twitter's 140-character limitation acts as a barrier that prevents users from creating a deeper, more descriptive message. They consider social media platforms like Facebook, Twitter, and Path with personal status and photo updates to be heavily personal, and describe users who tend to use such platforms as interested in self-presentation rather than common interest. For Kaskusers, the online community is about a choice of having multiple social media experiences. In Kaskus, thus, they tend to dwell in more than one (sub)forum.

For example, Sodron stated that at times he dwelled in the Kaskus Regional Forum Solo as much as in the Anime-Manga-Hentai Forum where he had initially dwelled. William was simultaneously active in the Kaskus Regional Forum Surabaya, while at the same time administrating a thread in the Linux Forum. In addition to having the ability to dwell in multiple forums, Kaskusers are also active on Twitter and Facebook. @Becomingmoon, Sodron's wife, proposed the following analogy, 'just like we like to read books. [Now that we like to chat online] does not mean that we have left books. We do still read books, right?'

She also admitted that their offline lives are as lively as their online ones. Thus, dwelling in a digital space does not mean leaving the offline space; instead, it is an act of multiple belongings to various social cluster(s). Prima, besides actively moderating his threads, is also a student activist and is involved in various other civil society organizations. Surandy moderates one thread while dwelling in several other threads; he is also a member of a Christian community and church activist. For Kaskusers, both online and offline world forms are enriching realities. This interpretation of multi-social sphere echoes Wellman and Gulia who argue that it is a misunderstanding to see online and offline engagement as a zero-sum game (1999: 180–182): Social skill facilitates an individual's ability to become 'members of multiple communities' that could provide various resources (Wellman and Gulia 1999: 183).

Kaskusers explained that although hanging out with those who have similar interests is easier than those who do not, they do not place any preference on their online or offline friends. @Becomingmoon described that going online is a pragmatic decision: 'it is just difficult to engage with the [offline] neighborhood since everybody is busy with their own schedule'. By contrast, with friends from Kaskus, the neighborhood is located digitally and can be accessed using a gadget 24/7 and is already filtered by chat subjects and forum interest.

## 2.2 Reputation and Online Militancy

Home is a place that needs to be cared for; in Kaskus this requires lively and continual chats and, at the same time, a location where feedback is expected. Although Kaskusers can have several online identities and take on multiple roles and characters, they all need feedback to be able to converse. I could try to pretend to become a cat in Kaskus, as an example, but when no one writes back to me, what is the point of being a cat and going to all that trouble? Consequently, to be in a chat crowd or public, a Kaskus member needs more than location; a Kaskuser requires the certainty that the readership will recognize what/who s/he is.

### 2.2.1 *Crafting Reputation and Visually Ordered Regime*

After becoming accustomed to location of conversation and the written language style, a Kaskuser also needs to learn how to gain quality feedback, that is, how to converse. Without feedback, no conversation could take place and no merriness could emerge. A Kaskuser with a good reputation tends to have more chatting partners and is more likely to receive more feedbacks. There are two reputation signifiers in Kaskus: the 'ribbon' (*balok*, trans. log) and '*Statistics* record'. Consequently, these two signifiers also function as a monitor of a member's engagement. While a ribbon measures a member's participation quantitatively, the reputation record shows all the conversation posted by a member and is thereby a qualitative description of how one is conversing with others.

A ribbon consists of square badges. There are two kind of badges in Kaskus: a red badge named 'red-brick' (*bata merah*) which marks bad behavior, and a green-badge named *cendol* which marks achievements. Like military awards and decorations, the number of *cendol* signifies the number of rewards achieved and posts that a user has made. When a Kaskuser is considered to post valuable information or answers, s/he might get *cendols* from others as a reward. As a *cendol* functions as a sign of achievement, Kaskusers nurture their own digital hierarchy of merit system-based chatting contributions. On the other hand, a comment that does not maintain the flow of a conversation or is perceived to be 'Out-of-Topic' (OOT) will likely be deleted and the writer of the message will be sanctioned with a 'red brick' (*bata merah*) by others. The *bata merah* is a minus point to the post count. Posting a message or becoming involved in a chat, therefore, is not without risk.

A newly-registered Kaskuser, or a newbie, will automatically receive a gray badge. When the cursor points on the grey badge, it will blink with a tag 'this user has no reputation yet'. The post-counter serves as a barometer with an ordinal scale of ranking of reputation. The first classification covers 0–99 posts, during which a Kaskuser will be assigned the reputation of 'Newbie'. The highest reputation is 'Made in Kaskus', assigned to those with more than 50,000 posts.

Within this range of 0–50,000 posts count, the 2000th mark is determinative. It marks when the gray badge turns green. With a green-badge, a Kaskuser is granted a user feature that allows them to transfer badges to other members. For this reason, the 2000th post mark is also called the ISO 2000. 'ISO' is a word play between the acronym of 'International Standard Organization' and a Javanese homonym meaning 'to be able,' or 'can', which both point to a new level of reputation standard that gives the user the ability to reward badges to others.

Since green-badges or *cendol* signify how quantitatively diligent and active a Kaskuser is, a Kaskuser with more green-badges is considered to have regularly dwelled in forum(s), willingly participated in and learned about various chat subjects, and is thus an experienced dweller. As such, traditionally, Kaskusers with many green-badges will be respected by other fellows. Their opinions could direct a chat thread, and their chat will gain more frequent feedbacks. Having more than one *cendol* is a sign of prestige for many members. A merchant with more *cendol* tends to gain additional trust from potential buyers. Having a good public image is lucrative.

Before Bitcoin, *cendol* was already a currency in Kaskus. A Kaskuser needing a certain service or information could post a request and offer (a) green-badge(s) as a reward to those supplying the most assistance. In the Kaskus Market, it also functions as a payment method. When agreed in a transaction, a Kaskuser could pay for a service or a product with a *cendol* instead of with actual Indonesian Rupiah.

Green-badges and red-bricks are sentimental items. Receiving or obtaining a green-badge evokes a sense of happiness, satisfaction, and pride. On the contrary, getting a red brick raises the sense of subordination and exclusion leading to disappointment. These virtual exchanges are mentally interactive and affect the emotional state of a Kaskuser. It is a sentimental experience that decodes the users' assessment of being in Kaskus. Thus, in Kaskus, emotion is not abstract but is a visually ordered regime.

Prima recalled a period when he had an online quarrel with some Kaskusers back in 2010. He felt anxious when he had to log in to Kaskus as he feared he might have been 'bricked' by them. Prima's eyes narrowed into a glare as he told me the story with some emotion and excitement while narrating the experience. Harya was once challenged to an offline physical duel by a fellow Kaskuser after a harsh online debate. The contender was enraged that Harya had sanctioned him with red-bricks, turning his green-badges count post to zero. A red brick is indeed virtual, but receiving it devastates the reputation and online identity—that a Kaskuser has built through conducting good conversations and creating rigorous posts—as a whole.

Kaskusers have an emotional attachment to their online identity and reputation. An online identity is like a house of cards: it is built carefully to gain reputation in order to gain trust from other Kaskusers and to present one's existence in the forum. The worst punishment that could happen to a Kaskus member is when his/her online identity, or username, is confiscated by an administrator to resolve a conflict or a problem. A defunct identity nullifies the long hours of dwelling effort, wipes out the online character a Kaskuser is trying to build, and annuls the merriness of being online.

The green-badge and red brick mechanism as a social control, however, has already been betrayed by corruption. There is a weakness in the reward system: it has no due diligence algorithm to check how a Kaskuser actually obtains a green-badge. The first challenge is concerning the accountability of the reputation system because Kaskusers can buy green-badges in the online market. Second, the system has resulted in the dark play of Kaskus chat namely 'speed posting'. This practice is common among '*junkers*' or spammer or troll who participates in a chat or discussion merely to collect the post count without giving an acceptable quality post.[3] *Junkers* move from thread to thread, from forum to forum, to post short messages and they do not read the whole content of the thread. The goal is simply to accumulate 2000 posts or more to obtain more *cendol*. Currently, the speed posting method has become difficult to apply as Kaskus dwellers have created neighborhood watches to monitor threads and track *junkers* and their vandalism. Such manual monitoring, however, does not completely eliminate *junkers* and they continue to spam in Kaskus.

In the end, since the circulation of *cendol* is not regulated, inflation is unavoidable. The green-badge has become a reification of a reputation and is considered an ineffective participation system barometer. For that reason, quantitative participation is today to be viewed less as a prominent signifier of a Kaskuser's contribution to the community, and this has led to an active appraisal of Kaskus members' participation through a qualitative assessment of the 'statistical record'. The name is not revealing. The *KaskusStatistics* database does not present the quantitative performance of a Kaskuser, but actually a record of a Kaskuser's chat history. It is a digital footprint. Each Kaskuser's post and thread is archived in the *KaskusStatistics* database. The archive includes the sign-up date, forum and group membership(s), posted messages, thread(s) started, list of friends in Kaskus, and track record of activities in the Kaskus marketplace. Reading Kaskusers' digital footprint eventually creates a sketch of his/her online attitude.

An assessment of a Kaskuser's *KaskusStatistics* or digital footprint, by reading each of his/her post, will cue whether a Kaskuser has collected green-badges as a *junker* (spammer, troll) or as a contributor. When a Kaskuser is considered a *junker*, s/he will be perceived to be a weak chatting partner as s/he is considered too lazy to engage in conversation. When a Kaskuser does not have a chatting partner, s/he would not have an opportunity to *ngeksis* (to exist), thereby cancelling the possibility of experiencing merriness of online dwelling.

Conversely, those actively feeding the discussions and chats with quality posts—which can only be measured by subjective reading on the *KaskusStatistics*—will gain recognition. The more a Kaskuser is able to offer information, particularly in terms of sources that are often difficult to retrieve, the more s/he will be respected by others as s/he will be considered as a person 'in the know'. As a sign of respect, other fellow online dwellers will collectively address such a Kaskuser as the 'elder' (*sesepuh*) or 'senior'. This status is not a virtual rank, has no virtual attributes, and has nothing to do with age; it is a social recognition and entitlement. There is no competition to achieve it.

### 2.2.2 Online Militancy, Hoax, and Cybersense

In a textual realm like Kaskus, conversation is an arena to gain reputation and recognition. Currently, Kaskusers prefer to trust *KaskusStatistics* more than any other virtual attributes, making the ribbon honorific values almost obsolete. Sodron, an owner of eleven decorated ribbons, which consist of a total of approximately 17,000 *cendol*, expressed: 'I wouldn't care if something happened to the server and somehow I lost all of my green-badges. People will know who I am from my posts'.

Sodron's statement not only refers to the sum of his utterance pattern, but moreover to what Kaskusers coined as posting 'militancy'. Militancy on this stage means the ethic of diligence in providing useful information in threads and becoming a responsive chatting partner. The 'elders' (*sesepuh*) or the seniors, are the role models of what is considered a militant person. This creation of terminology creates two poles of distinctive opposite typology of attitudes in Kaskus: between becoming a 'militant'—the most contributory Kaskusers—to 'junkers'—the least contributory.

This sense of militancy appraises chat contributions through the stability of informative contribution. A militant could be a Kaskuser who is responsible for a thread, such as a Thread Starter or an administrator, and is expected to monitor the chat traffic regularly within hours. A militant could also take the role of a chat participant who is expected to engage in the forum and maintain the flow of the chat, if the shared desire is to keep the subject of conversation alive. A militant Kaskuser is also expected to provide, among other things, unique information, help others to answer particular questions, bring humor to the conversation, and provide updates such as citizen journalism reports.

With the proliferation of social media, hoax or fake news became a major challenge for the digital public in terms of information validation. Kaskus' now-classic cyberpractices of militancy and due diligence have actually resolved this issue. Kaskusers always conduct background checks on the persona responsible for the post. Posted messages and *KaskusStatistics* become data to approximate Kaskuser's online and offline characters. A post from a Kaskuser considered to be less militant will not be bumped up, making it unlikely to become viral. Militant Kaskusers would consider posting hoax is a risky activity because they could get bricked and eventually lose public trust.

Consequently, the totality of anonymity of the online identity is no longer a feature. Kaskusers can read each other's *KaskusStatistics* and collect clues about fellow Kaskusers' characters and interest. Like digital forensic agents, those who are well-trained to recognize a Kaskus persona and to approximate the character figure of the person behind the screen could approximate a description of the offline character of the subject. Reading *KaskusStatistics* is a practice of profiling.

In an environment that promotes anonymity and role playing, Amakuzalek views this ability to become a sleuth or profiler, as a 'sense' or as he called it, a 'cybersense'. As he stated, 'we have begun to develop a "cybernetic sense" (*indera cybernetic*), a sense to recognize what kind of persona this Kaskuser is acting. Whether we can trust him.'

Unlike bonding with new friends in online games, which has the winning end as a goal, the goal of online chat forums is open-ended. To learn about other fellow dwellers is a continuous journey of sensing. As signing up for a Kaskus account does not require any offline identity verification, cybersense is useful for understanding the chatting partner's character or behavior. Such efforts will, in the long run, help in maintaining the flow of the chat and building trust between communicants. Those considered to have bad *KaskusStatistics* will gain no trust from others. Amakuzalek provided an example:

> When you asked to meet offline, I went to your chat track record. You were not my friend and I, as an informant, I would like to know you first. After I read your chat history, I guessed that you are alright and would be a nice person to have a chat with. From your chat subjects, I also had to guess how old you are, whether you are fun to talk to, or if you are a serious person or just fooling around. Remember our first meeting? We met for like four hours. Do you think two strangers could actually chat for four hours? And you were asking about stuff from years ago, so I assumed you have also read my history. We could connect ('*bisa nyambung*') right? With newbies [read: those who have no chat record] it could be difficult. But, with a *junker*? I would not waste my time.

Not only had Amakuzalek 'sensed' my online persona, he had also tried to establish my offline character. The sense of connection, as Amakuzalek said, does not necessarily have to be a reciprocal communication. For Amakuzalek, that night was not our first encounter, as his first contact with me was through my *KaskusStatistics*. When we met, I was no longer a distant object for him although I never had any conversation with him.

I had a similar experience when I met Harya. When we met for the first time, we did not start with an introduction but went directly to chatting about our subject of interest as he had already tracked my tweets. Because of this preparation, our first offline meeting was like a meeting between old friends. This practice highlights the complexity of the Kaskus online world as a Kaskuser has to understand both the online and perceived offline characters of the chat partner(s).

It takes skill for Kaskusers to determine how to use their 'senses' to approximate another Kaskuser's character. The mastery of such skill ensures that the purpose of the initial chat is not to simply receive feedback or replies, but is a starting point in order to route what is coming, which eventually sustains a stronger connection with the chat partner.

Such an understanding does not position connection or contact and sensing as immeasurable technique. Instead, it views sensing as the basic competence of Javanese communication of *rasa* (feeling), that is, the means by which a person approximates his/her perceptions, feelings, and possible reactions (see Benamou 2010; Magnis-Suseno 1988: 125–128, 145–164). In the context of musical communication, Benamou (2010) illustrates that *rasa* or intuition is not an abstract scale but could be grasped through a lifelong learning approximation. The process is not learned from a formal or direct correction but from understanding patterns of examples and interpreting the common good (Benamou 2010). In this light, Kaskusers' digital practice in reading *KaskusStatistics* as patterns of examples is an exercise of intersubjective experience. It is an effort to create contact with the other subject, the chat partner, as synchronization to the communication process through text and the imaginative narrative of the thread or forum.

Zygmund Bauman (1998) suggests that intersubjectivity should be approached as a process of understanding the other in its own rights and terms since a product of perception should be free from any preconception. In face-to-face communication, we tend to correct our body language and communication style according to the feedback from a lively face. In Kaskus, the context of expression should be perceived from the words on the screen. Thus, approaching, studying, or sensing, another user's persona through the *KaskusStatistics* and reputation offers a more exhaustive reading of the text on the screen as the object is unable to directly correct his/her persona accordingly. Cybersense as intersubjectivity is, then, to know the other by learning our chatting partner's online persona and offline character without predisposition, using nothing but the text s/he has offered to the community. Kaskusers' experience of forum dwelling is, then, defined by an evolving perception and its exposure to and exposure to diverse personas. It also requires that users be open to the different characteristics their online neighbors bring to the Kaskus neighbourhood.

The lack of physical cues in virtual spaces requires the development of skills to look for cues in the digital realm to approximate the character of others, and this could only be mastered after having regular life-story sharing in chats (Rheingold 2000). Since ill-conceived statements will receive improper feedback, paying attention to the detailed stories presented in the conversations found in *KaskusStatistics* facilitates Kaskusers' ability to predict how they could quickly bond with their fellow online dwellers. Online communication therefore requires as much time and effort as offline face-to-face communication. In the online world of Kaskus, the first step of bonding involves investment in understanding the others by exploiting this 'cybersense'.

Hence, as a procedure of consideration to understand the context of the text, the emotional condition of the writer, and the possible character of the post's messenger, Kaskusers will engage in a careful reading before writing or replying a message. There will always be a reflective question that antedates the chat: 'what did s/he mean by that?' Avoiding misunderstanding is urgent as Kaskusers need chatting partner(s). It is often that a Kaskuser will rewrite the message, change or add an emoticon, or even cancel the message accordingly. This time-distance between reading and replying to a post is what Du Bois (2009) frames as 'stance', or the space of reading. Stance is the space between the text and the reader. It is the reflexivity and the procedural interior responses of a conversant that involves intersubjectivity.

It is therefore a signifier of the mental landscape of each inhabitant. As Sodron expressed, 'when we chat with somebody in a thread, we are not only trying to understand the information but also wondering who is behind the screen; what kind of an actual person is this?' Such a process is what Kaskusers also point to as the merriness of being in an online community. Tom Boellstorff, from his experience in a virtual hangout community suggests that such a process constitutes the 'wonder' or the experience of having a better understanding of the other digital fellow (2008: 248–249). In the textual world of Kaskus, text as the scripted speech is the resource of wonder. Thus, *KaskusStatistics* as a chat record is a complete digital footprint of what a Kaskuser has ever expressed in patterns and a resource to approximate what s/he intends to convey and receive in the future.

### 2.2.3 *Rich Communication*

By tracing a user's digital footprint, a Kaskuser is not only able to track another fellow's movement from thread to thread and weigh the quality of his/her posts, s/he can also discover a communicant's communication style, and thus a certain online personal trait. Kaskusers have learned that the language style of an online persona and personal signs do not vary extensively; the user's use of certain words, writing composition style, thread location and subjects of interest, and the type of avatar all have patterns. They therefore believe that as chat, text is a visual identity.

This sensing is important not only to assess Kaskuser's reputation but also to present a holistic online character to establish bonding. Even a humorous post could be meaningful in building trust. As Celia Pearce proposes, 'humor is unique: it's spontaneous; it's like a fingerprint of the personality' (2009: 258). Here is an excerpt from a morning chat from @amakuzalek as an example:

| | | |
|---|---|---|
| Location | : | Lounge Regional Solo |
| Source page | : | http://old.kaskus.co.id/showthread.php?t=16750389&page=54 |
| Date stamp | : | 16/10/2012 |

*Post #1061 8.17 AM//Amakuzalek*: 'Morning horny everybody!'
[emoticon:cutie:]
*Post #1073 9.34 AM//Amakuzalek*: *[start quote from Rajawali's previous post] Is the commander awake yet? I would suggest that we have a blood donation drive. Brother Pongky will coordinate the event [/end quote]*
Deal :thumb emoticon:
But I just had a similar event [donating blood and charity event] a few days ago.
[emoticon: surprised]
*Post #1075 9.42 AM//Amakuzalek*: *[start quote from p0n6ky] it seems you are no longer horny...:D [/end quote]*
It is time to work [sic]. Should put the energy into our work.
[rock-music-sign emoticon]

From these messages, Amakuzalek presented a persona that is male, not a conservative in terms of humor as he inserted a sexual innuendo in his first post [Post #1061]; his heavy reliance on emoticons shows that he is an easy-going person, and his text reflects that he is an active participant in Kaskus' social engagement [Post #1075]. He is a white-collar worker who has mobile or Wifi Internet access at his place of work at 9 AM. His use of language also indicates that he is likely part of the urban middle class who also likes to use English. He likes to start conversations, or is, at least, in the habit of giving a morning greeting [Post#1061], and by the time he posted those messages, he had already had conversations with @Rajawali and @p0n6ky, the two other fellow Kaskusers he mentioned.

Kaskusers' *KaskusStatistics* investigation method echoes Judith Donath's (1999) findings in Usenet. She argues that although Usenet members' offline identity could be hidden, anonymity is never absolute since the digital persona tends to convey 'signals' that reveal information regarding the user's offline identity or character. As Kaskusers are trained to identify these signals, they, in turn, are able to describe the chat partner's characteristic pattern. Imagining the gesture, the facial expression, and the act of speech helps the reader to construct the person s/he is dealing with.

Currently, no digital algorithm could sense a Kaskusers' digital persona to the degree that humans can. In terms of interpreting data as an entire complexity coded through avatar pictures, local innuendos and references, and typos, among others, the ability of a human being, or in this case a Kaskuser, is still better than Kaskus' programming algorithm.

While each persona is indeed a result of role play, Kaskusers believe that their cybersense can predict the character of the person behind the screen because the person would have some language patterns including certain words, spelling mistakes, writing style, and subject of conversation. Amakuzalek expressed confidence that even if he were to login using multiple usernames, his/her main online persona would be revealed not least because of how the sentences and references are composed:

> No one changes that much! We would know that there is a different person behind the screen even when they use the same username or online identity. As hard as you try, I could not be you. Our sentence presentation would be different and others know this.

However, the practice is never simple. The complexity of assessment and interpretation is much greater when we face a thousand chat messages, not to mention whether they come from different threads, forums/subforums, emoticons, time stamp, and chat partner(s). Emotion itself engages in the everyday life online experience. In addition to the empathy that stems from following fellow Solo Kaskusers on their personal digital media, emotions change intensely as per the mood of the threads, as part of intersubjective experience.

In February 2012, for example, on one single page register of f=160,[4] Solo Kaskusers encountered a thread of condolences for Surandy who had just lost his wife to cancer [thread #6], an FR thread on 'PlayStation Competition and Having Fun' [thread #8], a thread congratulating Sodron and Becomingmoon on their newborn baby [thread #9], a thread for a charity organization [thread #14], and a thread reporting criminality in Solo [thread #20]. When, as such, a thread celebrating a newborn baby filled with pictures and forwarded wishes is listed right next to a thread dedicated to a mourning friend filled with poem and prayers, Kaskusers need to adjust their emotions within a matter of minutes.

They experience sadness, happiness, humor, severity, and anger or fear, all within an eye sweep of a page read (see Table 2.1). Their emotions change with a click. Within those seconds of thread-hopping, emotional adjustment is required as the user needs to imply a proper emotional reaction when posting a message or meme or emoticon, since it will affect the textual and

**Table 2.1** Emotion and threads

| *Thread/thread starter* | *Replies* | *Views* |
|---|---|---|
| For Kaskusers who like to hike and trek | 581 | 6956 |
| Happy camping to Cemoro Sewu | 141 | 1460 |
| Many Javanese are ashamed to admit their ethnicity | 605 | 6255 |
| Training in giving speeches in Javanese | 185 | 23,241 |
| Pandawa Water Park | 329 | 8040 |
| Goodbye Grandma Sur [RIP] | 113 | 1272 |
| [Invitation for Solo Kaskusers] community for charity | 70 | 1381 |
| Field report: 2012 playstation competition [fun, togetherness and frolic] | 161 | 1382 |
| Congratulations to Sodronezz and Becomingmoon for their new baby born | 66 | 1007 |
| Distant healing program for Solo Kaskusers | 238 | 3956 |
| 2012 playstation competition [fun, togetherness and frolic] | 708 | 8147 |
| Let's go to the annual *Sekaten* city fest | 209 | 2744 |
| List of participants coming to *Jenang* festival | 57 | 825 |
| Gathering and volunteerism (*bakti sosial*) from Depok Regional | 11 | 138 |
| Regional Solo Kaskus anniversary | 47 | 775 |
| Proverb of the day | 405 | 10,863 |
| Stories about traditional games and toys | 212 | 3680 |
| Happy 267th Anniversary for our Solo City | 60 | 1069 |
| News: Solo city's electronic-ID administration named national best | 188 | 2412 |
| Share/information on crimes in Solo | 183 | 2533 |
| First night diary of *Wedhangan*—joining offline meet-up | 633 | 8218 |
| Q&A: All about Microsoft Office. | 57 | 1244 |
| Q&A: Problems with software/viruses/crashing/programs | 214 | 2740 |
| For Linux user | 948 | 8941 |

Page 5 of 32 registered pages
Sort by newest
Source: archive.kaskus.co.id/forum/160/120
Accessed October 1, 2016

language presentation. It is therefore important for users to remember that each message should be personal for it is addressed to our friends; otherwise it will be considered a junk post or disrespectful. There is therefore no room for emotional confusion, which only leads to stagnation in replying to these threads. Kaskusers' members are well-trained in adjusting their emotions according to thread titles and updating the latest emotional state from the latest post since they know each other and each other's lives intimately through intensive chat. Here, online spaces and digital gadgets serve to compress reality and the compression of emotional ups-and-downs.

Chatting in Kaskus forums is therefore a rich experience. It requires digital skills and technological awareness, involving emotional interaction, social interaction, and exploiting our emotional and sensory capabilities. The entire routine of encountering casual communication, reading emoticons, investigating *KaskusStatistics*, sensing the text and character of the online persona, and the sentiment of being in the community, all refer to a condition where a mediated communication presence is an experience that requires significant investment and productive engagement over time.

These social productions of Kaskus community exercise Kaskusers' sense, perception, emotion, and social capacity. Mediated communication, thus, is not secondary to face-to-face communication as it requires mental and physical interaction. It is also procedural and a productive activity as part of being in a community.

### 2.2.4 *Exchange: Friends as Repository*

The feeling of being in a community at the same time has to be lucrative. It has to be tangible as intersecting activities between participation and bonding in exchange activities among Kaskusers' everyday chat. On one hand, there is an expectation to become militant, while on the other hand there is always uncertainty about running out of subjects to talk about, which could eventually risk the bonding in conversations. It is, therefore, important to build a potential repository, or 'databank'. A repository is a series of information or a directive of web links that could be used to supply information.

In the 'Scholar Corner' forum of KRS in October 2012, for example, a Kaskuser started a thread asking for a list of local colleges. The Thread Starter was in his final year of high school and he wanted to ask Solo Kaskusers' opinions about each college in Solo. The thread soon became a thread for compiling public reviews about local colleges where Solo Kaskusers' posted reviews or information they had heard about the colleges. The discussion started with reviews from random colleges in Solo. Icesusujahe, only two hours after the thread started, however, brought systematic order to the discussion by providing a complete list of colleges in Solo altogether with their national ranks and accreditation status, while asking the discussants to submit their reviews under each listed college. Prior to that day, Icesusujahe had never come to the Scholar Corner forum. In a private message, he told me that although the subject of education is not his main subject of conversation, he was able to provide such data because he already had the college data in his 'databank'.

Surandy explained that the common practice of 'databanking' in Kaskus emerged in the 1990s during the early years when Internet connections were slow throughout Indonesia. At that time, Internet cafe administrators who had better Internet connections used their free time to mine random data to help those needing immediate information, and other users later followed suit. Databanking as a habit is rooted as an act of altruism.

William, as another example, started the tutorial thread 'Linux How To' as he was moved by the fact that many Indonesian Linux users came to Kaskus without finding the help they needed. At the same time, they could not access the international Linux online forums because of their limited English. He described his experience:

> Some [Indonesian] users could not speak English so they could not simply go to Linux's Q&A. But, every time there was a Kaskuser who asked a Linux-related question, s/he would only get an answer like 'just Google it' If you don't understand [the language], it would be useless too. I felt pity (*kasihan*) for them, so I build it [the thread]. I collected all the Linux tips and tricks from the Internet. I spent not only hours, but days. [Indonesian] Wikipedia was not that informative that time.

When explaining his motivation for starting the 'Scholar Corner' thread, Superpekok expressed that he felt the responsibility to become an academic discussion partner for other fellow Kaskusers. Through offline conversations, he recognized that many fellow Kaskus members were in the dark when it came to academic research. As a university lecturer, he was then motivated to start a Q&A thread about the subject. The thread gained sudden popularity as it served a purpose for many Kaskusers who were in their college years.

Another form of militancy is in providing citizen journalism reports, or what Kaskusers dub 'eyewitness reports' (*laporan pandangan mata*). These reports comprise current local information on traffic, accidents, weather and various current event reports. Wahyu explained:

> I think it has become a habit to update [read: report] something, especially an emergency. Indeed, it is different [the reportage quality] but still, you could read the flow of the news (*benang merah*), and the links to other blogs or recent info.

He chimed in: 'Now, every time I experience something, I just immediately remember Kaskus, and to share my experience there. Every single member is a potential contributor'.

He recalled that during the shocking terror attack at the JW Marriott Hotel in Jakarta on July 17, 2009, independent reports and photos were available on Kaskus even before news outlets managed to provide coverage. The first report was posted by a Thread Starter who was working next to the hotel. Soon, other Kaskusers who happened to be near the location posted replies offering various reports of what was happening at the hotel. The thread also turned into an emergency board, collecting data about those who had been injured, offering descriptions of safe routes for traffic, and links to police reports.

At times of natural disasters such as when the Merapi Volcano erupted between October and December 2010, eyewitness report threads developed comprehensive report montages of the civil collective engagement. Kaskus threads also provided a live report about the civil organizations that were involved in crisis management, information about what was needed for the rescue efforts, who was doing what and where, the effect of the disaster, and connecting communities, organizations and groups of helpers.[5]

These reports, while maintaining Kaskus as a hub, linked Kaskus posts to all other available media. Twitter, messaging services and Facebook served as announcement media to enlarge the outreach and media circulations, and YouTube was set as a space for visual documentation archive. This also underscores the degree to which netizens like Kaskusers do not confine themselves to a single platform. Instead, they maximize the possible features of various media to form a bigger picture, or as Holden proposes, to 'extract message bits, constructing a lived whole' (2006: 18).

While the motivation to accumulate green-badges is always present, organizing threads, databank mining and reporting on events require significant effort of volunteerism, too. Helping Superpekok in answering the Q&A in his thread, I soon recognized that maintaining a thread requires high discipline, time management, and benevolence; all characteristics that Kaskusers define as part of being 'militant'. It represents a Kaskuser's commitment to becoming a reserve for the community.

At the same time, a personal databank prepares a digital dweller for becoming a random chat opponent. The greater the potential chat literature, the higher the ability to help other Kaskusers, which results in a greater possibility for a Kaskuser to make online friends in various forums; that is, the larger the archive, the higher the conversations level and, accordingly, the Kaskuser's exchange value. In short, a databank increases the possibility that a Kaskuser will widen his/her social network. Because of such ethics of exchange and participation, Kaskus was gradually viewed as a space for the community.

In the development, friends themselves also become a repository, as Kaskusers draw on their friends when they are looking for help online. Friends are the patches of our databank, our eyes for events, our ears for gossip, and our partner in the vast online space. Their participation in inquiries is expected to be certain as we know them as our fellow Kaskus dweller. Thus, their existence and their participation is our safety social network. Having as many online friends as possible is therefore a strategic move to set a safety net. In this light, online chatting can be seen as an emotionally comforting action; it keeps our problem solvers and our heroes close.

Because of the importance of knowledge, questions like, 'what do you do exactly?' make up many of the initial chat encounters among Solo Kaskusers. Such questions are not simply an effort to test the approximation of what someone had already figured about the chat partner's offline identity; instead, it serves mostly to identify common networking buddies. Questions like 'do you know this so and so? He works there too,' or 'he lives there too' would follow to fill in the degrees of separation.

More importantly, such inquiries function similar to Laserferguson's initial questions to me about where I dwelled in the threads. They are used to investigate the Kaskuser's interest and capacity as a potential patch of information in the future. Such questions therefore are used to determine a Kaskuser's value. Accordingly, the purpose of chatting in Kaskus is sometimes aimed at filling the databank with people who can provide random insights to the user and to whom a user might be able to offer an exchange as part of our exchange value within our common network. It is a 'pay-it-forward', reciprocal practice.

Newberry (2006) describes that a chat in a working-class neighborhood in Java is scheduled as an afternoon ritual that maintains family-like ties (*kekeluargaan*) as the core of the community-building and is only interrupted by a bath and dinner. The chat is a medium for information exchange through which a member of the neighborhood can express his troubles and gain help from others (see Newberry 2006; Guinness 2009). Both neighborhood chat as a safety net cultural practice and online chat present similarities that provide the historical basis for Kaskus chat and data mining. As it is in the offline setting, online chatting is considered a 'standard' manner, to borrow Newberry's (2006: 43) depiction on the corresponding practice in the Javanese neighborhood, where a Kaskuser's consideration to share his/her actuality is perceived as openness and a readiness to hear and help other community members. This illustration of exchange and readiness as a part of becoming a neighborhood provides insight into Solo

Kaskusers' cultural setting. Exchanges in an online neighborhood emphasize the imagination of being in a community, whereby imagination is not an impractical myth but is instead a context for strategic action.

Those who register and keep coming back to Kaskus are those that share the feeling of a need for a neighborhood and a community; a 'home' as Harya described it. This is also tied to the offline world: in Javanese, 'going back to the community' (*pulang kampong*) has the exact meaning of 'going home'. In his work on community, Zygmunt Bauman (2001) asserts that community exists between the duality of social support and the regime of demand. We come to a community because we are seeking a warm connection, but eventually we are required to act and comply with the collective goals that sustain the community itself. Community is shaped through a collective strategy as members face crisis and 'look for individual salvation from shared troubles' (Bauman 2001: 144).

Translating Bauman's assessment, to experience being online in the Kaskus community and to have some merriness is not without a cost. The fellowship of online conversation is the underlying foundation for empathy, like in William's above experience, responsibility, like in Superpekok's experience, and, at the end, social solidarity such as that found in threads dedicated to humanitarian actions during the Mount Merapi eruption. Furthermore, fellowship and solidarity require specific individual competencies: time management, data mining skill, and discipline. Kaskus, an online community that was intended to be simply a place to chat, has indeed become a community that demands commitment and militancy to participate in the information circulation.

## 2.3 What Makes an Online Community?

'Community' is a subject notorious for its diversity and may be one of the subjects most often exploited by scholars. Nevertheless, the subject of community is a popular point of discussion in digital media studies as the new medium enhances how people bond and are interconnected. The discussion is, however, often overshadowed by its two optimist and skeptic poles.

Those who are more optimistic about the online community present evidence from the field that indicates that digital media has helped to strengthen social networks and will therefore eventually shape a community. They call for the open possibility of a new form of community and underline the empiric definition of community by its members through the function of community. For example, Rheingold's (2000) descriptions on virtuality suggests that 'community' is an accumulation of interpersonal communication acts as a pool of support and consort. Quan-Hasse and her colleagues (2002) emphasize the role of virtual presence, which leads to intensified interactivity and evokes a sense of care as new media connectivity raises the network capital, civic engagement, and sense of community in North American society. Their research starts with the assumption that the Internet is no longer a distanced medium but is instead a space where people meet and share, thereby enhancing solidarity and cohesion (ibid.: 294).

On the other hand, studies also show that there is a problematic distinct separation and antagonism between a digital community and offline community. Wellman and Gulia (1999) argue that even though such a bond of community through the virtual cyberspace is intimate, it does not compensate for the question of informality. While no virtual bond should be undermined, they worry that informal interpersonal ties are weak in nature (Wellman and Gulia 1999: 182). Furthermore, Beniger (1987) warns of virtuality and its identity shield, which means that virtual communities could face the online community's greatest ghosts; trust and identity coherency. He therefore calls the online community a 'pseudo-community', which is unable to replace the transparent traditional community. Putnam (2000) warns that civic interest in the individuated technologies could explain why the number of offline associations in the United States is declining.

In the time of online connection, before we even consider the undecided formality of bonding, the transparent identity connection or the civic participation of an online community as these studies describe, we should first look at the uncertain access to the community and its space. Access to a gadget and Internet connection is imperative for Solo Kaskusers, as both function as the access point to touch the community. At one of our offline get-togethers, Rheanz politely excused himself and hurried to top up his phone credit. Just before he left, he declared, 'I must top up my credit, my (prepaid) Internet is void tonight!' Having phone and phone credit is essential for Kaskusers; it is (one of) the main capital to keep coming back to f=160. Therefore, ensuring the ease of finding a mobile phone credit vendor in the offline surrounding is imperative for Kaskuser's social connection. Since a community requires space, space and place are no longer confined to a geographical parameter, but are enlarged to where the interactivity takes place where the point of access connection should be secured first. For Rheanz, were he late in going to a phone shop when he had already run out of his data quota, the Kaskus community would have disappeared for the night.

Recent scholars have brought this debate into context by looking at how digital engagement works in relation to the community's presence. Bruhn (2011), for example, argues that with the non-discipline form of digital community such liquidity of a community is not so much a matter of choice and struggle but a connection and disconnection to trust and solidarity. To describe this condition, he uses the term 'community of limited liability' (ibid., 24) where members exercise their rights to exit a group, juxtaposed to the question of loyalty and outcasting where a community member would leave the community if the collective demand is not fulfilled.

By contrast, Barry Wellman and Caroline Haythornthwaite's (2002) rich compilation of cases shows that digital community engagement is quite related to how people engage in the community where they live. Their studies are examples of an attempt to avoid the simplified relationship between the user and the gadget, while investigating how digital users relate to others and to the media, rather than assessing its form of 'community-ness'. This approach is necessary since community itself is not naturally objective and functional. Community as a conformist unity is therefore a myth (Bauman 2001). Bauman (2001) argues that the notion of community as 'a "warm place" that both shelters and nourishes us in a dense web of family and friends' is imaginary and historically vague. Community is a pool where social relationships need to be certain and, thus, it tends to be restrictive for individual autonomy to secure safety. In his assessment, social agreement is engineered rather than natural (Bauman 2001: 10).

Recent scholars, therefore, prefer to view online community engagement without the dichotomy or dualism of attachment and detachment, and to approach the phenomenon as what community members do as a unit, both against the interior or to the external (Fuchs 2008; Pearce 2009). The impact that comes out of it is a complex world of the whole that depends on each virtual experience. This approach of practicality underscores that media engagement does not exist along a certain projection; instead, it evolves with what both the new digital media and the user have to offer. The user is required to develop 'skills and attitudes' to mine the potential of a resource, as the resource has its own world to be revealed (Burbules and Callister 2000: 20).

### 2.3.1 *The Itch and Belonging*

If we treat digital media as an active object, it should be seen as both a gadget that serves a certain function with functionalities to be revealed and an acting agent that has a role in how communication is mediated, including how it will impact our bodily experience. Merleau-Ponty argues that 'all consciousness is perceptual' (1964: 13) with sense and body as the presupposing entry point for recognizing the tactile nature of the object. He proposes that perception is a bodily process that connects the self with the world it observes. Sensory revelation marks the relationship between the perceiver and the perceived object, both as the subject recognizes the object and as the object reveals itself to the sensory. At the same time, our bodies, as the center of the consciousness and the perceiving subject, are within the world, just like the perceived objects.[6]

Merleau-Ponty's (1964) account could provide an understanding of why chatting is perceptual and sensory interactive: it requires Kaskusers to type, search for appropriate pictures, emoticons, and subjects related to their offline background, to name but a few. The interaction not only comprises the visual interactions with the screen, the imagined *voces paginarum*, the sonic experience, approximating the person behind the screen, and other possibilities of sensing, but also the experiences of hand pressing the screen or keyboard, maintaining the discipline to do databanking, and other bodily experiences.

When gadgets and the online forums are essential for securing the regularity of reaching out to friends, the body is required to feel the tangible merriness associated with being in a community. It is therefore frustrating when we are unable to connect to our social media platform or to initiate touch with our gadget. Failed connections, broken gadgets, or slow connections, or website down dubbed 'Kaskus overposting' ('*Kaskus kepenuhan*') create dissatisfactions as they block the development of the emotionally expected social connection. With the interactive digital gadget, friends and communities become omnipresent.

A gadget is, then, a rich medium of being in a community, as it helps to raise the awareness of community space, physical interactivity and body engagement while opening access to a further perception and sensation of chatting-with-people experience. A gadget that does not evoke merriness (Indo: *asyik*) will be quickly forgotten, and, consequently, no online journey could begin. Clicking the gadget is a perceptual experience of what the gadget delivers, or in this context, it is the gate by which the KRS community is accessed.

For Indonesians, such sensory touch is not a foreign perception experience of reaching out the others. De Grave (2007, 2011), investigating the martial arts *Pencak Silat*, notes that 'touch' as a perceptual experience in Java extends beyond mere body contact and could be a metaphysical experience as long as the subjects can feel the effects. For those having trained in the martial arts, he describes that sense of contact does not mean a direct touch between body-operant, as contact is never singularly isolated within the location of physics; it could be mediated and constructed. To translate such experience in the Kaskus world, when a Kaskuser types a message to the dwellers in the thread, s/he is touching them. The user could even already feel close to the chat partner as s/he reaches for the gadget.

At the same time, touch is only meaningful if it results in feedback. When feedback is non-existent, the initial igniting touch would be regarded non-functional, or the non-existence of the online community. That is why Kaskusers always go back to the thread by touching the mouse or pressing their smartphones to read the comments and the feedback to see if their message has successfully reached others. As Icesusujahe told me with a smile and excited expression:

> I tried to be away from KRS for two weeks, that was the longest, but then I missed them [friends in the forum]. I felt the itch to click (*gatel nge-klik*) and submit the post. I missed meeting them, I missed their language; I missed the persons, their play [online persona]. So now, even if it is only for ten minutes I would check it [f=160]. Maybe it is just a moment (*sebentar*) when you go online and enter the forum, read a discussion in which a certain Javanese word comes up, it makes me really happy, reminds me of home.

The relation of 'itch,' 'click,' and 'the feeling of lost' formulate the relationship between the gadgetry touch and the mental delight of imagining being among friends. While the gadgetry touch is physical, it is also virtually imaginative and sentimental. The result of clicking, that is, when the gadget responds to show the chat text, the pictures, the videos, the emoticon, and other online properties signify a form of social connection. As Icesusujahe explained it, home and the perception of being among friends are just a click away from being reached. Being away from f=160 foments the itch to click ('*gatel nge-klik*'); to submit a post as the digital friends are being missed.

Van Loon describes such experience as 'mode of transduction' and argues that, 'by operating on the basis of 'touch', digital electronic communications can form networks of relationships in which bodies become neurotransmitters of extensive, partly disembodied systemic life forms' (2008: 128). It is, in his conceptualization, 'simultaneous connections' of 'being there'. Van Loon's notion of touch correlates with the merriness associated with a gadget as an extension of the social; that is, the gadget is part of being in f=160. When I am not touching my gadget, I am not in f=160.

As Amakuzalek illustrated, Kaskus is where his friends are, and they are a group of significant others that will accompany him 24/7:

> What do most people do when *ngaskus* (visiting Kaskus web forum)? For those who are signed-in and dwell in a forum, most simply to chat. Today, we could quickly read online news, and at the same time to have conversations with my friends about what we are going to do. They [my friends] are all in my pocket.

The metaphysics of presence endures because of the gadget's presence. It is an artifact of the memory and experience of being in a community. It is a reminder of what the digital connection signifies. The gadget has access to a person's online Kaskus persona, and Facebook and Twitter accounts. Hence, the new media gadget is personal and intimate property. It can be awkward, for example, to borrow someone else's smartphone.

Eventually this leads to a mode of what I call 'intensive communication', an interaction between members on a subject that occurs continually, minute by minute, hour by hour, day by day, until the thread or the forum is closed, only paused by one's agency to stop to post a message. As Kaskusers never log off, most forum members practically never leave the forum. Most have even saved their passwords in their web browser or their mobile phone's social media application to make access to the page easier and faster since they would check it at every possible time and frequently exchange messages. They know that such a method is unsecure and has a greater risk of a breach and identity theft if they lose their gadget. Nevertheless, the urge to simplify access to the forum is greater.

For such avidity, Becomingmoon explained that it should not be considered an addiction (*ketagihan)*, but a 'social habit' (*kebiasaan*). Through these chats, fellow inhabitants collectively evoke the sense of a 'warm connection' (*akrab*) and the presence of buddies as they spend a great deal of time talking to each other. When a Kaskuser starts to write a chat line, s/he is not merely shouting into thin air, but is expected 'express a feeling,' or what Indonesians call '*curahan hati,*' commonly abbreviated *curhat*, in public space. For Kaskusers, intensive communication is about the care of sharing life stories.

Social media features not only the immediacy of technology, but the glorious modification of time and space according to a user's agency. The user has the control to manage how fast or slow a connection is. This control also enlarges our agency of when we will be in the community, when we reconnect with our friends in our pockets, how we keep them there, and how we can distance ourselves from our community. We touch the screen only when we need to; we will be among our friends only when we want to.

### 2.3.2 *Modalities of Online Community*

Kaskusers had to build their community from scratch: creating web pages, threads, rules of chat and cyberculture. Kaskus chatting has become a digital practice that creates its space and cyberculture through information exchange, language expression, emoticon presentation, obtaining badges, databanking and cybersensing, employed in community practices. These are the modalities of the making of an online community. Online chatting practices determine how members associate meaning with their digital property and how their digital properties affect both their social relations as well as their attachments. It is a set of practices that shape the perception of Kaskus and its forum as a home.

The relation of Kaskus as a cyberspace and Kaskusers' practices as cyberculture is mutually influential. The lack of software capability in monitoring green-badge due diligence, for example, has made Kaskusers creatively engage in *KaskusStatistics*. This also eventually led Kaskusers to pay more attention to *KaskusStatistics* data development than the green-badges. Such interactivity is what makes media interaction meaningful for users. Joost van Loon (2008) underlines that products of mediation constitute 'specific orientations and sensibilities' while regulating how participants see themselves in their belonging and 'being in the-world' (ibid.: 132).

What this chapter emphasizes, then, are the procedural elements that need to be considered by Kaskus dwellers as part of an online community and its relation to digitality. First, online chatting could be considered rich communication. Similar to face-to-face communication, online chatting requires the skill and capacity to manage the properties of communication and its intersubjectivity dimension vis-à-vis Kaskus as a space and other fellow Kaskusers. It is also emotionally engaging; the corporeality of online chatting forms and wraps the mental ability to practice *rasa* and realize the metaphysics of presence. All Kaskus practices are possible because online chatting is interactive, hitting all seven details of interactivity: it is imaginative and comical, it raises productivity (databank, citizen journalism), it is perceptive (reading, interpreting, wondering/cybersensing), it is emotional, it controls time and space, it is bodily and sensory interactive (sensory, touch, sense) and it serves the possibility for multitasking or multihandling the threads, forums, and friendships.

Second, going online is a productive activity that requires discipline and leads to other activities. Online chatting produces its own skills, practices, obligations, and norms through its cyberculture and cyberspace. Since dwelling is an interactive form of social relations and sensory experiences, which could create new terms of the relationship by exchanging information or through their mundane chat, Kaskusers feed the imagination of community. Furthermore, as Kaskusers have to pave their way to gain recognition through regular and tactical participation in a forum, interactivity and participation become the new decrees of agency in the realms of digital technology.

Similar to the consumption of the material culture of a gadget used to access the online world and its personalization, engaging in an online community is a life journey, or what Ingold (2000) terms 'wayfaring'. Within the course of a collective life, community wayfaring is the relationship between the space as a location and the group's dynamic, which is reciprocal, recursive, and poignant for both sides. The intersubjective relationship between Kaskusers and the online space, gadget, and digitality is an undesignated, processional operation, and is eventually a continuous revelation; no one signed up for Kaskus with the goal of becoming a digital militant, or adopting the habits of databanking, or eyewitness journalism.

In sum, being in the digital public eventually requires more than simply registering on a website. It requires a mode of dwelling, which, in turn requires consistently presenting the virtual self or an online persona to the public and participating regularly in conversations in particular forum(s). Online dwelling is a continuation of the initial step of going online, and it is a crucial transition from offline to online as it decides whether one will acquire the online forum's merriness or not. These are things that were revealed to them by circumstances and that they themselves have learned after taking the first baby steps of dwelling in a forum. These steps eventually led Kaskusers to the next experience of going online: going offline.

## Notes

1. www.reddit.com
2. www.xda-developers.com
3. In Kaskus, a troll or a spammer is called *junker*<!--junker-->. It is a person who posts a message which is considered out-of-topic, unrelated, or has no point. Such a message, material that does not fuel the chat, is called 'junk post'. A *junker* is not necessary a flamer. A flamer is what is internationally termed 'troller'. For further study on trolling, see: Judith S Donath, "Identity and Deception in the Virtual Community," in *Communities in Cyberspace*, edited by Marc A. Smith and Peter Kollock (Routledge: London, 1999), 27–58.
4. https://archive.kaskus.co.id/forum/160/120
5. Post by @Mbah_Soer with the title '[Official Kaskus Solo Peduli Merapi] Mari Menghibur dan Membantu Pengungsi Merapi'. Accessed March 5, 2013. http://archive.kaskus.co.id/thread/5811592/0#
6. Our entirety, body and mind, is a 'sensorium commune' (Merleau-Ponty 2002: 277) that will first dependently react to or reflexively recognize the object—not because we already know the object. Merleau-Ponty concludes that between the subject and the object, they are connected, rather than mutually exclusive elements. The perceived object is 'a totality open to a horizon of an indefinite number of perspectival views' (1964: 16). He illustrates that our body will transform into a car while driving as if we know it is 'in the hands' (ibid.: 166) and we do not think of the separation between the spatial direction of the car and the hand's sensitivity to tilting the steering wheel (Merleau-Ponty 2002: 165–166).

## References

Bauman, Zygmunt. *Work, Consumerism and the New Poor*. 1st Edition. Buckingham: Open University Press, 1998.

Bauman, Zygmunt. *Community: Seeking Safety in an Insecure World*. Cambridge: Polity, 2001.

Benamou, Marc. *Rasa: Affect and Intuition in Javanese Musical Aesthetics: Affect and Intuition in Javanese Musical Aesthetics*. Oxford: Oxford University Press, 2010.

Beniger, James R. "Personalization of Mass Media and the Growth of Pseudo-community." *Communication Research* 14, no.3 (1987): 352–371, accessed March 1, 2014. DOI: 10.1177/009365087014003005.

Ben-Porat, Amir. "Split Loyalty: Football-cum-Nationality in Israel". In *Fringe Nations in Soccer*, edited by Kausik Bandyopadhyay and Sabyasachi Mallick, 106–121. Oxon: Routledge, 2013.

Boellstorff, Tom. *Coming of Age in Second Life*. New Jersey: Princeton University Press, 2008.

Bruhn, John G. *The Sociology of Community Connections*. Second Edition. Dordrecht: Springer, 2011.

Burbules, Nicholas C. and Thomas A. *Callister Watch It: The Risks and Promises Of Information Technologies for Education*. Colorado: Westview Press, 2000.

De Grave, Jean-Marc. "L'initiation Rituelle Javanaise et ses. Modes de Transmission: Opposition Entre Javanisme et Islam." *Techniques & Culture* 1, no. 48–49 (2007): 85–124. Accessed March 1 2014. DOI: 10.4000/tc.3032.

De Grave, Jean-Marc. "The Training of Perception in Javanese Martial Arts." In *Martial Arts as Embodied Knowledge*, edited by D. S. Farrer, 123–144. New York: SUNY Press, 2011.

Donath, Judith S. "Identity and Deception in the Virtual Community." In *Communities in Cyberspace*, edited by Marc A. Smith and Peter Kollock, 27–58. London: Routledge, 1999.

Du Bois, John W. "Interior Dialogues The Co-Voicing of Ritual in Solitude." In *Ritual Communication*, edited by Gunter Senft and Ellen B. Basso, 317–340. Oxford: Berg, 2009.

Fuchs, Christian. *Internet and Society: Social Theory in the Information Age*. New York: Routledge, 2008.

Guinness, Patrick. *Kampung, Islam and State in Urban Java*. Singapore: NUS Press, 2009.

Hill, David T. and Krishna Sen. *The Internet in Indonesia's New Democracy*. Oxon: Routledge, 2005.

Holden, Todd Joseph Miles. "Theorizing Media in Asia Today." In *Medi@sia: Global Media/tion In and Out of Context*, edited by Holden, Todd Joseph Miles and Timothy J. Scrase, 1–22. Oxon: Routledge, 2006.

Ingold, Tim. *The Perception of the Environment: Essays on Livelihood, Dwelling & Skill*. London: Routledge, 2000.

Ingold, Tim. "Epilogue: Towards a Politics of Dwelling." *Conservation Society* 3, no.2 (2005): 501–508.

Ingold, Tim. *Lines: A Brief History*. Oxon: Routledge, 2007.

Irvine, Judith T. "Formality and Informality in Communicative Events." *American Anthropologist* 81, no. 4 (1979): 773–790. Accessed March 1, 2014. DOI: 10.1525/aa.1979.81.4.02a00020.

Irvine, Judith T. "Ideologies of Honorific Language." *Pragmatics* 2, no. 3 (1992): 251–262.

Lim, Merlyna. "The Internet, Social Networks, and Reform in Indonesia." In *Contesting Media Power: Alternative Media in a Networked World*, edited by Nick Couldry and James Curran, 273–88. Maryland: Rowman & Littlefield, 2003a.

Lim, Merlyna. "From Real to Virtual (and Back again): Civil Society, Public Sphere, and Internet in Indonesia." In *Asia.com: Asia encounters the Internet*, edited by Kong-Chong Ho, Randy Kluver and Kenneth C. C. Yang, 113–128. London: Routledge, 2003b.

Magnis-Suseno, Franz. *Etika Jawa: Sebuah Analisa Falsafi Tentang Kebijaksanaan Hidup Jawa*. Jakarta: Gramedia, 1988.

Merleau-Ponty, Maurice. *The Primacy of Perception: And Other Essays on Phenomenological Psychology, the Philosophy of Art, History, and Politics*. Evanston: Northwestern University Press, 1964.

Merleau-Ponty, Maurice. *Phenomenology of Perception*. London: Routledge, 2002.

Newberry, Janice C. *Back Door Java: State Formation and the Domestic in Working Class Java*. Toronto: University of Toronto Press, 2006.

Olson, David R. *The World on Paper: The Conceptual and Cognitive Implications of Writing and Reading*. Cambridge: Cambridge University Press, 1994.

Pearce, Celia, and Artemesia. *Communities of Play. Emergent Cultures in Multiplayer Games and Virtual Worlds*. Massachusetts: MIT Press, 2009.

Preece, Jennifer J. and Ghozati, K. "Experiencing Empathy Online". In *The Internet and Health Communication: Experience and Expectations*, edited by R. R. Rice and J. E. Katz, 237–260. Thousand Oaks: Sage Publications, 2001.

Putnam, Robert D. *Bowling alone: The Collapse and Revival of American Community*. New York: Simon and Schuster, 2000.

Quan-Haase, Anabel, Barry Wellman, James C. Witte, and Keith Hampton. "Capitalizing on the Net: Social Contact, Civic Engagement and Sense of Community." In *The Internet in Everyday Life*, edited by Barry Wellman and Caroline Haythornthwaite, 291–324. Malden: Blackwell Publishers, 2002.

Rheingold, Howard. *Virtual Community*. Originally published by Addison Wesley, 1993. Massachusetts: MIT Press, 2000.

Siegel, James T. *Solo in the New Order: Language and Hierarchy in an Indonesian City*. New Jersey: Princeton University Press, 1993.

Van Loon, Joost. *Media Technology Critical Perspective*. Berkshire: Open University Press McGraw-Hill Education, 2008.

Wellman, Barry and Milena Gulia. "Virtual Communities as Communities: Net Surfers Don't Ride Alone". In *Communities in Cyberspace*, edited by Marc A. Smith and Peter Kollock, 167–194. London: Routledge, 1999.

Wellman, Barry, and Caroline Haythornthwaite. *The Internet in Everyday Life*. Malden: Blackwell Publishers, 2002.

CHAPTER 3

# Going Offline, Order and the Environment

It was on a Saturday evening at a street food stall, or what is popularly called '*lesehan*' in Javanese, when I joined the Solo Kaskusers' offline meet-up for the first time. After establishing f=160 as a chatting forum, Solo Kaskusers began having weekly offline meet-ups there every Saturday where they could order local finger foods, snacks and drinks. The food stall is located directly in the city center and is considered a strategic meeting point that most Solo Kaskusers could reach. It is only 300 meters away from one of the largest malls in the city, Solo Grand Mall, as well as shops and various city landmarks, and 200 meters away from the mayor's official residence. Directly facing the city center's prominent street, Jalan Slamet Riyadi, the food stall shares a corner wall with the city's oldest football stadium, next to the oldest recreational park complex, Sriwedari. It occupies the pedestrian sidewalk and is illuminated only by street lights.

Every Saturday night, the *lesehan* manager reserves a spot for Solo Kaskusers to hang out starting at 8 p.m. It was one of those Saturday nights when Armin and I arrived a little bit earlier than the regularly scheduled time. As the first to arrive, we had the duty of preparing the plastic mats for sitting, just two meters away from the condensed city center's Saturday night traffic. Armin reached his Blackberry and tweeted, 'I am already here. Get moving!' He ended the tweet with the KRS hashtag, mentioning @KaskusRegSolo. He then strolled through several forums on Kaskus to get himself up-to-date.



A. Seto, *Netizenship, Activism and Online Community Transformation in Indonesia*, DOI 10.1007/978-981-10-5397-9_3

Minutes later, KRS members started to arrive. With the exception of Kris and Surandy, who are older than forty, most participants are younger, ranging from teenagers to those in their early thirties. Half an hour later, we were a group of eighteen, six of whom were women. Kris had asked his wife and daughter to come, while Harya, the Regional Leader, came with his girlfriend.

We all sat on the floor making a circle and started to chat with each other. The conversation would usually begin with the currently trending subjects in f=160 or from Kaskus general forums. Solo Kaskusers exchanged actualities from the threads and forums where they dwell while also chatting about other random subjects. Coming to such an event is always beneficial for keeping up with the news from other threads and forums. During the offline meet-ups, Solo Kaskusers also sometimes chit-chat about their personal lives, a subject that sometimes does not surface in f=160 but comes up during personal communication. Some Kaskusers often offer rides home to those who came on public transport. Thus, over time, Solo Kaskusers began to learn where the others live in the city; information that would not normally be obtained if the conversation remained online in Kaskus' shielded-identity world. By going offline to the meet-ups, Kaskus friendship transcended the reality of Kaskus threads.

That night, Prima and Plerdisk started to discuss about the preparation for the upcoming community's *Iftar* (fast-breaking during Ramadan, Ind. *buka puasa bersama*, abv. *bukber*) during which they would visit an orphanage and organize a charity dinner. However, Mochi, the appointed project officer for the event, quickly moved away from her sitting place and left the conversation, expressing her objection to the topic of chat. She that the evening's meet-up was intended to be a relaxed gathering instead of an organizational meeting of an event.

In the other corner, Prima, in his 30s, was playing a Sony PlayStation Portable he had borrowed from another Kaskuser, Hanung. Next to him, Kris sat with his family. Others had dispersed into small chatting groups. We all stayed at the food stall until about ten o'clock when Surandy excused himself to go home to care for his ill wife. We paused our conversations abruptly and expressed our best wishes for Surandy's wife, as she had recently been diagnosed with cancer. Shortly after that, other Kaskusers began to say goodbye and left the meeting. Harya, as a Regional Leader (RL), stayed until the last person left the meet-up. While there is no regulation that states that an RL should stay until the end of the meet-up, Harya just wanted to be the host.

For Solo Kaskusers, the weekly offline meet-up is an extended dwelling of the online forum. The food stall is the offline form of f=160. There, we greeted other fellows, located ourselves in a sitting spot as if dwelling in a thread, and eventually joined a discussion or a conversation that interested us. When the conversation did not suit our interest, we could, like Mochi did that night, move around to find a suitable group. At the end of the meet-up, we left the spot knowing that we would return next week, just like the habitual practice of signing back into Kaskus. There is no obligation to attend the meet-up regularly, yet, the event is held regularly each week simply to provide a space to those who will come.

This offline meet-up is typical for Kaskus forums across the archipelago, some take place weekly, monthly, or based on the forum's mutual agreement. It is a get-together evening without a specific meeting agenda other than hanging out. Such offline meet-ups of an online community are widely known in Indonesia as *kopdar*—the commonly used portmanteau of *kopi darat. Kopi* is an Indonesian homophone, meaning either 'coffee' or 'copy'. While the first represents an activity of having a coffee together, the latter is a procedural confirmation-speech from walkie-talkie communication practice indicating that a listener could hear the transmitted message. *Darat* is a homograph, meaning 'ground' as opposed to 'air', thus it means 'off-air'. As a compound, *kopi darat* means off-air meet-up, or having a coffee together while off-air.

Indonesian off-air meet-ups are rooted in the 1980s, the heyday of amateur radio communication such as Community Band (CB) radio service and the walkie-talkies. Recalling his own experience, Surandy explained that even when the CB radio service could only cover smaller residential areas, such as a Kampong where communicants already knew each other, they were nevertheless keen to have a face-to-face off-air meet-up. Off-air meet-ups, he said, became an event where radio-communicants would gather to chat about subjects they had yet to talk about on-air. 'Today, you could read all the chats in the thread, so if you go offline for a day, you still could catch up the actualities simply by reading what's online. Back then, there was no Internet, so you would miss actualities from the neighborhood if you didn't turn on your CB radio. That's why we had *kopi darat*', he clarified.

*Kopdar* is a common event among Indonesian online groups and each Kaskus forum has one, with its own name. In KRS, it is called '*Wedhangan*', a Javanese term for having a warm drink. The verb and the noun denote the social act of having a drink with other people and cannot be applied to a single person drinking alone. In Central Java, like in Solo, the term is strongly associated with the activity of drinking and chatting in *lesehan*.[1] The food stall is the Javanese café; here, locals gather at lunchtime or after work during suppertime to exchange news or to simply enjoy finger food (Rukmana and Purbadi 2013).

Offline *wedhangan* meet-ups are not only held in Solo but also in Jakarta to accommodate Solo Kaskusers who live in the capital city metropolitan area, around 550 kilometers away from Solo. Icesusujahe, one of the Solo Kaskusers based in Jakarta and the person who was responsible for organizing the first *wedhangan* in Jakarta, explained that a longing for typical hometown finger food and chatting in Javanese while having an *Iftar* meet-up were the two reasons why Solo Kaskusers who lived in Jakarta organized their first offline meet-up in October 2007. They eventually agreed to meet up and find a *lesehan* in Jakarta. Ever since, similar to the regularities in their hometown, Solo Kaskusers in Jakarta have organized regular *wedhangan* events every Saturday. The event has become popular with participants from various other forums attending, and was later dubbed the Jakarta Chapter Wedhangan for Multiregional Kaskusers.[2]

In Solo, the offline meet-up was initiated a year earlier simply because some Solo Kaskusers wanted to hang out together. As Armin explained when he was trying to remember what the motive was for the initial offline meet-up in Solo: 'There was no reason at all. I guess because coincidentally it was a weekend and we had nothing to do'. Nonetheless, these mundane meet-ups have become the disciplining regime as a dimension that solicits community members' obedience to internal solidarity as this chapter illustrates.

## 3.1 The Procedures of Going Offline

At first, offline meet-ups in Solo were simply irregular events with no official invitation. The meetings were completely spontaneous and arranged by some Kaskusers through the IM chat platform Yahoo!Messenger, not on Kaskus' thread. Armin explained that during that early era of offline meet-ups, most occasions would end with Solo Kaskusers getting drunk while hopping from food stall to another food stall and sometimes from bar to bars. The meet-up became widely known as a 'boy's event', he added. This is the period Prima dubbed as an era of '*viva hura-hura*' or 'long live the party.'

Armin recounted that it was not until 2008, or two years after the establishment of f=160 and the first *wedhangan* night, that offline meet-ups became regular and were intended to be a second forum for the online community to see each other. In June that year, Prima, a camping enthusiast, started a thread asking whether anyone would like to join him for a hike or a 'picnic' as he called it.

'I like to hike, and I was asking simply if anybody wanted to join me. Also, I was simply curious to see how far an online persona could differ from the offline character. I simply thought at that time that it was exciting to meet a Kaskuser [in the offline] in-person,' he said. The idea of having a picnic with a group of friends whom he never met face-to-face intrigued him. He assumed that during a highly engaging activity such as a picnic, he could know (*mengenal*) more about the other Kaskusers above the daily practice of *cybersensing*.

The thread soon gained a great deal of attention and many replies. It was listed as a hot thread and listed on f=160's front page. Some Kaskusers offered to arrange the logistics and some others expressed their opinions regarding options for time and location. Soon figuring out the details became complex—it is important to remember there were no web applications for scheduling, such as Doodle, at that time—and Armin suggested that they should all meet offline to make a plan.

From more than twenty Kaskusers who had posted their eagerness to join the picnic, only five Solo Kaskusers (Prima, Armin, Pikomon, Diablos, and Flew_meneer) showed up to the meeting. This low attendance prompted a fear among them that online enthusiasm was not an equivalent to concrete offline participation. When Prima recounted the experience, he still seemed disappointed: 'it was supposed to be our first event together. Unlike the casual meet-up to get drunk, we had to prepare the hike thoroughly. But, nobody showed up!'

### *3.1.1 'Messy Online, Messy Offline'*

The meet-up that night, which was initially intended to prepare for the picnic, eventually shifted to a discussion problematizing the meaning and purpose of offline meet-ups. During the meeting, Armin expressed his concern that the contents of the online threads and the activities in offline meet-ups at that time had created a depiction of Kaskus as a location where people tend to condone crass talk, making sensual jokes, and getting drunk. Accordingly, he and the others worried if the picnic—and the offline meeting to arrange such a thing—had been depicted and predicted by other Kaskusers in general as a similar event, and thereby the likely reason for that night's low turnout.

Indeed, those who did not come for the meeting that night actually shared the same concern. For instance, Surandy, a devoted Christian who does not drink alcohol, recalled that the uploaded visual documentations of previous *wedhangan meet-ups*, at that time, had constructed a certain public image that KRS was becoming a space for young men and their parties, which led him to feel excluded.

The discussion went further, as the five Solo Kaskusers correlated the trending Kaskus online content with the minimum rules of dwelling in Kaskus. Armin expressed in the meeting: 'It was a messy disordered online; it was a messy disordered offline'. He described the relationship between online conduct and offline attitude during the interview in 2012:

> At that time, [some] attended *wedhangan* only to get drunk together and was just pointless (*nggak jelas*). At the same time, some people began to avoid the [online] forum because of the unregulated explicit inappropriate posts [like the pictures from the *wedhangan*]. Although I joined the party, I was also one of the very few to warn other Kaskusers [about their explicit posts]. I started to feel bad because they are also my friends. On the other hand, it was becoming apparent that there was no order among us. When there are no strict regulations in the online space, of course there will be also no proper conduct in the offline meet-ups. People will just do what they want.

Armin added that he, to avoid being considered 'playing the saint' by the others, preferred that the forum be regulated collectively rather than taking on the role of vigilante to scold those posting explicit contents.

Explicit content with harsh language and adult pictures were commonly found in Kaskus' early years because of the loose interpretation of 'online freedom'. When it was first launched in 1999, Kaskus was hosted on a server located in the United States and it was common at that time that a US-based website would have a disclaimer stating the Dotcom's ideology of freedom of expression or speech.[3] The disclaimer denied Kaskus' responsibility for any liability in terms of what Kaskusers were posting. It states:

> KASKUS is providing freedom of speech. By using KASKUS, you agree to the following conditions; the User expressly agrees that the use of KASKUS is at the user's own risk and it is not the risk of the owner or the web host. The User specifically acknowledges that KASKUS is not liable for the defamatory, offensive, or illegal conduct of other users or third-parties in

cases including but not limited to any interactive communication on or through the site and that the risk of the former rests entirely with user(s) [sic]. (www.kaskus.co.id)

Kaskus' disclaimer, written at the bottom of every page of the web forum, was, however, not intended to be a political ideal or to advocate any sort of liberal practices. Instead, as founder Andrew Darwis explained, it served simply as a warning to visitors that they should not blame Kaskus if they were offended by chats in the online forum as content management was minimal. He was motivated to include the disclaimer as he recognized that Internet users at that time tended to openly express their voice in online forums as they were celebrating the Internet as a new medium with fewer constraints. He was therefore worried that he or Kaskus might be subjected to litigation by some offended visitor, Kaskuser, or other parties while reading content they deemed to be inappropriate. Although young technocrats and the Indonesian government had attempted to promote the Internet as a space for educational resources since the mid-1990s, early Indonesian net goers at that time would simply depict that the online sphere is simply a censor-free space, Darwis explained.

Surandy illustrated that some Kaskusers interpreted such environments as a chance to escape general Indonesian constraining social norms in the offline world. As Armin put it: 'Suddenly, you could talk about sex, write anything explicitly, and make sensual jokes; things that you could not do offline'. In its initial years, Kaskus traffic was filled with materials and communications that would have been difficult to find in the offline world: pornographic materials, images, and video sharing were hosted in BB17 Forum (*Buka-bukaan* 17, trans. Stripped 17); illegal and pirated software in the hacker forum of '*Cara Curang dan Program Pembajakan*' (abv. CCPB, trans: Tricks and pirated software); and the 'Fight Club' (FC) debate forum, which allowed the use of explicit language and became a location for politically incorrect or culturally insensitive slanders.

Instead of developing further into a student bulletin as Darwis had intended, Kaskus rapidly became popular because of these notorious forums.[4] Its existence was quickly spread by word-of-mouth in the Indonesian online sphere. Coincidentally, it was also around the time when mobile telephones with cameras became increasingly popular and inexpensive. As Harya generalized: 'We have to admit, when you meet a Kaskuser with an old join date, say early 2000s, and that person happens to be a male who does not seem to be a religious man, then you suspect that he had joined Kaskus merely for downloading or sharing pornographic materials. It was simply a common fact'.

The circulation of BB17 pornographic content and FC harsh language could not be confined locally in those two forums since many members would bring the popular subjects, images, sexual innuendo or other explicit messages to other subforums and locations in Kaskus. Such circulation could also be found in f=160. Threads with sexual content were commonly found and even became popular. Threads such as, 'Who's on top of you?', and 'What is the color of your or her underwear today?' remained on the f=160's main page for three years.[5] Even the thread 'What would you do if you had a sexy housekeeper?' lasted for four years after it was started.

The general chatting lounge was also dominated by sensual messages and it was not rare for a Kaskuser to post adult pictures. For their avatar, some Kaskusers would have an image or animated image in.gif format of a naked person or persons performing sexual acts. Sensual innuendos were also common in the threads. '*Selamat pagi*' (good morning), for example, was often written as '*selamat vagi*' (greetings to the vagina) where '*pagi*' (IPA: pagi) and '*vagi*' (IPA: vagi) almost sound the same. These comprise a few examples of how BB17 affected online chats throughout f=160 and other subforums throughout Kaskus' first decade.

Solo Kaskusers attending the meeting for the picnic preparation then assumed that the minimum regulations for chats and the simplistic interpretation of 'Kaskus' online freedom' had directed the '*viva hura-hura*' mode of offline meet-ups, with the latter immiating the first. They feared that there was a tendency among Kaskusers to transfer their loose understanding of freedom, which they grasp from the online sphere, simply to the freedom of excessive alcohol consumption during the offline meet-ups.

Assessing the situation at that time, the five Solo Kaskusers pointed out two risks of unregulated chat. First, explicit posts would spread across the forum and dissuade new potential members. Although he did not attend the meeting, Sodron shared the same opinion that the way Kaskusers had interpreted 'freedom', as a censor-free environment characterized by explicit language at that time, had resulted in a backlash against the forum because those who are not accustomed to the harsh expression in their everyday lives would avoid f=160.[6] He felt that this sociability was problematic as it could keep potential new inhabitants away:

> We all know that it is virtual, and people could do whatever they want on the Internet, but we all have to realize that swear words keep people away from Kaskus.

Second, the minimally regulated chat also conveys inexplicit messages to (a) junker that sanctioning is absent from the forum. As such, everybody voiced a common concern at the meeting that there was a growing tendency that f=160 was becoming a junk web forum. Harya expressed that as a *junker* himself, he missed having orderly (*keteraturan*) online threads since many threads were interrupted by various unrelated posts or harsh and crass comments, which was devastating to the 'flow of conversation'. The meeting, which was initially meant to prepare a picnic, eventually ended with the overarching conclusion that if the online chat was not regulated, Kaskus' freedom of speech would only become a justification for digital vandalism.

That evening, the five Solo Kaskusers eventually concluded that both the online sphere and the *wedhangan* should be first organized to lay the groundwork for promoting any further common activities such as picnics. They agreed to the new premise that as a precursor to higher participation in KRS activities, an inviting online space that suited the general public needed to be created. They concluded that, community members' online and offline participation needed to be tied to a certain discourse of order, which would require a reorganization of the chatting procedure in f=160. Armin stated the formula: 'the more people are well organized [in f=160], the more they live in order. That way it would also be easier to organize activities'.

These changes and the notion of order did not come from thin air. 2008 was also the year when Andrew Darwis was determined to reorganize the forums in order to re-launch Kaskus as a company.[7] Kaskus' management planned to move all Kaskus' servers to Indonesia. Such a move also meant that the site needed to comply with the regulations of the Indonesian Ministry of Communication and Information, which required that: (1) the BB17 adult forum be terminated because erotica is illegal in Indonesia; (2) that the CCPB hacking forum be closed down to adhere to the copyright protection law; and (3) that the FC be deleted to comply with the national law on anti-blasphemy and religious defamation.

That year, BB17 was closed down completely and its digital trace was locked and deleted. The CCPB was remodeled to become a learning center for software-hardware, game tricks, and IT-related discussion forums. Having more forum moderators installed, FC was renamed 'Debate Club' (DC), which demands that Kaskusers should participate in the debates in a more scholarly manner, strictly forbidding any slander against SARA,[8] and banning any explicit language.

Accordingly, with such changes in the general Kaskus website, forum and sub-forum moderators began to post discussions about how they could regulate their forums. That year, nine years after the first launch of Kaskus, the regional forum Administrator, *@Lord_nara*, set up the first online regulation, 'General Rules for Kaskuser Regional' [sic].[9]

These regulations inspired the five Solo Kaskusers to apply a similar crackdown on crass posts. The meet-up ended with an agreement to put the picnic plan on hold and three decisions to overhaul the KRS Forum: (1) to reorganize f=160 by prohibiting adult content in posts as an effort to create a 'comfortable space for more general members,' to use Harya's expression; (2) to regulate the weekly *wedhangan*; and (3) to appoint a RL that would have the power to monitor f=160 and the authority over the stick-and-carrot mechanism. The RL would be given the power to delete posts and organize threads while also taking on responsibility for organizing offline events.

As Armin was the person who had proposed the idea to organize the online chat practices, he was elected with acclamation to become the first RL. That Saturday evening after the offline meeting, the five Solo Kaskusers returned home having put in place a new RL for their online sphere. The next day, Armin began organizing f=160. He firstly posted the online chatting regulations he had taken from Kaskus' basic online chatting regulations and from the meeting the night before. The crackdown against deviant posts was democratic because he also started a thread for Solo Kaskusers to discuss how they would like to regulate themselves and take complaints from those disagreeing with the changes.

With the advent of the new regulations, five new principles guided the reorganization of the chatting forum. First, discussions and conversation regarding sensuality, alcoholism, and other adult subjects were localized (*lokalisir*) to a thread, Nightlife Experiences. Second, any message or thread with adult or offensive language outside that forum was subject to deletion. Third, Solo Kaskusers who wanted to chat but had no specific topic were only permitted to converse in the Lounge Chat. Any conversation that did not correspond with the thread's title was subjected to direct deletion. Fourth, as a consequence of the second principle, message posts were required to feed the discussion, and any troll, hustler, flamer, or junker would be warned, bricked, and eventually banned from the forum. Fifth, to tackle junkers, those who wanted to dwell in f=160 should register themselves in the Dweller List. Accordingly, those who are not registered would be neglected and his/her post would gain no feedback.

This set of regulations eventually became larger than simply a means to tackle explicit posts; it quickly became a scripted normative order on online dwelling in f=160 and how to become a Solo Kaskuser. These transformations continue to guide Kaskus: today, chatting in Kaskus is a subject-oriented activity and junkers, with their hoaxes or nonsense post, are harshly sanctioned. This compliments what the previous chapter has identified as the first two disciplines that a Kaskuser needs to learn to be able to dwell in Kaskus, as complying with these new regulations is the third discipline to become a Kaskuser.

The decision to appoint Armin as RL was groundbreaking for the Kaskus realm in general as his was one of the very first RL elections that transpired through an offline meeting. It was a landmark of how both online and offline realities affected the organization of digital dwelling in Kaskus. At that time, there was no obligation for a regional forum to have a 'Leader'. Since an RL possesses the strategic power to lock threads, many Kaskusers at that time associated such powerful functionality with the presence of a watchdog for formal chats—a policy that both Kaskus management and Kaskusers were hesitant to adhere to, lest it makes the online forum less liberated.

With his duty as RL, Armin became a digital authority and gained access to lock threads and to delete posts. This new administrator right became Armin's new capital and power to remove posts that he found to be unfit based on the regional forum's regulations and subjects of discussion. Solo Kaskusers dubbed this time as the 'cleaning (*pembersihan*) period'; a transition period to the current model of communication in Solo Kaskus.

Armin underlined that the supremacy of the new regulations nevertheless, did not simply arise from the sanctioning power he had, but mostly from complying thread starters and administrators who were mainly respected senior members. The five senior Solo Kaskusers who had discussed and initiated the reorganization of KRS during the picnic meeting happened to be senior and respected members of Kaskus. Even though the KRS Forum was intended to be an egalitarian space, senior members of Kaskus gain more respect because of the quality of their *KaskusStatistics* as the previous chapter describes.

Since senior members have green-badges (*cendol*), they also enjoy the technical access and 'power' to brick others.[10] This means seizing their support could ensure political back-up in case there are spam protests objecting to the new regulations. As they clearly supported the changes, it would not be strategic for other members to resort to protest as protesters would risk being bricked by senior members and losing their green-badges (*cendol*). Furthermore, since senior members are viewed as competent chatting partners as Chap. 2 describes, they usually have a large number of chatting partners, whom they could persuade to agree with the importance of the change, both through off-page communication or private messaging.

As the person with the duty to reorganize the chats, Armin credited the five senior members of Solo Kaskus, who not only took the initiative to delete trolling comments in the threads, but also administered and started to change their communication or language style to set an example for the public. Prima described that most Solo Kaskusers recognized the change almost immediately and that 'there was something happening' as the five Kaskusers started to post messages with 'more polite language, with no sensual jokes'. These technical and behavior supports were effective in mainstreaming the narrative in chats in terms of what was required of the community for its new order.

### *3.1.2 Organizing the Text*

Since Kaskus is a realm of text, the greatest challenge in reorganizing the forum was to revise how text is presented in posts. At that time, the new spirit of Kaskus regulation was in direct conflict with Kaskus chat's common practice in communication style and language use respectively. Accordingly, while the online regulations provided a clear identification of what and where a Kaskuser should post, the communication style and content did not swiftly change overnight. It took more than terminating subforums and erecting online posting rules to transform popular communication in Kaskus, especially when these subjects were already incorporated in the frolic of general chat since the forum's birth. This was further compounded by the fact that Kaskus management did not have censorship and surveillance technology that could digitally monitor the chats.

Solo Kaskuser admitted that it took them almost another half a year to eradicate threads and posts with adult content and for them to avoid the use of explicit language. Since there was no computerized algorithm for censorship, a complete termination of such practices was challenging. Thread administrators had to rely on reports from fellow Kaskusers; they could not monitor the chats minute-by-minute, especially during office hours while they were at work or at school. Eventually, text organization consequently became a collective action of public monitoring and prosecution where obedient Kaskusers eagerly reported misconduct.

In this new Kaskus world, Kaskusers would give thread administrators a notification of deviant chats. Take, for example, a post from @Puspithamartha in October 2010 in protest of the thread, 'What Would you do if you had a Sexy Housekeeper', which had been started by @Randy and had been around for two years before the complaint.[11] @Puspithamartha protested that the thread had managed to escape censorship and deletion despite Armin's campaign and criticized that, although the thread starter did not upload any pornographic pictures, the title of the thread was a sexual innuendo that attracted derogatory comments against women and housekeepers. @Puspithamartha stated:

> The comments are very destructive; it is pornographic, beyond expected decorum (*diluar kepatutan asas bicara*). Kaskus is famous for its support of individual dignity, even if that person is only a housekeeper, you should not look down on them [...] Please, housekeepers are also a human being like us, do not make them into an object.

The protest was written in formal Indonesian, which distanced the writer from the playful art of the casual *ngoko* Javanese language written in f=160. It also did not contain any playful emoticons. @Puspithamartha also copy-pasted the same post to all @Randy's post in Kaskus. This is what in Kaskus is dubbed as 'stalk-posting' to annoy the post writer. Since no posters contested Puspithamartha, Armin the then-RL, eventually closed the thread.

Not all demands for text reorganization were uncontested. Mochi, the administrator and offline coordinator for the Women's Thread, recounted her experience in 2011 when one of her campaigns sparked some protests. The story started that year, when she began to realize that women Kaskusers' participation, especially in the offline activities, was declining. Reaching the conclusion that the digital f=160 home needed to become more suited to women, she argued that the forum not only needed to be regulated according to the content, as Armin had already started in 2008, but also the communication style. She suggested that the language used also needed to be adjusted: to be politer. For her, more eloquent language usage would provide a good halo-effect and bring more potential visitors, especially women Kaskusers, to the forum. 'After all, what ideal home would be one where people use explicit language?', she argued.

On February 1, 2011, Mochi, therefore, started the thread, 'Do You Agree with Making Changes to Invite More Kaskuserwati [Women Solo Kaskuser] to Join?' Mochi argued in her post that simply organizing the content of posts was insufficient; to successfully attract new Kaskusers, she contended, posts should be written in 'proper language' avoiding crass talk and lavatory or offensive humor for the public. The thread stayed live until March 9, and gathered 1387 responses. In terms of responses, 1022 messages (73.68%) supported her suggestion.

For some Solo Kaskusers who agreed with Mochi, the delivery of eloquent posts was not a matter of censorship, but presented a means to keep bullies away, as ineloquent language and offensive jokes were considered a bullying technique. Sodron, who was the Solo Lounge Chat administrator, echoing Mochi's call to regulate the presentation of language style, explained that the idea of restricting offensive statements in any subforums should be understood as common courtesy, a means to avoid 'hurting each other's feelings'. This also required, accordingly, the creation of a comfortable chatting environment.

Sodron's argument pertains to the problematic arena of digital 'dark play' (Boellstorff 2008: 194) that makes the flow of the chat fragile. Sodron argued that although online forums and media are intended to be a liberated space where users can be expressive, Kaskuser should also cater for the hope that 'freedom of speech' does not become a means of exclusion and permit 'abuses of power'. In a text world where everybody could write something offensive, it was feared that crass talk was an oppressive medium to bully others. Explicit language as 'dark power', to use Sodron's term, can lead to a particular reality: bully or be bullied.

He added that such patterns of social relationships and crass talk could offer the permissiveness to be violent and disrespectful toward others. 'Simply like a gang member', was his analogy. Experiencing the plurality of the community, those in support of Mochi's motion believed that regulating Kaskus chat would keep the home stable and avoid the risk of conflicts emerging from misunderstanding. Eventually, therefore, controlling the language style or message delivery became about 'organizing Kaskusers to become thoughtful (*santun*) and respectful', explained Harya. As Sodron stated, 'a communicative home shouldn't be hurtful. Offensive jokes and mockery are becoming common, and that is dangerous; we became ignorant of other's feelings'.

Support for the change was, however, not unanimous; 365 (26.32%) posts objected to the suggestion. Surprisingly, the detractors were mostly women Kaskusers. In Kaskus, apparently, it is not always the case, as is classically common, that explicit language and derogatory remarks represent an arena for men. @Tompiloverz, for example, wrote as Kaskuserwati on the thread that if Mochi or any other Kaskusers did not feel comfortable in f=160, she should move out and find another forum. Another woman protested to Mochi privately, arguing that she never objected to the crass talk and that she also expressed herself using such language style. Both woman protesters argued that the initial unregulated Kaskus world, which presupposes a shielded-identity that masks class, educational background, physical appearance, location, ethnicity, and gender, had made it possible for Kaskusers to behave however they wanted and to be away from the constraints of society in the offline world.

Apparently, contrary to popular belief, these women Solo Kaskusers considered f=160 as a place where they did not have to exercise their socially-expected offline gender role. In Kaskus, they could become a persona without worrying that a woman should behave in a refined (*halus*) manner, which is socially expected in offline Javanese interactions. For these Kaskusers, the possibility to have the space in which they could express themselves explicity, regardless of the gender order, made f=160 a home for them.

Some male users actually also objected to the strict regulation on language style presentation, but they did not dare to present their objection through online posts because they were afraid of being accused of being gender insensitive. They simply shared their disgruntlement in personal communication with other like-minded Kaskusers or during the offline meet-ups, while defending the idea that explicit language is not all about vulgarity but is instead about language play indicative of the close relationships among Kaskusers. For example, Icesusujahe believed that, 'home is not a public space, but a place for those who are willing to accept who we are'; it was thus expected that inhabitants provide *freedom* for fellow users. Similarly, Harya stated in an interview,

> A newbie or an outsider might feel irritated and consider us an uncultured gang. But here, because we post and talk every day, it made us closer. I know [the people] who are there [in the forum/thread]. It is impossible [for me] to curse [read: to use explicit language] anywhere [read: other thread] else, [because] it is not my home. If people have become so close and there is no distance, it would not be a matter and maybe all of those swear words would be taken as jokes, also because it is [so] in Javanese [language]. [Those who mind] could just simply disregard it.

Kaskusers like Harya and Icesusujahe did not find offensive or explicit language to be insensitive; instead, for them it was simply an expression of ridicule.

Anthropologists and linguists have identified that explicit language used at the right moment can be a sign of intimacy, affection, and humor. The folklorist Alan Dundes (1989), for instances, has investigated how Germans use the word 'shit' in their colloquial communication, even to the degree that the word marks a strong relationship between communicants. He records that Germans use the word '*Scheiß*' (drops) abundantly in riddles, name-calling, and proverbs, despite the fact that the German language has layers of politeness as an imperative norm. Similarly, Agnes Brandt, in her research among the Mãori-Pãkehã in Aotearoa, New Zealand, documents that the function of explicit communication such as sensuality and politically incorrect jokes are not merely for social intimacy, but are also psychologically lucrative. There, she reported, such words of choice are considered leisure, which 'releases the burden from everyday life' (2013: 134).

In Solo, the offline environment of f=160, both explicit and sensual humors are a common outburst in folk wit, parodies, or witty puns (*plesetan*) among close friends. They are an art of play as a swinging pendulum between 'refined' (*halus*) and 'crass' (*kasar*; or inelegant) demonstrated in art or entertainment performances (Sears 1996; Siegel 1993; Pemberton 1994; Richter 2008; Perlman 2004).[12] The textual play between refine and crass was also a common finding in f=160 before Mochi's campaign. Each Solo Kaskuser who decided to dwell in the forum and accept the communication style had to train themselves until they gained the competence to sense 'the mood of the message', to borrow Amakuzalek's term. With the new regulations, however, sensing the mood of the message and the flexibility of being eloquent become secondary since message delivery and its presentation style were regulated.

Regardless of protests from those who objected to the control of communication style, and since the majority of the responses were supportive, the formalization of language style had to be quickly constructed. Failing to uphold the majority's opinion could damage the dignity of the forum management and the regulations Armin had erected two years earlier. The order for language then was added to the online regulation, regardless of the explicit women Kaskusers' objections.

Sodron recollected that to support Mochi, he set a new motto as a banner on a thread: 'not to limit freedom but to secure common convenience (*kenyamanan bersama*)'. He argues that he had underlined the word 'common' to emphasize the solidarity needed 'to create a mutual space' as it is 'our home'. The idea of home and the expectation to create eloquent conversation highlights the second major textual and visual change for Solo Kaskusers: the regulated language used.

### *3.1.3 Going Offline and Moral Vocabulary*

In such effort to create a home, Solo Kaskusers also agreed to create an index of dwellers in f=160s as per the fifth regulation stated by Armin. Since then, Solo Kaskusers have been required to introduce him/herself in the Dweller List thread,[13] including revealing some of their offline identities: parts of their real name, a photo, and occupation. Those who do not register in this thread would be deemed an intruder.

The thread is not meant to be used to reveal Solo Kaskusers' complete offline identities, as this would dismiss the shielded-identity role play altogether. Instead, this registration process is considered a symbolic action that represents loyalty and submission to the community. As Amakuzalek explained:

> You don't have to submit a passport photo, it's just like a test whether you are opening yourself to this community or not. Of course, you could lie about your information also, but we would see that you are not committed and we will not consider you trustworthy (*terpecaya*). We still have the cybersensing capability to track your profile anyway. Usually, *junkers* would not register.

He argued further that revealing one's offline identity would not change the playful communication style since each person is expected to understand the separation of the online persona and offline character. Similar to

Amakuzalek, Sodron stated that limiting the conditions of anonymity should not dismiss 'the alter ego play':

> We still could be somebody else [*in f=160*]. If you play with your online persona, we will talk to your online persona. If you want to be your real self in the offline world, we will talk to your real character. And, of course, you will do the same [for me].

Mochi, who appeared to be religious in wearing a hijab, relaxingly echoed Sodron's account of the Dweller List thread while telling a story:

> You could see Icesusujahe's avatar [note: the avatar show's an anime character who holds her large breasts], we all know his jokes and how he can be [politically] incorrect with his comments, but I have nothing against him. When we meet offline, it is all casual, and we are good friends. So, I know all about his offline identities; it does not affect our friendship. When we are online, I would be me, and let him be what he wants to be.

Here, to recall the intersubjectivity between the online persona and the offline character, and between online persona and the environment, just like dwelling in Kaskus and using other new media platforms, such recognition of each role is neither an overlapping juxtaposition nor a zero-sum game. This separation of online persona and offline character, or going offline, is not an antithesis; instead, the distinction represents an ordering that requires greater engagement or responsibility. Hence, revealing anonymity at home as a part of a communal solidarity is not a submission of play but a form of trust-building.

One fundamental aspect of organizing trust is a common vocabulary that everybody understands. When the online cyber practice was no longer sufficient to justify the effort, they had to find other sources, and at that time the closest source of justification was their Javanese vocabulary. During these evolving experiences in transforming f=160 into a home, KRS organizers employed several Javanese terms as common imaginaries. The first two Javanese words that they used to organize the forum were the normative words of *guyub* (together, attuned, collective) and '*nggenah*' (to be proper, to be in order, to be correct; Ind. *teratur*), which were used more often by Armin and other senior members to justify the new online chat policy. While *guyub* denotes the notion that the reorganization of KRS should become a collective effort, *nggenah* highlights the collective expectation that each Kaskuser should have the self-control to generate proper conduct.

Unlike the formal use of *guyub*, which was set as a title for a thread, nobody in Kaskus Solo tracked the record of who brought the term *nggenah* (orderly) to the surface. Armin tried to remember and suspected that he found the word simply in one of the digital posts on f=160. He did not bother much about who generated the word as long as the Kaskus public could understand the intended goal captured by the term. He stated, 'let's see it this way, if there is a newcomer and s/he sees the room [f=160] is neat and in order, then it would be nice. It will attract more Kaskusers and chatters to stay'.

Like cybersense, to be correct (*nggenah*), is another form of intersubjectivity. In Javanese, *nggenah* represents the idea of proper manner and correctness based on the relation to the contextual others. Consequently, to be incorrect or improper (*ora nggenah*) would be considered insanity. In Javanese communities, 'insanity' is not a psychological terminology, but instead connotes a form of failed compliance whereby an individual does not uphold the normative order and is perceived to be a human error. Thus, an insane person would be socially outcast. With the exploitation of *nggenah*, those who are not—the junkers and the offenders of the online regulations—are directly depicted as pariahs and excluded from the sane community; those who are incorrect are those who would be considered unfit for society.

Different from sense, or *rasa*, *nggenah* is to be understood within a regulatory framework and operates within rigid procedural conducts. Thus, all the guidelines for the behavior perceived to be *nggenah* is no longer an individual choice. Instead, it is clearly determined like the chatting regulations that Armin scripted. Since the regulations are detailed, those who do not comply with social expectations are perceived to be those who do not have the ability to recognize the guidance, or are 'insane'.

Furthermore, in Solo, where Javanese eloquence or being refined (*halus*) is socially expected, *nggenah* has an essential connotation as a point of control between individual agency and the social as a structure. Any non-compliance with the term or nonconforming behavior would be depicted as antisocial. Hence, the whole textual reorganization of f=160's communication acted as a treatment to make Solo Kaskusers 'sane' and compliant.

The import of the Javanese aphorism of correctness to the online sphere and such governing interpretations proved to be strategic. The terms were greatly common in everyday Javanese life, making it easy to be understood by Solo Kaskusers. Accordingly, Solo Kaskusers also started to assert the relation between 'correctness' and 'common good'. That way, the understanding to be 'sane' was not an abstract matter, but tangible since it could be visually seen. Armin explained:

> It was not easy [since all posts and chats containing explicit content were due to deletion]. I was also a *junker*. Prima lost 1500 post-count [thus also loosing some green-badges, as the badge is a sign of post-count acccumulation] since the thread where he had troll posted was deleted. But it was also surprising that no one contested these changes. [...] I was fearful when I began to post the rules. I stayed online all the time to read the newest comments as soon as possible, it was nerve racking (*deg-degan*)! But it went peacefully and it seems that everybody understood that it was for the common good (*kebaikan bersama*).

Icesusujahe and Surandy expressed that sometimes they miss the prankish 'old chaotic chat days' or the days when they did not have to be careful about the content and word choice of their posts. At the same time, they are also convinced that change is needed 'for the common good', that is to create a convenient home for a larger public, while hoping that one day there will be more participants in the offline activities.

Both Javanese terminologies became a regime when compliant behavior started to become a signifier for Kaskusers' membership maturity. Harya asserted that orderly behavior is a sign of 'growing up' as a digital being. As Harya and I discussed the matter:

Harya: What is changing is a factor of how they are growing up (*pendewasaan*). Again, back to our intention to dwell in Kaskus, we are here to find new friends.

Me: But you had your time and chance to become a junker, and now newbies do not have that privilege?

Harya: It is about developing. Our Kaskus ID has the attributes of green-badges generated by the number of post-count and join-dates, but they are not the genuine achievement. If we meet these green-badges highly-decorated people, but then they turn to be passive in participating in our offline activities, it means that they could only play their alter ego.

Me: You mentioned the word development (*pembangunan*), what does it mean to you?

Harya: Back then I regarded things [in Kaskus] lightly, now [as RL] I have become a facilitator for friends with similar hobbies and region. I have changed during my leadership time as a Regional Leader. It is about giving my best responsibility for my 46 voters. During this time as a RL, I have also changed how I see the world and the way I think; now I think that it is my duty to serve the KRS, the community. It is all started by the quality of my post. I have to think before I click the 'send message' button.

Me: How did you change? And how do you expect other people to change? It seems that you define 'growing up' as self-restraint (*mengalah*).

Harya: The definition of growing up is to minimize egoistic conduct in ourselves and to be more considerate of other people. Less compulsive. Does my post add something to the conversation or just an utterance? When I talk about online flaming, now I feel that I could do more than flaming, I could moderate a regional forum. For us, being an adult is to be able to restrain ourselves, but not simply to restrain, but to be able to see something larger [read: to be part of the community].

Solo Kaskusers like Armin, Harya and Prima believe that most Kaskusers were longing for 'order' themselves because unregulated chatting would only result in Out of Topic (OOT) chat that would hinder the development of online conversation. As such, the transformation represents the nature of order itself; that is, the limit of personal autonomy when a community eventually reaches common terms. In a community, things tend to be functional (see Bauman 2001). The use of moral vocabularies in KRS is, therefore, not a traditional turn, but a pragmatic unprompted decision to keep f=160 as a functional chatting space. 'We are not on Twitter where everybody talks, we are in a community,' explained Sodron regarding the notion of order in Kaskus communicative exchange.

After some months of regulating the online threads and making other Solo Kaskusers accustomed to the new regulations, Armin started the thread 'Guyub Offline' (Offline Together) on June 5, 2009.[14] Meaning togetherness, '*guyub*' became the second Javanese normative term with which Solo Kaskusers formally engage. The term was also heavily used to stimulate Solo Kaskusers to attend the offline meet-ups. Although not mutually exclusive, exercising 'togetherness' as a normative word is significant for three separate reasons. First, it creates a sense of bottom-up participation inclusive to the individual agency instead of a sense of top-down reorganization. Second, unlike the term '*kopi darat*,' which merely reflects the urge to meet those behind the screen, 'togetherness' is more mutually intimate since it reflects bonding within a collective; it conveys a message concerning the relation to the other. Third, it is a Javanese vernacular, which is closer to communicants' everyday life.

As Sodron imposed, 'I want to know (*kenal*) you [thus I will *guyub* and go offline], I want to have offline interaction with you, why wouldn't you [come offline and meet us]?' Going to *wedhangan* or offline meet-ups has shifted from simply revealing offline identity to a symbolic action of reciprocal caring and solidarity. Solo Kaskusers view face-to-face communication not as a physical meeting, but as part of the completeness of becoming a member of f=160 or to be participative. Going offline has therefore become a self-attestation of loyalty to friendship.

In the post-reorganization era, to accommodate this togetherness, the meet-ups are held regularly on Saturday evenings at 8 p.m. at the family food stall in the city center described earlier in this chapter. The food stall was picked carefully to convey the notion of community reorganization and the change in offline purpose. Unlike the previous irregular meet-ups that mostly ended with a party, the current meet-up location is intended to be a spot for family-friendly meet-ups. As it is with the online reorganization, in this new offline setting, alcohol and adult entertainment are prohibited from the premises. Choosing a food stall that does not serve alcohol is therefore decisive. It should also be in the city center to be fair to everyone in terms of travel distance. The time and environment are set to attract potential individuals from different backgrounds.

For most Kaskusers, the first experience of going offline evokes the dilemma between protecting the shielded-identity and coming-out-of-the-closet as part of submissive loyalty to community. Therefore, regardless if a Kaskuser goes offline out of curiosity or because of peer pressure; the first offline surfacing is always a momentous experience. Going offline for the first time is emotionally engaging and is dubbed 'Consummation' (*malam pertama*).'[15]

Whenever Solo Kaskusers told me about their *offline consummation* experience, they always did so with an engaging facial expression. They always recalled the nervousness, the awkwardness, and the uncertainty of the reception from other Kaskusers. An offline newcomer, regardless of how long s/he has been in f=160 as an online inhabitant, would be uncertain about how they should behave during the offline encounter. Self-representation is always a challenge: should I be my online persona or just be my offline character? Harya described his experience:

> I was a bit afraid at that time to come to the meet-up because I was new [in the meet-ups] and might get excluded from the group. What if they don't like me? I would no longer have somebody to chat [online] with. If we are lucky, however, in contrast to other online groups, some of us have already actually met, as we have had (online) chats before.

He explained that he was a flamer and a troll in f=160, and he believed that if he had behaved like his online persona during the offline meet-up, the chance of being punched by another Kaskuser was not small. Going offline for the first time is therefore not effortless.

For Solo Kaskusers, going offline for the first time is sacred, as sacred as their first marital intercourse as the name signifies. It marks a user's trust with other community members letting them know our offline character, or body-operant, and giving them the chance to assess the difference between our offline character and online persona. Each user's experience with going offline for the first time has been well documented in the Consummation Diary thread.[16]

*Kopi darat* has become an important feature for Indonesian online communities, as it marks the community members' effort to make time for the community and to reveal the offline identity; thus, a sign of transparency and loyalty to the community. Although coming offline is socially endorsed and expected, it is not imperative. Since Kaskus is a space that honors shielded-identity role play and the representation of an alter ego, Solo Kaskusers also honor each person's choice and agency in whether s/he will surface offline. However, Solo Kaskusers tend to chat only to those who eventually go offline and join the meet-ups.

Despite the fact that there was no certain meeting agenda or if the weather was challenging, Armin explained that Solo Kaskusers would consistently seek to hold the weekly offline meet-ups as part of the community's responsibility to ensure that offline activities continue to exist. The RL, or the appointed deputy, would be responsible for organizing the meet-ups.

Bonding needs proper (*nggenah*) discipline to be practiced regularly, both online and offline. Take, for instance, one experience during a weekly meet-up in 2014. It was raining shortly before eight o'clock that night. The air was chilly and the road was still wet. Yet, a group of twelve Solo Kaskusers attended, five of whom were women. 'See, it like this, we are all together (*guyub*)!' said Fajar humorously commenting on the togetherness regardless of the weather. The statement was not only a reminder of the norm, but also a credit to his other fellows, expressed in the offline, as they had shown their discipline by attending the weekly offline meet-up.

During another *wedhangan* meet-up, one of the Solo Kaskusers reminded us that we had to leave early since we already planned to visit Surandy's wife who was in hospital. Harya counted how many of us would be joining the visitation and made sure that there were enough motorcycles available. With the exception of two Kaskusers who already had something planned, everybody went to the hospital despite the fact that some of them, like Via who also went visiting, had never actually met Surandy's wife or had a close relationship with Surandy himself. Knowing the person or not knowing the person is irrelevant in this case as visiting sick relatives is always a correct (*nggenah*) manner. Furthermore, as Surandy is a Solo Kaskuser, visiting his wife in the offline world and not only wishing her well through online chat represented a gesture of togetherness (*guyub*).

Evoking normative terms represents a reality that Solo Kaskusers could understand and experience. Such normative terms have to be perceptual; Kaskusers need to be able to experience them. In Kaskus' textual online realm, the discipline of expressing the common normative terms and inserting them into the community's activities and properties will tie the solidarity. Such terms belong to the collective since they are not foreign or extraneous, and they are regular terms that are commonly practiced in everyday life. Looking at Via's visit to Surandy's wife, as an example, she did not hesitate or question whether she needed to visit Surandy's wife for such action is indistinguishable from the notion of 'togetherness' (*guyub*). Such ubiquity of practicing *guyub* makes the term understandable.

Each term of the community's order is intended to retain the sustainability of the merriness of experiencing a relationship with others as well. The merriness of KRS is eventually defined by the existing togetherness assessed collectively by all members. Those who do not comply with such norms will be left out of chats. Here, the incorporation of new norms in the online community does not fall into a singular tendency of adoption and it is also not used merely for the purposes of communication; instead such norms are reproduced accordingly for each experience in KRS. Solo Kaskusers are always assessing whether being *guyub* and *nggenah* is productive for the community's cohesion.

How the properties of the offline world have become resources for Solo Kaskusers to reorganize the chat, code of conduct and the community comprises is what I call 'offlining the online'. As their immediate resource, Solo Kaskusers have therefore reproduced Javanese properness from their offline cultural environment. Terms like '*guyub*,' '*nggenah*,' '*pendewasaan*' (coming of age) and aphorisms such as '*kebaikan bersama*' (common good) were exploited from everyday life expressions. The terms were considered to be common enough that Solo Kaskusers did not further investigate their clarity. It seems uncritical, but in this case, it was strategic and helped Solo Kaskusers invite collective participation. These terms are pragmatic as they become the patch for each other. In this case, the sophistication of a community, thus, relies on the repertoire of normative terms already circulating around the community and not on the ones that they generate. At the same time, the production of order in f=160 was a contingency to assure the existence of collectivity in Kaskus, the heart of which was just a desire to organize a simple picnic.

## 3.2 The Context of Cultural and Political Geographies

The offlining of the online continues as long as Solo Kaskusers can recognize the relation between the two realities. After its success with the picnic and organizing regular offline meet-ups, Solo Kaskusers started to have the urge to be able to explain the community from a historical perspective, as other people often asked them about it.

Eventually, on one evening during a *wedhangan* offline meet-up in March 2009, the issue became the subject of chat. Prima, as the one who started the f=160 chat page, narrated the story of how the first Solo Kaskusers gathered in one Kaskus thread. During the conversation, the participants realized they were only three months away from KRS' third anniversary. They eventually came to an overarching decision: Solo Kaskusers should commemorate the forum's anniversary that year for the first time. They agreed to organize an event to celebrate the 'anniversary of the community'. Armin recollected, 'we wanted to make something special; things that we don't get in our everyday life, or not just simply a weekly offline meet-up.'

After setting the date, the next challenge for the Solo Kaskusers was to decide on a name and theme (*judul acara*) for the event, as it is common to have such banners for such public gatherings in Indonesia. Instead of using the popular term *kopi darat* or the already used *wedhangan*, Solo Kaskusers gave the event an English name, 'Gathering', colloquially abbreviated to 'the Gath'. Harya, who helped arrange the venue, explained that the term was chosen simply because it was already popular among Indonesian online communities. For the first Gathering, Solo Kaskusers eventually agreed on a theme: 'No Seniors Among Us'.

The theme was intended to become a slogan to initiate a campaign ensuring equality in f=160. In the realm of Kaskus, even with its *Freedom of Speech* and casual language, virtual attributes like the green-badges, online ranks, join-date details, post-count, and a long history of dwelling in a forum—which is very well tracked in the *KaskusStatistics*—had become ways to identify seniority. Unlike Danet's (2001) optimistic description of how the digital inhabitant becomes more classless, Kaskus' cyberculture was unable to abolish social stratification since the badges reflected how deep a Kaskuser had been involved in the community as well as his/her level of deserved respect. This presumed stratification was suspected of making newbies and average Kaskus members reluctant to hang out with senior members. The theme of the event, then, was intended to tackle this issue. Senior members, such as Prima, Armin, Kris, and Harya, also took on an active role as event organizers—a symbolic gesture from the seniors to endorse more participation from newbies and make the campaign for equal membership stronger.

To mark the theme, the event, the fellowship, and the community, the Solo Kaskusers created their first f=160 offline artifact: a Gathering T-shirt. That day, each Kaskuser in attendance received a T-shirt as part of the ticket to the event. The black T-shirt was decorated with the words, 'Regional Solo Kaskus', the year of the event, and the *Gunungan*—the mountain in Javanese shadow puppet's theater. During the Gathering, everybody wore the same T-shirt to signify their unity. With a smile and looking proud, Harya described, 'everybody went home with it [the T-shirt]. It is memorabilia; a reminder (*pengingat*) of what we had that day'.

Since that year, the preparation of a Gathering has always involved designing a T-shirt collectively through a thread. For Solo Kaskusers, it is a source of collective memory of the year's event. The T-shirt has a different color and graphic design each year. Accumulated annually, these T-shirts have become collectibles. In an online community where green-badges could be bricked by other Kaskusers and a thread could be deleted or locked by the administrator or the server infected by a virus, Kaskusers' genuine possessions are, by contrast, not virtual ones but are instead a physical artifact: the Gathering T-shirt. It is also a traditional artifact of membership that can be kept and touched. Most importantly, Harya's statement also implies that a Gathering T-shirt is not simply a consumer 'good', but most importantly a signifier of participation and belonging. Collecting T-shirts is like collecting green-badges, with the former being permanent private possession.

When we chatted about the T-shirt in Armin's studio bedroom in 2012, Kris asked Armin to show me one of the stocked T-shirts from the previous year that he kept for other members who had yet to pick it up. Armin, however, replied that he was reluctant to do so because he had not obtained permission from the T-shirt owner to remove it from the stack where it was kept, underscoring the personal attachment that had been attached to the Gathering T-shirt, as the personal property of its owner.

Each T-shirt, with its specific annual design, is its own story of community participation. The T-shirt is like an athlete's lucky jersey; it is sacred.

The first Gathering took place on July 5, 2009. Fifty-nine Kaskusers showed up to join the commemoration. Compared to the five members who had shown up to the hiking preparation meeting, such a large number signifies the degree to which the reorganization of text actually worked to gain more offline participants. The event was held at a family restaurant in one of Solo's suburbs. Bands and karaoke were the main entertainment to go with the lunch buffet. During the week of the Gath, some Solo Kaskusers changed their avatar, replacing it with the Gathering's logo. During the month when the event is held, three threads are set on top of the first page of f=160: a thread for discussing the preparation, another for the program description and registration, and one thread is reserved for field reports and documentation.

In addition to the online coordination, Solo Kaskusers usually also meet offline, exchange private messages, or private online conference. Some weeks before the Gath, Solo Kaskusers also create a Twitter Hashtag for digital promotion to reach the digital public beyond Kaskus. On the Gathering day, a moderator is responsible for broadcasting the event across all social media platforms used by Kaskusers. During the event, more Solo Kaskusers replace their personal avatar with icon pictures of the Gathering, and posts are filled with diverse and declarative party emoticons, such as the emoticon blowing the paper pipe or the emoticon raising a beer. Kaskusers use colorful texts to post their best wishes or to comment on the event. To host the visual documentation of the event, a Field Report (FR) thread is created so Solo Kaskusers and other Kaskusers who attend the event can upload their pictures, videos, and stories. Those who attend the venue can also post their stories of experience in the FR. These participations shape and document the events, making the thread a montage of collective reports. Some individuals will retweet and repost the live report as well. All together, Kaskusers are not simply online spectators but have become agents of the event; they decide how the Gathering should be presented.

The sequences of events are thickly reported in timeline details. The FR thread also serves as a digital log book for those who could not attend the event but want to send their best wishes and congratulate KRS. Visitors can virtually follow the event through the pictures that are posted online along with uploaded videos, all of which are available to download. Starting in 2017, the event is also transmitted live in real time through FacebookLive. KRS's Facebook account functions in the same capacity as the FR thread.

The FR usually manages to gain enough attention from the general Kaskus world so that it is normally indexed on the Hot Thread List on the main page, side-by-side with the 'News of the Day'. Even though the offline celebration only lasts one day, the online celebration on the FR thread usually lasts at least a month. Reading these threads, Solo Kaskusers can follow the drama and struggles associated with bringing the event to fruition; how the organizers came up with the idea for the annual theme, how they faced technical challenges, how one is criticized and others are praised, how fellows dispute the event details, how they engage and disengage in the event, as if they are present in the making of the event. Each Kaskuser can pick their heroes and villains, single out their most memorable moment and the most disappointing ones.

The drama could extend itself not only on Kaskus, but also on Facebook and Twitter, and to the offline meetings. At this event, everyone can be perceived by their fellows based on their effort and ability to give feedback to the community. For Solo Kaskusers, the reality show is not behind the screen but around their own everyday life, between friends, and in the locale they know. They have the agency to interfere with the course of the event. They can also join the discussion and comment, and see themselves on the screen, in pictures, together with other fellow members experiencing the event.

The Gathering allows members to perceive themselves both in the offline world and on-screen; the threads are the medium by which they experience their community. The common virtue: Gathering is an alignment ritual, which involves the bodily experience and emotional participation through which we are part of the event and express our membership integrity to the community and its offline projects.[17]

The decision to celebrate the anniversary of the digital space in the offline space is not some sort of irony for the online community; instead it is a materialization that, as is the case of ***kopi darat***, marks community members' effort and time to celebrate the community. The Gathering is also a key accomplishment in the acquisition of a second space for Kaskus as an online community: the offline space. Unlike the animated 'drinking virtual champagne' after a PCBeth online theater performance by virtual actors on IRC (Danet 2001: 113), the peak of the annual celebration of Solo Kaskusers' Gathering is the offline *Tumpeng* rice cutting ceremony.[18]

### *3.2.1 The Gathering and the City*

A year after the 2009 Gathering, Solo Kaskusers were better prepared for the event and had created a special thread for it. When they started to discuss the preparation, they realized that choosing a theme for the Gathering should not be an arbitrary move because it had to give meaning to those willing coming to the offline event. In the thread and during offline meetings, Harya started to flame the discussion.[19] He cynically compared Kaskus' Gathering with school festivals, challenging Solo Kaskuser to organize an event that could 'give meaning' to those 'not within the Kaskus' realm', Prima recalled. Recalling the story, Harya energetically explained:

> I said [write] to the forum, 'if we are just going to do karaoke and eat out, a junior high student could organize that!' So, we should think of something that represents us as Kaskusers. We ended up with 'Solo.' We are Kaskusers from Solo, it means that we have a certain association with the city, whether that be 'currently living in the city,' or 'once studied or worked here', or 'loving the food'; whatever, but what does it mean to have 'Solo' as our Kaskus name?

Responding to Harya's challenge, Solo Kaskusers started to chat about how their community identity could be related to the city of Solo beyond the geographical association. Talking about the city in f=160 is an unavoidable reality as part of the Solo Kaskuser's everyday life to begin with. Regardless of the online location of dwelling, Solo Kaskusers locate their online persona and memory within the environment where the body was or is located: in the city of Solo. As such, it has become the material source for Solo Kaskusers' imagination of belonging. The chat eventually transformed into an overarching reflection about the actualities of the current city government programs. Prima recalled:

> At that time when we thought about Solo, we thought directly (*langsung*) about the city government (*Pemerintah Kota*). The mayor was trying to organize (*menata*) the city. What can we do about it? We realized eventually that as Kaskusers we should help the city government in promoting our city. As the commons (*warga biasa*) that was the least we could do.

The chat found its context in the city government's new slogan 'Solo: The Spirit of Java' as part of the mayor's tourism branding strategy. 'As a citizen of the city', Harya explained, Solo Kaskusers started to discuss how they could support the campaign; 'to be part of the city', he expressed. They were optimistic that with their spamming ability they could attract public attention to the mayor's campaign. Starting that year, the subject of 'promoting the city' (*promosi kota*) became a general directive theme in KRS Gatherings.

Concluding the three-week long online chat, Solo Kaskusers eventually agreed to translate 'promotion' as drawing public attention to the city's monuments, landmarks, or objects of heritage that were considered to be lacking public attention. They considered that such an approach would differ from the common method of advertising the city's best feature and would raise local citizens' awareness of their surrounding environment.

Before 2010, Solo Kaskusers had actually already formed indirect contact with the city's activities. The first thread that echoes such activism can be traced back as early as October 28, 2009 when Sodron initiated a thread called 'SOLOis.Me.'[20] The thread was made to support a website with the same name that operates as a repository for the city's promotional activities.[21] Even though it was administrated by five Solo Kaskusers, SOLOis.Me, the website, was hosted independently from Kaskus.[22] @Chidori_07, one of the website administrators, posted a call on the Kaskus thread and wrote:

> 'Show your love to the beloved city of Solo, (show that you are able) [sic] not just to post junk but can bring better posts and content here.'

Sodron explained that the website was intended to become a site of information constructed using netizens' contributions, including the oral history, pictures, and stories of how they experience the city.

The 2010 Gathering eventually focused on promoting the city's old steam train and the Sriwedari recreational park which were considered to have diminishing appeal in the public's eyes. Harya, the Project Officer for the event, described the role of KRS in promoting both city landmarks was to 'raise the pride of being Solonese':

> In 2010, we held the Gathering in Sriwedari [the city's oldest amusement park], which at that time had been abandoned (*terbengkalai*). Before going to the central venue in the park, we took a train ride with the *Jala Dara* steam train. People were saying that the train ticket was expensive, but in our opinion, [those who voiced such opinions] could not yet see and appreciate that it [the train] is our pride (*kebanggaan*). It is the only steam train in the world that still travels across a city.

> We tried to create a record in the Indonesian Book of Records by going online on Kaskus (*ngaskus*) on a moving train while documenting the experience of the train ride. We were hoping that it could raise Kaskusers' awareness about documentation, and would also promote the Jala Dara across Kaskus at the same time. Unfortunately, this second goal was cancelled because the Internet provider feared that the signal would not be strong enough.
>
> [...] The grand finale, the happening, was the *Woyo-woyo Campursari* (pop folk music) performance show. Here, we tried to promote the urban culture, Kaskusers should be aware (*sadar*, lit. conscious) that they should not only be concerned with new technologies, but also return to their roots, to their Javanese culture. We could not deny that the soul of Indonesia is actually the music; it is the mass product. [...]
>
> We also had presentations of folk culture (*kebudayaan rakyat*), for lunch we had traditional foods such as *brambang asem*, *ketoprak*, and invited the Indonesian Red Cross to collect blood. From there, the spirit of togetherness was being created.

Altogether, that year's Gathering covered: promoting the city's tourism assets and heritage, a campaign about local history and about the importance of documenting the city's everyday life, drawing public attention to the city's steam train, a production of performing arts, and participating in a blood donation project with support from the Red Cross. It was a hybrid festival.

On f=160, the travel documentation, the exposure of *Jala Dara*, and the festival in *Sriwedari* gained great popularity. The FR thread, which presented massive amounts of pictures and various stories and reports, was listed on the Hot Thread Index at Kaskus Home page for two weeks. Some blogs reposted the articles and several local newspapers covered the community's effort. The city government, its transportation, and tourism boards expressed their gratitude and appreciation for the effort, and even rewarded Solo Kaskusers with certificates of contribution. That day Solo Kaskusers went home with a new understanding: the event is a reaffirmation that Solo Kaskusers could play a certain role as citizens of the city. Thus, Solo Kaskusers started to view that citizenship is not an ascribed but an achieved status.

This experience of reaffirmation is important for three reasons. First, they had a feeling of reconnection with other actors outside Kaskus. Second, they experienced an offline event dedicated to the city's promotion.

Third, they attracted attention from the media and their fellow netizens to the project. The 2010 Gathering marked a milestone in terms of the successful materialization of the myth and hopes that Solo Kaskusers had imagined of how online communication would act as a medium for networking that was once virtual. This cooperation with other actors in the city—as networks of actors—formed a new perceptual experience for Solo Kaskusers: the belief that it is possible to collaborate with those in the offline world. Solo is no longer an empty space and the network is no longer anonymous, it is now a landscape filled with relevant actors connected to f=160 although they are not Kaskusers.

Forming connections with offline actors has since then become routine. For the following Gathering in 2011, Solo Kaskusers focused on the theme of family and education in the green city. That year's Gathering was held at the city's worn out Zoo, Jurug. For this event, KRS members refused to take the offer for discounted tickets, and fundraised instead to donate to the Zoo for its maintenance. The event also pushed forward the issue of family for the first time, asking Kaskusers to bring their family members and/or relatives. The program was set with outdoor and educational games.

The 2012 annual Gathering took place in the Surakarta Palace (*keraton*) with 'People in the Palace' as its theme. Around the troubles surrounding the traditional Kingship succession, KRS held a symbolic event that underscored that the people should consider the palace as part of their cultural heritage.[23] Therefore, Solo Kaskusers' campaign that year focused on how Kaskusers could become a heritage society by reporting on the cultural events taking place in the palace, explained Hanung, the event's coordinator. In contrast to the chosen aristocratic location, KRS celebrated the anniversary by inviting a *ketoprak* folk theater to perform and made it a free public event.

Promoting the state-owned Radio Republic Indonesia (RRI) Solo was the 2013 theme. Solo Kaskusers believed that RRI city radio had been declining and losing listeners since competition from the more hyped private radio stations. The goal of the event was to attract younger listeners to RRI, explained Harya. The annual celebration peaked with a live radio show at the radio station's studio.

The 2014 Gathering adopted again the theme of family while promoting another city park. In 2015, Solo Kaskusers opted to organize the following year's Gathering in a mall for security reasons because they invited a local band known for its satirical lyrics about social and political issues to perform. Furthermore, the 2015 Gathering also marked a year after the 2014 Presidential Election in which Indonesian voters were polarized, split between two strong candidates. Corresponding to the political polarization, that year's gathering's theme was, 'We Are Still Together'.

By 2015, the annual Gathering had grown larger. Attendance had increased from fifty-nine registered Kaskusers in 2009, to 214 in 2011, 156 in 2012, and 480 participants in 2013. Although the event attracted lower registered participants in 2014 (108 registered participants) and in 2015 (117 registered participants), the actual attendees are still increasing since each registered person could bring more than two other persons, such as their family and friends. The organizers recorded that they had to prepare 500 meal boxes in 2014 and 350 meal boxes the following year. In 2014, Amakuzalek explained that, like himself, there are several other Solo Kaskusers who fly regularly to Solo to join the Gathering. 'When others talk about it, and we chat about it in the thread. It intrigues us to come, to see the end result', he said.

Door prizes as collections from members also increased from less than 10 items in 2009 and 2010, to 26 items in 2012 and 2013, 44 items in 2014, and 35 items in 2015. The Gathering also attracted more sponsorship; from 2 sponsors in 2009, to 5 sponsors in 2010, 8 in 2012, 12 in 2013, 43 sponsors and donations in 2014, and 26 donations in 2015.[24] Hanung, who had the experience of becoming one of the coordinators for the Gatherings, said that Solo Kaskusers' ability to organize the event regularly has attracted more sponsors. Besides the enlarging network of KRS, the second factor that contributes to sponsorship, he added, is because there are more Kaskusers who have advanced in their careers and are able to ask their company to become a sponsor themselves.

Armin and some other Kaskusers have noticed that since the first Gathering, more newbies or Kaskusers have registered themselves in the introductory thread. He counted that new membership on the Registration Index Page has grown fourfold, from an average of 3 new members every month before the first Gathering to the average of twelve new members monthly after the 2010 Gathering. Weekly meet-ups have also gained new participants. Since the first Gathering, Armin explained, he has had to reserve not two but three mats for the weekly offline meet-up.

The 2010 Gathering preparation thread gathered forty days of chat with 511 posts (avg. 12.78 post/day), while the following year's preparation thread attracted 478 posts in thirty-eight days (avg. 12.57 post/day); there were 419 (avg. 4.7 post/day) posts in 89 days for a similar thread in 2012, and 1659 posts for 103 days (avg. 16.10 post/day) in 2013. In 2014, the preparation thread gained 20.05 posts/day (762 posts in 38 days), and 11.18 posts/day (175 posts in 7 days) in the following year (Table 3.1).

**Table 3.1** Comparison of Kaskus Regional Solo gathering statistics

| | *Theme* | *Campaign* | *Location* | *Number of participants* | *Door prize items* | *Number of sponsors* | *Gathering preparation thread traffic (post/day)* | *Gathering preparation thread views (views/day)* | *Gathering preparation response intensity*[b] |
|---|---|---|---|---|---|---|---|---|---|
| 2009 | No Seniors Among Us (*Jangan Ada Senior di Antara Kita*) | Internal solidarity | Bale Padi Restaurant | 59 | No records | 2 | No records | No records | No records |
| 2010 | Collectivity/ Togetherness Brings Good Well-being (Guyub Rukun Agawe Sentausa) | City heritage and cultural awareness | Steam train *Jala Dara*, Recreational Park *Sriwedari* | 56 | 18 | 5+ | 12.78 | 122.12 | 9.55 |
| 2011 | Kaskus Gathering in Jurug (Kumpul Kaskus ing Jurug) | Family, literacy campaign, and library donation | *Jurug* Zoo | 214 | No records | 7 | 12.57 | 196.65 | 15.64 |
| 2012 | Kaskusers' Cultivated Togetherness (Guyub Berbudaya Kaskuser) | City heritage and cultural awareness | Surakarta Palace | 156 | 26 | 8 | 4.7 | 85.88 | 18.27 |

| | | | | | | | | | |
|---|---|---|---|---|---|---|---|---|---|
| 2013 | Cultivated and On-Air (Berbudaya dan Mengudara) | Nation building and media information | Studio of Radio Republic Indonesia in Solo | 480 | 26 | 12 | 16.10 | 412.95 | 25.14 |
| 2014 | Eight (Sewindu) | Internal solidarity and social awareness | *Balekambang* Park Surakarta | 108 | 44 | 43 | 20.05 | 447.73 | 22.33 |
| 2015 | We Are Still Together | Nation building and politics | The Park Solo Baru Mall | 117 | 35 | 26 | 11.18 | 720.143 | 28.81 |

[a]2009 Gathering hardly has any records because all the threads have been locked

[b]Average of each post after number of views. Smaller number shows faster response intensity

The preparation thread of the 2010 Gathering managed to amass 4885 total views with 122.12 views/day. While the preparation thread for the 2011 Gathering was viewed 7473 times (avg. 196.65 views/day), the similar thread in the following year gained only 7644 views (avg. 85.88 views/day). The event preparation thread for the 2013 Gathering was viewed 41,708 times (avg. 412.95 views/day). The preparation thread gained 17,014 views (avg.447.73 views/day) in 2014 and 5041 (avg. 720.143 views/day) views in 2015.

When data from the total views and posts on the preparation thread are compared, there is an apparent tendency toward instability in the online participation discussion for preparing the Gatherings. In 2010, there was a post every 9.55 views, but only one post emerged for every 15.64 views in 2011. The number declined further: one post for each 18.27 views in 2012, one post per 25.14 views in 2013, one post per 22.33 views in 2014, and one post per 28.81 views in 2015.

Gatherings' organizers have provided two reasons why online discussion participation is unstable. First, Solo Kaskusers are becoming more accustomed to off-page communication, whether through private or closed groups' networks, such as WhatsApp and Blackberry Messenger, or through offline communication. Second, Solo Kaskusers are also becoming more comfortable with the technical patterns in the preparation of the event, making them well-prepared and well-anticipated; organizing such events has become a skill that requires fewer chats about the details. In 2015, for instance, Surandy as an RL, only created the preparation thread a week before the Gathering day because the technicalities for the event had been constantly discussed during the *wedhangan* offline meet-up and through a WhatsApp group.

Solo Kaskusers have assessed that all the troubles of organizing the Gathering and reconnecting with the city are not misdirection from the initial leisurely online chat. Instead, it is seen as an augmentation of the merriness of being in an online community. 'You could not see how proud and happy we are when we are done with a project. It's touching (*menyentuh*)', said Vida.

Gatherings, therefore, are not carnivalesque for two reasons. First, the intention to reconnect with the city and the happiness of its success appear beyond the event and they are present in Kaskusers' everyday life through their chats. It makes the community become more tangible after the event, in that Kaskusers feel that they can carry out an activity in the offline world together with their fellow members. Second, for Solo Kaskusers, Gatherings are a materialization that Kaskus could prevail both in an online and offline world at the same time, and this is what the notion of *guyub* has evoked: a non-conflicting appropriation of both worlds.

The ubiquitous digital media interconnectivity prolonged the imagination of being-in-a-community not only through virtual spaces communication, but also when the content of the communication offered the possibility of physical offline activities. In the old mass media, one could only see or hear what and where an event is taking place; in the era of social media, one can participate directly while the event is reported on the screen. Digital media has made it possible for the user to acquire what the friend or interconnected subject is currently experiencing and learning his/her life story followed by physical repositioning of support.

This real time connection between users under the same project—whether it be organizing a thread online or Gatherings in the offline world—resolving geographical and time limitations, raises a degree of intense mental closeness. It is an affirming medium of event through which they feel and tangibly experience a connection with other Kaskusers in both online and offline realities, in addition to their involving environments, such as the parks, the city landmarks, city civil servants, the zookeeper, journalist of other online media covering the Gatherings, the Red Cross, and so on. As community members have to meet offline and work together, Gatherings have transformed the merriness of online chatting into bodily engagements. The online-offline experiences give Kaskusers both mental and physical visibility. Going offline, thus, should be viewed as part of a rich experience of going online.

To this point, then, being in the online community is a rich experience not only because it is a mediated reality but moreover because a Kaskuser can reach all the properties of the online and offline worlds simultaneously.

### 3.2.2 *The Problematic Interpretation of Gathering*

Reflecting on the 2010 Gathering initiative, a general understanding emerged among Solo Kaskusers that the event should not just be about communal bonding, or coming together for the community, but also about citizens' contribution to the city—a sentiment that has attracted increasing participants each year. Such narrative of a moral tenet is, however, problematic for two reasons. First, Gatherings as a contribution to the city do not simply function in altruistic terms, but also as a manifestation of a successful self-assurance of being a citizen. Second, the theme KRS selects for each annual Gathering does not necessarily signify the genuine motivation behind adopting a particular theme, as such decisions might generally be influenced by different hidden agendas each year.

Organizing cultural events as a bonding medium and community ritual to seed solidarity is actually a popular citizenship practice in both Java and Indonesia (see Pemberton 1994; Ricklefs 1974). Although they are collectively organized events, Javanese rituals are not necessarily bottom-up phenomena. They could be generated by the state or local elites—through political brokers—to appropriate the symbols and values of the Javanese court's cultural product as part of political strategies to win the heart of the masses (see Foulcher 1990; Pemberton 1994; Sears 1996). In such forms, performances during the event become the medium by which certain actors with power convey their political agenda and moral messages, through which the notion of community solidarity is adjusted accordingly (Pemberton 1994; Anderson 1991; Sumarsam 2013).

In other cases, on the other hand, community and cultural events become mediums of struggle, negotiation, and contestation through which contesting actors—including the state and non-state actors, or the performers and the audience—struggle to mainstream their reflections on society (see Hughes-Freeland 2008; Sears 1996). This can, accordingly, result in an event that is the product of negotiated symbolism or a mixture between all possible principles that could attract larger audiences or participants and negate assumptions of Javanese moral messages as an isolated production of the cultural core or the locals (Sears 2005).

To give another perspective to such assessments of Javanese events, it is also important to uncover organizers' pragmatic intentions, regardless of their idealistic aims in conveying the moral message through an event theme. Rather than simply assessing whether each Kaskus' Gathering could impact the offline world or the public, it is therefore necessary to view such events also as a ritual that could be meaningful for all the participants in their everyday lives and could continually stabilize or change their community.

The driving force of the Kaskus Gathering is therefore twofold. On one hand, it is indeed a materialization of a organizational agenda from certain senior members to further establish the community's identity by connecting their activities to the development of the city. On the other hand, while arguing that their online dwelling could have a social impact on their offline society, the Gatherings has become the reason for participants to continue to dwell in Kaskus. Gatherings therefore have become the moral basis for spending more time chatting in Kaskus and a means to deflect the depiction that online chatting's value is simply that of personal leisure.

By comparing the messages in the event preparation threads with meetings protocols and talking with Solo Kaskusers during offline encounters, it is evident that not all Kaskusers share the same depth of engagement in the production of such events. The event organizers have a greater role in decision-making and shaping the event theme. Thus, they also take on larger roles in asserting certain messages about the community's values. Such roles are, however, organizationally inevitable for managerial reasons because some Kaskusers, such as the project officer and his/her team, are responsible for making technical decisions on the spot and they are the ones who have to make the event happen. For instance, the decision to hold the 2015 Gathering in the mall, and not in the city's landmarks, was made because the organizers had to find a closed and secure location for the band's political protest music, not that they valued 'malls' more than 'city's heritage landmarks'.

Such an example makes it clear that it would be an oversimplification to jump to the conclusion that Kaskus' events as rituals are the result of how the elite members of the community—such as Harya, Armin, and Surandy as RLs—are steering the group's solidarity. In fact, the opposite is true: the Gatherings are the manifestation of collective participation as the preparation threads, offline meetings, field reports, and their documentation are open to the public as a form of transparency.

For each Kaskuser, reading these threads is self-assuring. Reading the event preparation thread and chatting about the event preparation is comparable to a production setup. In this drama, Solo Kaskusers direct themselves to reflect on their role as both a Kaskuser and a Solonese, both online and offline. It involves routine participation to maintain the flow of the chat and a collective forming of an event that could act as a bridge between f=160 and the city. There is an intersubjective process in these dramas where a Kaskuser attempts to understand the other's opinion regarding their state of community and their relation to the city as each Kaskuser has their own opinion on what needs to be done to better their city. Consequently, the production process becomes the narrative of Gatherings, and not the themes of the events or the event presentation. It is an operation of revelation for the interior to reach out to the exterior. For this reason, the Gathering is reprogrammed annually and requires a new subject each year as new subjects bring a further realization of what a community can do. Gathering preparation and consolidation in this sense are the ritual, where the ideal should be experienced, both online in the thread and offline on the event location site. In the visual world of Kaskus, to see the ideal be achieved—to become part of society—should be visual as well.

Du Bois (2009: 322–337) argues that reading text and solitary speaking are actions of dialogue that offer the possibility for readers to reach out the exterior (ibid.: 337). If we want to trace the dialog in Kaskus, we would first look at the interactions that take place on-screen between the messages and, second, in a member's vast imagination of the realm in which they are active. Reading fellow Kaskusers' comments is not only part of the imagination of being in the public, but is also, following Du Bois, similar to reaching out to the social, that is, to Solo and the surrounding Javanese culture. These are the two main subjects of the chats during the preparation for the Gatherings. Accordingly, such text reading in Kaskus' forum has provided Kaskusers a basis for reaching out to the larger community, to those included in the perception of being in Solo.

Du Bois underlines that such reading could be understood as a ritual as it is a method of aligning the reader within the world they try to imagine and understand. He identifies that between the subject and the text there is a 'stance,' which consists of a 'triplex act' in which the speaker as subject (1) evaluates an object, (2) positions a subject (canonically the self), and (3) aligns with other subjects (Du Bois 2009: 333). This eventually builds 'the structure of engagement' between the subject and the narrative (Du Bois 2009: 333). Thus, the whole schema is a ritual of 'reflexive engagement' between the subject and the narrative (ibid.: 337). The chats and threads preparing the Gatherings are, therefore, not simply a matter of visual organization, but most importantly an intersubjective experience in navigating a connection with the city and its culture.

What Solo Kaskusers understood as 'culture' is, however, problematic. Recalling the events of the 2010 Gathering, Harya was confident that presenting Javanese culture is a part of how Kaskusers are 'coming back to their roots'. He started his illustration that traveling with the city's unique steam train was part of a campaign to 'raise local pride'. While describing the event's closing with a pop folk music performance, *Campursari Woyo-woyo*, he concluded:

> Here we are trying to promote the urban culture, Kaskusers should be aware (*sadar*, lit. conscious), they should not only be concerned with new

> technologies, but also with coming back to their roots, to return to their Javanese culture. We could not deny that the soul of Indonesia is actually the music; it is the mass product. [...] Besides that [the music], we also have the presentation of folk culture (*kebudayaan rakyat*), for lunch we have traditional foods such as *brambang asem*, *ketoprak*.

Contrary to Solo Kaskusers' views on 'cultural promotions', Javanese literati might find such variety events in the name of culture discomforting, simplistic and arbitrary. In their simplicity, Kaskusers failed to understand, for example, that *Campursari* is a product of recording strategies that were considered, contrary to popular belief, unrefined by Javanese traditional musicians (Supanggah 2003); eating traditional food has become a tourism or nostalgic commodification of the everyday life meals leading the locals to be alienated from their own common menu (Ramshaw 2016); and that such cultural events are no longer have tradition forms but have instead become hybrid presentation of shows (see Wallach 2008). This underscores, from an outsider's perspective, that what KRS members perceive as 'culture' is a product of a less cautious representation on the subject of culture.

No thread was ever created to cater for such an advanced discussion. Although some Solo Kaskusers actually had the possibility of digging further into literature sources to deepen their chats on 'Javanese culture', Harya, Amakuzalek and Mochi for instance, who were students of social science, were not aware of the need to investigate the subject of the culture they were presenting. They also did not consult with 'those-in-the-know' as they often do when they practice data patching inquiries on Kaskus threads as the previous chapter describes.

While this is ironic in terms of the expectation that the Internet and online discussions should provide access to vast potential educational resources, the Gathering actually became an event in and on its own terms as the context of how Solo Kaskusers' understanding of culture is embedded in their everyday life realities. Although the interpretation of 'tradition' presented at KRS's events among Solo Kaskusers seems to be deliberately arbitrary, it is a genuine account of what Solo Kaskusers—as the commons—perceive. A Gathering is a presentation of what they know about their culture. Any fallacies contained in what they were trying to construct is a result of what they encounter in the popular familiarities in their everyday lives.

It is, therefore, problematic to criticize Solo Kaskusers' understanding of the 'promotion of Javanese culture', for three reasons. First, they went home that day with a feeling of being closer to their culture. Second, Gatherings as a cultural junction between being a Kaskuser and being a citizen of Solo, seems to be working as Gatherings attract increasing numbers of participants. Third, the accuracy and study of culture were not the goals of the Gatherings, because Solo Kaskusers sought to 'promote' the culture they know. Gatherings should therefore be assessed as an effort to construct Solo Kaskusers' identity and materialize their imagination of home and the Javanese culture using their everyday life resources at that time. While the interpretation of the event might be problematic for Harya and the rest of Solo Kaskusers, the Gatherings are a series of complete dedication to Solo. They are the event organized for the city government, for those in need, and for their culture.

### 3.2.3 Against Alienation: The Practical Function of a Gathering

Through nine Gatherings, KRS continues to vigorously define its social role within the city each year. When I asked why users go to all the trouble of organizing such a labor-intensive and costly event, Prima convincingly answered:

> In life, we should be proud of something, and this is all we as an online community could do for the city. It is imperative (*keharusan*), it is an education for young people to have social awareness. Our love for the city has to be represented in our actions (*perbuatan*).

Such a statement might sound idealistic, but it affects how the community operates. Kaskus Gatherings are therefore an alignment and filter of ritual and online-offline contextualization events. Participating in preparing Gatherings reflects an experience of connection and relatedness between the twofold: between Solo Kaskusers themselves, and between Solo Kaskusers as citizens and the city.

The first pragmatic function of the Gathering is nonetheless to raise relatedness within Solo Kaskuser and eventually select the core members of the community. Although they refer to themselves as a 'community', Solo Kaskusers needed more than community rules and online participation. With the ease of leaving the online community, Solo Kaskusers realized that the community's future is uncertain if it relies simply on living within the membership. With the Gatherings, senior members of Kaskus established an annual ritual through which younger or newer members of the online community should recognize their own presence within the connection to what the community could do for the city of Solo.

Through this online-offline engagement and experience, the process of membership alignment and filtering takes place. Those who are not participating in the organization of the Gatherings will miss some chats and actualities among Solo Kaskusers. Those who do not come to the event will be left out of the documentations. Gatherings filter who will be considered an active member of the community; a Kaskuser that is willing to go offline and participate in the various activities.

Such filtering, is a search to find activists to be recruited as the next organizers or the backbone of the community. Those who are seen to be more active will be asked to administrate a chat thread or even to coordinate an event by the RL or others who have already become chat administrators. This merit-based relatedness is not only limited to the number of presented texts on the threads but also weighted through Kaskuser's capability of organizing offline events. By knowing each other's competencies and working style, Mochi expressed that offline experiences like organizing events have made her 'feel close' to her fellows-in-arms (*teman seperjuangan*) in f=160. Thus, for Solo Kaskusers, going offline and enlarging their activities in the city is also a medium to acquire a retrospective experience to affirm the online intimacy.

Senior Kaskusers like Harya and Prima admitted that they rely on these events as mediums of 'working together' through which they filter to whom they can offer their trust. Mochi underlined that through such experiences she could 'learn of how they need each other'. Offline events are another medium for repositioning against those we considered to be close.

The second function of the Gathering, therefore, is to become a medium of assessment through which Solo Kaskuser repositions their capacity to the city. As a community, Kaskusers needed recognition both from within their own consciousness and from the recognition of the offline world or the society in the city—that is, that Kaskus is present within the city in which they live. Gathering is a strategy against the problem of alienation.

Gathering is a method to give the online activities some relevances in the setting of the offline world. The link between the two realms lies in the perception of caring or 'social awareness' (*kepedulian sosial*), to reinvigorate

Prima's statement. Gathering is an outlet through which Solo Kaskusers perceive that they have the medium to be part of the dynamic of the offline society, allowing Kaskusers to revive themselves as citizens. Starting as an act of curiosity and a sign of loyalty to the online community, the 2010 reflective chat sessions have made going-offline into a materialization of citizens' contribution to resolving the city's problem; a medium for Solo Kaskusers to take on the role as city dwellers.

Such imperativeness of the action, as Prima stated, is what Solo Kaskusers later further described as being militant. With the annual Gatherings, militancy is no longer confined simply to the online forum with its participative chats and databanking, but it is also manifested in civic participation in the offline society. It has constructed an understanding among Kaskusers that such participation is a part of becoming a good Solo Kaskuser, thus being a good Solonese, a good citizen and a valid member of society.

Gathering, as an offline event, is an effort to authenticate the presence of the online community within other realities, such as the offline city. The steam train, the city park, the music, the food, and the blood donation campaign, were strategically chosen cultural objects and activities that have the capacity to relate Solo Kaskusers to their city and their society. For Solo Kaskusers, it was a pragmatic decision, rather than cultural. It was to reach out and seize what the social environment has to offer.

Beyond a one-way interaction, however, the Gatherings are also event(s) that act as a space and possibility for Solo Kaskusers to position themselves in the offline world and to prove their value to their host community. The intent here is not to study, but to promote, not only culture and the city but also to attract attendees and to ensure the variety of events. This is also evident in how KRS measures the success of an event: media coverage, thread view counts, and visitor counts, especially by users from other cities and other Kaskus forums as previously described.

Researching Solo's neighboring city of Yogyakarta, Wallach (2008) offers an approach that an event in Java does not have to be a cultural event that has the sophistication of a scholar or literati. Instead, he sees it as 'an arena in which the competing socio-moral visions of music genres, cultures, nationalities, classes, genders, and taste publics are displayed, parodied, and juxtaposed' (2008: 246). Through his observation, Wallach argues that the intention of these popular folk events is hardly sophistication; instead, they present a means to sustain cohesion. Examining a public musical performance in Yogyakarta, he proposes that cultural origins and comprehension are secondary to the goal of community-building:

> It is the role of the performers, the audiences, and the mediators to collaboratively make sense of this exuberant cacophony of 'alpha cultures' and in the process to forge an ephemeral but deeply gratifying solidarity community of participants. (2008: 246)

The sense of solidarity that has emerged from Gatherings is not only an internal one, but also a sense of bonding with the external, that is a way for KRS to bond with both the society and city. Again, to cite Harya, it is a way for Solo Kaskusers to 'come back to their roots'. In such an understanding of ritual, Gathering's offline could become less accurate in presenting Solonese culture, but it should be cultural since it represents the 'Solonese-ness' of Solo Kaskusers.

David Bell (2001), following Baudrillard's (1994) concerns about simulation and hyperreality, warns that the proliferation of media will bring a mediated self 'living through screens or as screens,' as what is constructed on the screen might become a model for the life beyond the screen itself. This is where going offline to the Gatherings becomes mentally influential for Solo Kaskusers. As the chats about specific Gatherings accumulate the narrative that the Gathering is a manifestation of becoming a concerned citizen, Solo Kaskusers worry that it will make them less Solonese or perceived by others as 'less Solonese' if they do not come. Since the risk is high, the choice of the Gathering's theme and its organization should be made within the scope and ability of KRS; a Gathering should be successful otherwise Solo Kaskusers have failed to attain the feeling of becoming citizens.

### 3.2.4 The 'Early Base of Citizenship'

While joining KRS offline meet-ups, it was common to hear a story of how Solo Kaskusers, through the Gathering and other social events, have managed to establish a cooperation with the city's elites, like the state apparatus and prominent business people, or those who are usually depicted as elites and difficult to be reached by the commoners like Kaskusers.[25] Solo Kaskusers reflected that the Gathering is a bottom-up project as each component of society relies on each other's capacity to form a collective cooperation in an equal manner. Thus, the Gatherings are viewed to be a point where the commons and the elites of the city can reconnect themselves to the greater society.

Prima stated that citizen's initiative, like the Gathering, is more effective for reaching out to other members of the city to create a cooperative citizen's network. It is a form of social awareness and responsibility. Reflecting on the experience throughout the Gatherings, Harya expressed himself: 'in the end, all we can hope is that we make ourselves better people, as we are reminded with all the lives surrounding our chats. Going offline was our early base of becoming a citizen.'

This view could be understood as a reaction to the Indonesian social-political reality after the fall of Suharto's authoritarian regime, especially the estranged relations between the citizen and the bureaucrats or government (see Crouch 2010).[26] Picturing himself as a father while projecting the whole nation as a family, Suharto took the traditional role of father figure in the Javanese Wayang epic (Emmerson 1999; Tomsa 2008). This Javanese leadership model brought about a centralized governance model where the centre idealizes a harmonious state of social management based on consensus by keeping disagreement away (Geertz 1961; Mulder 2005). Consequently, the Indonesian bureaucratic culture under the new order regime drifted public communication away from the citizen (Santoso 1993).

Nevertheless, relating to others, both human (state official, the mayor, fellow Kaskusers, etc.) or non-human (city's landmarks, the Jurug Zoo, Javanese culture, Radio Station, gadget, etc.), goes beyond democratic moral obligation of being a citizen as it materializes the pragmatic exercise of cyber practice, that of being in the community which formed one's socialization. To this point, Solo Kaskusers' relation to the offline society or with the city is not a form of 'active citizenship'; instead, it is a formation of 'citizenship' itself emanating from their awareness of their community's uncertainty and discomfort. There is no 'passive' and 'active' binary in this sense since Solo Kaskusers consider the connection to the offline world as marking a new revelation each time. They call this online-offline enlarging activity a 'process' and 'coming of age' (*pendewasaan*) to recall what Sodron, Harya, Armin, and Amakuzalek said.

This path of coming of age is possible since, unlike in civil society organization, in an online community where a member's role and future interests are not fixed or pre-defined, Kaskusers have the entire agency to meet such identity revelation as changes in the community or its future are not yet foreseen. In this case, their wayfaring with new revelations about 'being Kaskusers' and 'being Solonese' could only continue after they recognized the practice deficiency in reaffirming the two identities.

To them, undergoing a coming of age not only required a reorganization of the digital space, but is also related to the offline possibilities. The path to citizenship here is not a positivistic relation between public discussion and the public sphere, but rather of the dynamics of revelation or consequences of being digital. As such, to have some connections with the landmarks and other citizens in Solo is a consequence of the pragmatic choice of using 'Solo' as a name, and for they know that Solo Kaskusers could participate in the city's current challenge.

The process of 'coming of age', to recall Harya's terminology, is not without its challenges. They had to dismiss their 'undergroundness' and reconstruct Kaskus' '*freedom of speech*' to form a space suitable for a greater public engagement. As this chapter explains, to undergo the coming of age process, to relate with the city and the society, Solo Kaskusers had to firstly reorganize their online community. Each Gathering or online chat regarding the city, therefore, is a digital ritual to adjust Solo Kaskusers to their offline surrounding and a reminder of their previous successful coming of age. Each Gathering is not only a good deed of promoting the city, but also a hope that Solo Kaskusers will manage to reattach their presence to the city and the offline environment. It is for this reason that the discussions about the Gathering's theme will take weeks or months before a theme is decided upon. In the Gathering preparation thread, Solo Kaskusers try to capture the aspects of the city that are seemingly relevant for them or those to which they have a connection. In this view, being a citizen is not simply a result of speaking the local language or living in a common geographical region, but instead requires affirming their identity as 'Solo Kaskusers', as 'netizens'.

More importantly, the hope and the pursuit of offline social activism could only be seeded, not simply proceeded, after Solo Kaskusers became aware that KRS has succeeded in creating their own digital city of f=160. Data patching, citizen journalistic reports, the Gatherings, and activism, in Kaskusers' view, are demonstrations of the highest individual capabilities of responsible citizens in a collective. These procedural experiences and disciplines comprise various trainings to relate to other fellows in their digital homeland, and moreover, to present confidence in their ability to initiate the citizenship project.

Each change in community practice, thus, is an online revelation and perceptual experience. Kaskusers form their own experience of rituals as an opportunity to have a dialog with the environment while juxtaposing it with their search for identity. That said, how Kaskus is interpreted and how its activity is perceived to be meaningful for Solo Kaskusers depends on their pragmatic contextualization of the community with their resources of presence in its surrounding. It is, however, important to note that if the investigation of the struggle of being a citizen is to be set within the dynamics of the community's wayfaring, the question should then be intended for the construction of the collective production of ethics to establish a durable notion of citizenship, as the following chapter discusses.

## Notes

1. Previously a domain for older men, nowadays *lesehan* food stall visitors are diverse in age, gender, and class. A common simple mobile food stall will only have three benches for customers, which makes the seating area rather cramped. Consequently, due to its limited space, participating in small talk between customers is anticipated; sitting in the food stall without greeting other visitors would be considered rude.
2. https://www.kaskus.co.id/thread/000000000000000011374955
3. Freedom of expression was the chant of the early Internet era at the end of 1990s, as it was part of digital activism that Internet moderators were advocating to create public space (Levmore and Nussbaum 2010). Going online was soon perceived as a manifestation of independent space where controlling institutions, such as the state and its apparatus, were absent.
4. Some Kaskusers exchanged pornographic images or videos of their own sexual encounters in 'Indo Girls Only' forum under BB17. In a country where both the pornographic industry and circulation of adult videos is forbidden, such new activities were considered to be an alternative way to acquire pornographic materials.
5. Weblinks could not be provided since these links are today obsolete. Information on the threads' title was obtained from Armin and Harya.
6. During the first decade of Kaskus history, adult language was commonly used in messages. Kaskusers would use explicit words like 'dog' (*anjing*), or 'monkey' (*monyet*), or 'scumbag' (*bajingan*) to those who were in conflict with him/her.
7. This decision also ended the first era of Kaskus' organization that was maintained as a pure collective as a product of a college project.
8. 'SARA' is an abbreviation of 'Suku' (ethnic), 'Antar-Ras' (interracial), and 'Agama' (religion). The three subjects, which could form sectarian cohesion, were considered socially and politically sensitive by Suharto's construction of nationalism (see Crouch 2010).
9. *First*, it regulates the 'post's subject and demands that it should stay discursive within the local subject matter ('lokal content'): any post should be related to the 'thread's title, any thread should only discuss local issues

while national issues are discussed on 'Kaskus' general page, and subjects dealing with other regions should be registered under the related regional forum. *Second*, subjects that are not related to the 'lokal content' should be posted in Casciscus Forum (trans.: Bla bla) and Loekeloe Forum (trans.: You to You). *Third*, every specific subject should and will be merged with a more general forum. For an example 'Red Honda Civic 2nd Gen' was merged with the general 'Honda' forum. *Fourth*, non-specific chats and ads will be relegated to one thread. *Fifth*, green-badges could only be given to those who participate in conversations and could not be given for free. Those who posted an out-of-the-topic chat and unnecessary picture or emoticons will be directly sanctioned, and all the chatting threads in Kaskus were condensed and streamlined.

10. See Chap. 2 about assigning virtual bricks as punishment in Kaskus.
11. http://old.kaskus.co.id/showthread.php?t=942433
12. In the Javanese tradition, sensuality has been greatly influenced by the Indic culture on the depiction and symbolism of sexuality. Sensuality is a subject of spirituality (de Balzac 2010: 62; van Bemmelen and Grijns 2005: 107–107; Hughes-Freeland 2008: 138) or as wittiness of a conversation or in a comical cultural performance (Sears 1996: 281; Sumarsam 2013: 71).
13. http://kask.us/gWjxE
14. http://old.kaskus.co.id/showthread.php?t=2027526
15. The term, 'consummation' (*malam pertama*), is taken from the ritual of the first night of a marriage where the couple is expected to have sexual intercourse for the first time.
16. http://archive.kaskus.co.id/thread/2241069/560; http://kask.us/2241069
17. For ritual communication as community alignment mechanism see Ellen B. Basso and Gunter Senft, "Introduction," In *Ritual Communication*, edited by Gunter Senft and Ellen B. Basso, 1–20. Oxford: Berg, 2009.
18. *Tumpeng* is a saffron rice dish shaped as a cone to symbolize a mountain where the spirits of ancestors live and where the prosperous agriculture originates.
19. http://archive.kaskus.co.id/thread/4454172/
20. http://archive.kaskus.co.id/thread/2491261/0#
21. The title of the thread is wordplay on 'solo is me' and 'soloism'. Soloism is a colloquial term that was coined to depict the distinction between the Solonese culture and that of its Javanese neighboring court-city of Yogyakarta. Both courts originated from the same Mataram Kingdom and share numerous cultural products. After their dissolution following the Treaty of Giyanti in 1755, each Sultanate tried to enforce their own cultural material (Sutton 1991). Today, the antagonism between Solo and Yogyakarta has become part of daily life humor and the Solonese tradition and lifestyle is referred to as 'soloism'.

22. www.solois.me is obsolete per January 2014. Kaskusers involved in developing the website is @aristdudutz, @SodroneZz, @areMean, @cHidori_07, @xhandhekx.
23. After the death in 2004 of Susuhunan Pakubuwanan XII, the Sunan of Solo, two of his sons fought over the crown because he previously did not declare a crown prince. The conflict was resolved in June 2012. (Suprapto and Sodiq 2013).
24. Gath 2010—FR: http://archive.kaskus.co.id/thread/4760797/
    Gath 2011—FR: http://old.kaskus.co.id/showthread.php?t=9751910
    Gath2012—FR:http://old.kaskus.co.id/showthread.php?t=15253846
    Gath 2013—FR: http://kask.us/hd310
    Gath 2014—FR: https://www.kaskus.co.id/thread/536b86168807e7c9088b46f7/pendaftaran-gathering-akbar-sewindu-kaskus-reg-solo-2014-di-balekambang-surakarta/
    Gath2015—https://www.kaskus.co.id/thread/55a9a6d5529a45bd0b8b456b/undangan-gath-regional-solo-9th-and-still-together/
25. Solo Kaskusers depict themselves as the commons (*rakyat biasa*) to describe that they are not those in political, economic, or cultural power, like state actors, the Solonese King, the market key players, NGOs, or activists.
26. In Indonesia, or Java in this case, home does not merely consist of a nuclear family. It could host some extended family members or their closest acquaintances. The Javanese home relies on a functional distribution based on hierarchy. Each home dweller is expected to sustain the operation of the house.

## References


Anderson, Benedict R.O'G. *Imagined Communities: Reflections on the Origin and Spread of Nationalism*. First published in 1983. Revised edition. London: Verso, 1991.

Balzac, Honoré de. *My Journey from Paris to Java*. Translated by Barry Winkleman. Paris: Editions Didier Millet, 2010.

Basso, Ellen B. and Gunter Senft. "Introduction." In *Ritual Communication*, edited by Gunter Senft and Ellen B. Basso, 1–20. Oxford: Berg, 2009.

Baudrillard, Jean. *Simulacra and Simulation*. Translated by Sheila Faria Glaser. Ann Arbor: Michigan University Press, 1994.

Bauman, Zygmunt. *Community: Seeking Safety in an Insecure World*. Cambridge: Polity, 2001.

Bell, David. *An Introduction to Cybercultures*. London: Routledge, 2001.

Bemmelen, Sita van, and Mies Grijns. "What has Become of the Slendang? Changing Images of Women and Java." In *The Java That Never Was*, edited by Hans Antlöv and Jörgen Hellman. Münster, 97–132. Lit Verlag, 2005.

Boellstorff, Tom. *Coming of Age in Second Life*. New Jersey: Princeton University Press, 2008.

Brandt, Agnes. *Among Friends? On the Dynamics of Māori-Pākehā Relationships in Aotearoa New Zealand*. Göttingen: V&R Unipress, 2013.

Crouch, Harold A. *Political Reform in Indonesia After Soeharto*. Singapore: Institute of Southeast Asian Studies, 2010.

Danet, Brenda. *Cyberpl@y: Communicating Online*. Oxford: Berg, 2001.

Du Bois, John W. "Interior Dialogues The Co-Voicing of Ritual in Solitude." In *Ritual Communication*, edited by Gunter Senft and Ellen B. Basso, 317–340. Oxford: Berg, 2009.

Dundes, Alan. *Life is Like a Chicken Coop Ladder: A Study of German National Character through Folklore*. Detroit: Wayne State University Press, 1989.

Emmerson, Donald K. *Indonesia Beyond Suharto: Polity, Economy, Society, Transition*. New York: Asia Society and M.E Sharpe, 1999.

Foulcher, Keith. "The Construction of an Indonesian National Culture: Patterns of Hegemony and Resistance." In *State and Civil Society in Indonesia*, edited by Arif Budiman, 301–320. Clayton: Centre of Southeast Asian Studies, Monash University, 1990.

Geertz, Hildred. *The Javanese Family: A study of kinship and socialization*. Michigan: University of Michigan Press, 1961.

Hughes-Freeland, Felicia. *Embodied Communities: Dance Traditions and Change in Java*. New York: Berghahn Books, 2008.

Levmore, Saul, and Martha C. Nussbaum. *The Offensive Internet*. Cambridge: Harvard University Press, 2010.

Mulder, Niels. *Inside Indonesian Society: Cultural Change in Java*. Third edition. Yogyakarta: Penerbit Kanisius, 2005.

Pemberton, John. *On the Subject Of "Java"*. Ithaca: Cornell University Press, 1994.

Perlman, Marc. *Unplayed Melodies: Javanese Gamelan and the Genesis of Music Theory*. Berkley: University of California Press, 2004.

Ramshaw, Gregory. "Food, Heritage and Nationalism." In *Heritage Cuisines: Traditions, Identities and Tourism*, edited by Dallen J. Timothy, 53–64. Oxon: Routledge, 2016.

Richter, Max M. "Other Worlds in Yogyakarta: From Jatilan to Electronic Music". In *Popular Culture in Indonesia: Fluid Identities in Post-Authoritarian Politics*, edited by Ariel Heryanto, 164–181. Oxon: Routledge, 2008.

Ricklefs, Merle Calvin. *Jogjakarta Under Sultan Mangkubumi, 1749–1792: a History of the Division of Java*. London: Oxford University Press, 1974.

Rukmana, Deden, and Djarot Purbadi. "Street Vending in Indonesian Cities: Their Characteristics and Activities in Yogyakarta". In *Transforming Asian Cities: Intellectual Impasse, Asianizing Space, and Emerging Translocalities*, edited by Nihal Perera and Wing-shing Tang, 123–136. London: Routledge, 2013.

Santoso, Priyo Budi. *Birokrasi Pemerintah Orde Baru: Perspektif Kultural Dan Struktural.* Jakarta: Raja Grafindo Persada, 1993.

Sears, Laurie Jo. *Shadows of Empire: Colonial Discourse and Javanese Tales.* Durham: Duke University Press, 1996.

Sears, Laurie J. "Intellectuals, Theosophy, and Failed Narratives of the Nation in Late Colonial Java". In *A Companion to Postcolonial Studies*, edited by Henry Schwarz and Sangeeta Ray, 333–359. Malden: Blackwell Publishing, 2005.

Siegel, James T. *Solo in the New Order: Language and Hierarchy in an Indonesian City.* New Jersey: Princeton University Press, 1993.

Sumarsam. *Javanese Gamelan and the West.* Rochester: University Rochester Press, 2013.

Supanggah, Rahayu. "Campur Sari: A Reflection" *Asian Music* 34, no. 2, Spring—Summer (2003): 1–20.

Suprapto, Hadi and Fajar Sodiq. "Kisruh Panjang Keraton Solo, Apa Sebabnya?" *VivaNews,* August 27, 2013. Accessed August 27, 2013. http://fokus.news.viva.co.id/news/read/439386-kisruh-panjang-keraton-solo-apa-sebabnya.

Sutton, Anderson. *Traditions of Gamelan Music in Java: Musical Pluralism and Regional Identity.* Cambridge: Cambridge University Press, 1991.

Tomsa, Dirk. *Party Politics and Democratization in Indonesia: Golkar in the Post-Suharto Era.* New York: Routledge, 2008.

Wallach, Jeremy. *Modern Noise, Fluid Genres: Popular Music in Indonesia, 1997–2001.* Madison: University of Wisconsin Press, 2008.

CHAPTER 4

# Netizenship: Between Ignorance and Prudence

Going offline as a medium to reconnect the online community and the offline world is an open-ended journey. Once Solo Kaskusers decided to enlarge their activities to the offline world, they could no longer confine their community experience. They had to open themselves to the new activities the offline world demanded. It makes their community wayfaring more tensed. Through such awareness, Solo Kaskusers became acquainted with the voluntarism they now call 'social activism'. Such experience is a continuation of what they previously described as 'being a member of the city'. Only this time, 'the city' is not merely the space Solo Kaskusers live in, but also the offline individuals they could encounter along the way as this chapter describes. This 'othering' is an access to recognition that leads to social reconnection.

Eventually, as they expanded their scale of activities to the offline world, establishing the online community could no longer simply be confined digitally within their internal retrospective. Moreover, this is related to their perceptual experience of reaching the external as the responsibility for having the power of being a netizen. In dealing with these dynamics of experience, Solo Kaskusers started to realize the importance of producing the ethic of netizenship.



A. Seto, *Netizenship, Activism and Online Community Transformation in Indonesia*, DOI 10.1007/978-981-10-5397-9_4

## 4.1 The Production of Ethic in the Time of Crisis

Solo Kaskusers' social activism as a method of reconnection to society in the offline world is rooted in 2010. On July 25 that year, at 6:25 a.m. just around the time when Indonesians start to check their social media accounts, Suromenggolo started a thread, 'Please help with any necessary means! Thank you'.[1] In the post, he reported about an eight-month-old child who was suffering from 'swollen bleeding rashes'. Suromenggolo described that Ilham, the child, came from a poor family and did not have access to healthcare. They lived in an underprivileged neighborhood, without steady work and income. The baby was actually checked at a local hospital but the doctor was only able to complete a limited medical examination and inconclusively declared that the rash was symptomatic of a 'rare cancer.' The hospital redirected Ilham to the city's hospital which has better diagnostic equipment. His parents, however, could not afford to finance any further treatment. At that time, there was no public health care in Indonesia. Suromenggolo underscored the urgency: 'Currently the baby is crying in pain all the time, could not sleep and does not have the appetite to eat'.

Solo Kaskusers were moved by Suromenggolo's detailed description of the matter and the thread rapidly gained attention. Half an hour later, the post had been reposted to other forums by Andykendil. Half a day later, the thread was listed on the general Kaskus Hot Thread Index. At 2:10 p.m., Lientank reported that the thread's link had gone viral in other Kaskus chat lounges, forums, and on Facebook (Post #4). At 2:41 p.m., Brutallica, one of the initiators of the weekly offline meet-up, suggested that Kaskus dwellers should start a fundraising campaign (Post #6).

While addressing Brutallica's call for a fundraising campaign, Surandy requested that concerned Solo Kaskusers should meet on Yahoo!Messenger (YM) for a quick chat to discuss the matter: 'sign in to your YM, let it be light (*sumet*; Jav.)' (Post #14). The reference to '*sumet*', meaning to evoke light connotes the Javanese shamanic practice when a sacred fire is started as a spiritual medium or to solve a problem through spiritual effort.

Surandy and Brutallica then agreed to start the first response: a site visit to the sick child. The next day, Surandy, Johar, Prima, Sodron, and Armin visited Ilham. This site visit was historic. Unlike the Gatherings, it was the first time that Solo Kaskusers had initiated activism that was not related to Kaskus internal activity. After the visit, Surandy posted a report:

> When we came there, a lot of people thought that we were a bunch of reporters looking for news. We, however, then cleared the air and explained to Sri Rejeki (the child's mother) and father that we are a bunch of Internet

> people (*'sekumpulan orang internetan'*) who were touched by the story and want to help Ilham. We could not promise anything, but we also conveyed that we will do our best. (Post #62)

In the next post Surandy identified the challenges for further action: fundraising, admitting the child to the hospital, medical advocacy, and assisting the family during the treatment process.[2] The responses to the report were a choir of support.

An ad hoc team was rapidly initiated with Surandy and Prima appointed to helm the offline team providing assistance to the family during treatment. This team was responsible for providing support for the family in the hospital and communicating with the medical authorities as most of Ilham's family members could not speak formal Indonesian. Surandy was also asked by Kaskusers to manage the financial arrangements and cash flow. Amakuzalek was given the task of organizing fundraising in Jakarta and on the online network. PlinThenG was assigned to coordinate the offline fundraising in Solo as well as mobilizing fundraising on the streets. Suryomenggolo took the initiative to do online research on the illness and to bring information to f=160. The then Regional Leader, Johar, was appointed to manage the general online fundraising, online networking, online coordination, and mobilization.

Directly on the next day, a bank account was set up to receive the donations. A thread was created to track the progress, enriched with visual and video documentations. On July 27, Surandy and the team contacted the local Red Cross. It responded quickly and contacted the National Department of Health. Two days later, Ilham was admitted to the city's hospital and underwent his first advanced medical examination. The doctor later was able to conclude that the eight-month-old baby was suffering from Haemangioma, a rare type of tumor. A series of medical treatments was urgently required to keep the tumor from spreading rapidly.

The collective action gained media attention and attracted donations from several local business people. The National Department of Health and Red Cross also guaranteed that they would keep the medication expenses at nearly zero. After undergoing two sets of surgery and spending almost six weeks in total at Kasih Ibu Hospital, Ilham was allowed to leave the hospital on September 28 to continue the care at home. Solo Kaskusers continued to assist the family for a full month afterward until Ilham's health improved.

During these two months, Kaskusers not only furnished financial support, they also catered for the family's daily needs, including meals, clothes, daily logistics, and closely assisted the family in dealings with the Red Cross, doctors, local philanthropists, and the press. They also managed to find employment for Ilham's father in order to secure the child's future. All activities were recorded and reported live on the thread, which had been 'pinned' on Kaskus' main page.

The action was memorable and became a milestone for several reasons. First, it marked the production of ethic in handling the offline world. Second, it was the time when Solo Kaskusers realized that once they go offline and relate to the larger society, as the previous chapter illustrates with the Gatherings, they could no longer limit their community's activity. Accordingly, their community reflexively changed. Third, as it was an activity that started with an emergency call to action, Solo Kaskusers began to realize that they could become a responsible 'pool of assistance' (Geertz 1961) to those in the offline world.

### 4.1.1 *Prudence and the Consequences of Being Online*

Although Solo Kaskusers had previously initiated the annual Gatherings as a medium to reconnect with the offline world, their first ethic of being a Kaskuser in the greater society was agreed only after a strained relationship emerged between Prima and Harya on one side and Johar on the other during the Ilham campaign. During that time of crisis, Prima and Harya criticized Johar, the then Regional Leader, for being slow in responding to Ilham's family's inquiries and in facilitating the offline team's inquiry, resulting in disorganization. At the same time, while he was considered to be failing to keep up with his responsibility in moderating the thread for the action and coordinating those responsible, Johar was spotted chatting on other threads. Surandy eventually had to step in to replace Johar as the person in charge of the online communication.

Prima recollected the problem two years later still with an angry tone. He shook his head with disgrace, put his cigarette down, and with disappointment stated:

> He just left us. What do you think of a person like that? We needed an organizer and a leader…for things like arranging the shifts to visit Ilham, to organize food supply, to determine who could provide what, and other things. We needed that fast. One can say, [he] did not do [his] work. We lost our coordination. Eventually I posted a message on the thread trying to

> remind everybody and I wrote the sentence in red characters that 'it is ok to be playful in Kaskus, but we also have to be prudent' (Jav. '*Cengengesan ya cengengesan ning yo mbok sembada.*'). You could chat as much as you can, but please maintain your role (*dilakoni*) when you have a responsibility.

Sodron, who was then the administrator of f=160's Chatting Lounge—the thread for the subjectless everyday life mundane chat—contacted Prima through Yahoo!Messenger after the post and expressed his intention to adopt his post as the forum's code of conduct. As he explained: 'It was just [the] correct (*bener*) [thing to do]. We cannot just fool around (*main-main*) during a time of crisis. It is part of coming of age (*pendewasaan*)'. Starting that night, 'playful but prudent' ('*Cengengesan ning sembada*') became the maxim and normative order for the online community.

The campaign for Ilham ended at the end of September 2010, but the assessment of the community's engagement continued, and Johar's behavior was perceived to be hurting the community. As a Regional Leader, he was depicted as failing to set a good example for his other fellow Kaskusers. While he was a prolific online chatter simply for his own leisure, he failed in two roles: for not becoming a responsive member of the community which needed him as a coordinator, and for not becoming a responsible member of the society that needed him to save Ilham. His neglectful attitude toward Ilham as a person in an emergency situation was described as a 'sin' and was not forgotten.

Harya started to digitally stalk Johar in each thread and forum. Harya contested his posts and disrupted the flow of the chat; an act of flaming. When Johar conveyed his protest, Harya publicly bullied Johar and brought up his lack of response during the Ilham campaign. Prima explained that Harya's flames were backed by several other members and his posts were not considered 'junk posts', which saved the flaming posts from deletion. Through off-screen communications, Harya and Prima started to organize a digital mass protest to replace Johar.

Johar was not alone; he too had his supporters who objected to Kaskus' new activism as their membership in Kaskus had been motivated simply by an interest in having a leisurely chat. Nevertheless, after countless intimidations, on December 26, 2010 Johar eventually submitted his resignation as Regional Leader and since then his avatar is no longer active on f=160.

This incident appealed to Solo Kaskusers to consider what it takes to be a Kaskuser in correlation to the offline world. Johar's late response to the campaign, while he maintained his other online chat, was depicted as self-centered and a form of ignorance toward the emergency in the offline world. Eventually these depictions were equated with the character of an individualistic conspicuous consumption on a leisurely online chat. On the other side of the spectrum, Kaskusers viewed that Kaskus as a community has a certain role for the offline society. This polarized depictions of the two worlds led Solo Kaskusers to further discuss the connection between the online and offline realm, urging them to find a justified operational mechanism for activities in both worlds.

The use of '*sembada*' as Solo Kaskusers' first ethic is innovative since the terminology had never been mentioned previously in any threads on f=160. When asked about the word choice, Prima and Sodron simply answered that *sembada* was the word that best described the expectation of being coherent and prudent as a Kaskuser in the offline sphere and at the same time a citizen in the offline world.

The word *sembada*, nevertheless, is a popular word in everyday life conversations, both in Javanese and in Indonesian, albeit with different meanings. As *sembada* does not have a direct English translation, three related meanings are of importance here. First, in Indonesian, the term refers to 'sufficient'. It is commonly used as a compound, for example, '*swasembada*' meaning 'self-sufficient'. Second, in Javanese, *sembada* refers to a sense of prudence and fairness in the act taken. For example, a child is expected to be fair when playing a game and not to cheat. If the child is caught behaving inadequately, s/he ought to be *sembada* and willing to accept the punishment; or, one is expected not to complain when injured after being consciously involved in a quarrel during a game or in a risky game.

The third interpretation of the term comes from a Javanese compound of '*dora sembada*'. It derives from a Javanese mythology of Dora and Sembada, the loyal assistants of the mythical King Saka. The Letter of Aji Saka (*Serat Aji Saka*), a letter describing the historical account of the foundation of Java, depicts that Aji Saka invented Javanese letters in memory of them. The story starts when the prince of the mythical kingdom, Bhumi Majeti, initiates a quest to discover Java. Before leaving, he asks Dora to accompany him and Sembada to guard his sacred saber (*Aji Pusaka*) at his palace. He warns Sembada that no one should ever lay hands on it except the prince himself.

At that time, Java Island was ruled by the Giant King, Cengkar, a cannibal. When Aji Saka landed on Java and learned the story of King Cengkar and his favorite meal, he asked the chef to introduce him to the King. Aji Saka eventually kills the giant during the meeting and takes over his power. Reigning in a new kingdom, Aji Saka asks Dora to pick up his saber back in the old kingdom. Coming back to Bhumi Mejati, Dora is welcomed by

Sembada. However, being loyal to the task he was given, Sembada refuses to give the saber to Dora. Dora, on the other hand, being loyal to the mission refuses to go back to Java without the saber. The consequence was that the two ended up in a battle and died.

Learning the news, Aji Saka mourned the tragic fact and regretted his absence. A personal letter or a letter of assignment, he reflected on the tragedy, would have avoided the misunderstanding. Thus, learning his lesson and to honor the two late assistants, he created the alphabet, which marked the dawn of Javanese literacy and civilization. The alphabets, a form of pangram, are now known as *Hanacaraka* (Sutardja 1917; Santoso and Pringgoharjono 2006: 22; Ras and Robson 1991: 119; Endraswara 2006; Humboldt 1836). Several interpretations of the story underscore the notion of order and consequences. Sagar (1992: 158) predicts that prior to the time of alphabets, social norms were not codified, and there was thus no single governance on the island. On the subject of intersubjectivity, Sindhunata (2007: 92–92) interprets the story as a message for 'understanding people' within their context as the first priority before making any response, as it is only in that way that the consequences of action can be fully understood and thus the fairness to the action. Thus, being prudent.

These illustrations of *sembada* imply several dimensions of prudence. First, prudence is a skill to have the presence of alertness as a basic part of the procedural steps of action while respecting the consequences. Second, it denotes the ability to calculate and anticipate any consequences as a distant object that might emerge as a result of an individual's action. It is an investigation of an individual's agency and capacity for the course of action in order to be able to bear the reciprocal consequences, and, thus, to have concern or care while relating with others or objects. Such calculations, accordingly, are considered to be the fairness of valuation between the act and the endured consequence. Third, in sum, it requires the ability to take responsibility while encountering the external. *Sembada* as 'prudence' requires self-awareness on the coming, both predicted and unpredicted, occurence.

Harya described prudence (*sembada*) as an attitude that is weighted fairly between self-oriented activity (*diri sendiri*) and the role (*kebermanfaatan*) of the community or society, between the online and the offline, between leisure (*senang-senang*) chat and social obligations. 'To have a role for others, not only to be playful (*cengengesan*),' he said. These dualities are the consequences of having the ability to 'play' in the online sphere according to Amakuzalek. He emphasizes the ethic of online dwelling as follows,

> We can be playful but we also uphold the consequences (*cengengesan ning sembada*). When we meet online we could just be a playful being and just have fun, [we are] not making anything; but in the offline, we should make something, we 'are becoming.' (*dadi*, to become, to take shape)

This account implies two preconditions of being *sembada* in f=160: the further recognition of the distinction between the online and offline, which had previously emerged during the organization of Gatherings, and a sense of failure or guilt if the consequences of being a netizen could not be met. Again, this understanding of netizenship implies the three dimensions of *sembada*: alertness, fairness, and responsibility.

### 4.1.2 Digital Power and Being Alert

The notion of 'balance' and consequence of being netizens, as Harya said, was recognized after Solo Kaskusers experienced that online dwellers had two potential capacities during the Ilham campaign: network-building and speedy responses. Within four days (the speed dimension), KRS managed to build a cooperation (the network dimension) comprising the Red Cross, the National Department of Health, mass media, and donors while, at the same time, securing Ilham's first medical treatment. This ability to respond to and initiate acts within the frame of speed and network is what eventually formed trust and reliance. These experiences show that such speedy actions could define how a network could further develop. They realized that both speed and network are, subsequently, what they can generate to mobilize and to change the course of offline society and the common good. It is a form of 'digital power', Sodron said.

It was in that two months of social activism that Solo Kaskusers revealed that possessing digital online power could affect those in the offline world, and that with great power comes great responsibility. In this context, once Kaskusers dwell in the online, their speedy response is recognized as a passionate engagement and a sign of solidarity to the larger society. To recall the Ilham campaign, in a social setting where—at that time—there was no health insurance, and hardly any protection from economic uncertainty, each member of the community and society should be helpful. After the event, Solo Kaskusers reflected that as netizens with digital power, they could be relied upon to sustain the life of the exterior, whether they be other citizens of Solo or any other citizen. Relating with others as an effort to become a node in the network is a continuation of the trainings that Kaskusers are familiar with in the databanking habit as Chap. 2 illustrates.

Speedy responses therefore act as signs of the exercised of power to care for others living beyond Kaskus; this signifies social responsibility. Caring is a dimension of dwelling. Solo Kaskusers' offline activities, like Gatherings and social activism, rely heavily on their recognition of the exterior, that is, the neighborhood where their offline and online bodies dwell. On this point the perception of neighborhood and dwelling has been redefined three times: First, when a Kaskuser started to chat and recognize the merriness of the online forum (Chap. 2). Second, when Solo Kaskusers started to reconnect themselves with the city of Solo as they could not avoid the geographical attachment (Chap. 3). Third, by discovering new neighborhoods as a sphere that could be impacted by Solo Kaskusers' activity. The life of Solo Kaskusers as members of an online community shows that the change in their digital activities and activism are revelations of recognizing their new environments, which in Solo Kaskusers' case are the city and its society, and the willingness to care for those included in the environment.

Different from the Western classic sociological notion of urbanization and modernity, Indonesian and Southeast Asian cities are still characterized by a traditional network of *kampong* (neighborhoods), which influences urban social relationships (Newberry 2006; Evers and Korff 2003). Contrary to the fear of urban social disconnection (Tönnies 1887), Southeast Asian urban settings are spaces where urbanites readily seek out a closer relationship with others since it empowers economic and social capital (Newberry 2006; Evers and Korff 2003).

In this view, the *kampong* is not merely a location but is, most importantly, a network of livelihoods. This is what Hildred Geertz identified half a century ago as a 'pool of relations [which] can be drawn on for assistance' (1961: 25). The *kampong* is a social safety net and a reservoir of assistance; neighbors are considered specialists who are expected to be ready to provide assistance unconditionally, that is, to be reliable. Unlike the specialists from the next *kampong* or from a city that is far and sometimes beyond our reach, our neighbors in the *kampong* are near and visually present.

The construction of f=160 as a home, therefore, relies on: (i) mutual reliance and a pool of assistance, and (ii) the notion of power in Kaskus or in an online community, which refers to individual skills within a collective reliance. Therefore, when Johar failed to complete his duty, the punishment was fatal since he was considered to be a broken spoke in the wheel of the community's competence and destructive to Kaskusers' anticipated role at home. In Kaskus' network of reliability, such conduct is an anti-social behavior that destroys the intimate family at home and in the community.

Understanding Kaskusers' view on power is, therefore, a mark that shapes the perception of the disparities between the online and offline realities, on one hand, and guilt, on the other. These are the two preconditions for being *sembada* in Kaskus. Social activism could be viewed as a justification that being in Kaskus is not simply self-serving and for the 'ego' while leaving 'the society' (*masyarakat*) behind. Each social activism is a mutual practice of self-affirmation of being online and offline. It is a relationship that perceives all realities as 'real'; to make Solo Kaskusers 'sane', Sodron said. In this notion of ethic, the feeling of guilt is not the opposite of 'right,' but of 'ability' and 'coherence'; good in this sense is not simply the opposite of 'bad', but is the opposite of being 'selfish' or 'ignorant'.

In Kaskus, this reckoning of the entirety of action can be traced back to the initial perception of online activity as a self-centered playful activity. Online chat is considered to be a sphere of play, leisure, and individuation, advocating the online persona and 'alter ego' as Chap. 2 describes. As a consequence, if Kaskusers want to dwell in the online sphere, they are expected to show the same commitment to matters in the offline sphere. In this formulation, being *sembada* represents the effort to maintain fairness to the social, after being 'individualistic' in the online sphere.

Such construct on social relations and social responsibility, nevertheless, could only be revealed after two procedural perceptual experiences. First, Solo Kaskusers recognized the disembeddedness between the 'online community' and the 'offline society'. Here, again, othering is a means to access recognition, which leads to reconnection. Second, Kaskus activism as a social reconnection could only be revealed after a successful experience in creating a digital home (Chap. 2) and after the experience of reconnection during the Gatherings (Chap. 3). These experiences are pivotal in layering the confidence for the enlargement of the online community to include the offline sphere, culture, and network. The community ethic of social activism, accordingly, is not simply a moral tone, but most importantly procedural perceptual revelations.

Kaskusers' sense of *sembada* and guilt or the fear of being guilty is different from the guilt associated with traditional and religious norms, which are introduced to a subject before one experiences the error. Kaskusers' guilt was recognized after an experience took place and Solo Kaskusers underwent a reflexive dialog. After the Ilham activism, for example, guilt was redefined when Solo Kaskusers revealed the digital power they possess and after recognizing the offline-online partition.

Accordingly, being prudent in relation to circumventing guilt is a new reinterpretation and not simply a duplication of the traditional Javanese value. Again, it is procedural.

In this mental operation, society in the offline world is set as the exterior while the online properties—Kaskus, Kaskuser, shielded-identity, online chat—are set as the interior. For Solo Kaskusers, living between the two requires a weighted fairness. With the realization of social activism—through which Kaskusers could bodily experience the notion and function of community they have built in the online—such juxtaposition no longer recognizes the offline world as a foreign entity. Instead, it has become part of Kaskus' online environment.

This interpretation of Kaskus activism contests Bell's (2001) formulation on the formation motive of an online community. Bell (2001) argues, that the creation of community is meaningful for its members since they have previously longed for a community connection that has been absent from their offline urban society. Kaskusers' experience shows that this online-offline reconnection and relation is neither straightforward nor automated. It needed, instead, reflection on random unforeseen historical events, like the thread about Ilham and the actions that came after. The online to offline transformation of an online community is thus not necessarily a genuine digital urge since the origin of a community connection relies on the result of reflective evaluation about how Kaskusers, as online community members, see themselves as part of the offline world.

As such, participating in both online and offline spheres is a feedback routine which is a sign that Solo Kaskusers are making an effort to become a reliable node in the network between the two realities. In this notion of relatedness as reality—although they are not part of any threads and live completely apart from the Kaskus realm—Ilham and his family members have eventually become parts of Solo Kaskusers' offline community, or the neighborhood (*kampong*).

### *4.1.3 The Feasibility of Social Activism*

Being *sembada* in Kaskus, thus, is also about exercising digital power to help those outside the realm of the online. Accordingly, Johar's online unresponsiveness was a failure of the operation of power among Kaskusers. Through this experience, Solo Kaskusers came to the conclusion that the interaction with the digital practice should always be 'fair' to the offline world: their online merriness of chatting should also be useful in helping those offline. This means that, in the world of Kaskus, citizenship is not simply an ascribed status, but is shaped through the continuous discipline of netizenship, which requires swift participation.

At this stage, the efforts to exercise digital power as a fair treatment in the offline world became another value-added dimension to Solo Kaskusers' notion of 'sanity' (*nggenah*).[3] It is only then that an exercise of digital power is acceptable and defined through Kaskusers' interpretation of prudence. Returning to digital power, with such a high collective expectation of exercising power, failing to recognize guilt, as Johar did, is perceived to be 'insanity' (*ora nggenah*). To recall the magnitude of togetherness and sanity for Kaskusers, a failure to bounce back or to re-embed themselves in society would be defined not only as imbalance but also insanity or 'delusional' according to Kaskusers. Sodron explains the view:

> In the virtual (*maya*) world, our *alter ego* could go out [read: to become prominent]. What we wanted to say in the tangible (*nyata*) world but couldn't, we could do that in the virtual world. [...] a conflict can occur because we could not differentiate between virtual and real. For example, somebody who has a lot of posting counts and reputation in Kaskus could feel as if s/he is an 'elderly' [read: senior member of a society] in the offline. You could go online for your needs, but in the real world [read: offline world] you might not have [achieved] anything.

Kaskusers' view on bouncing back to the offline reality as a formula to tame the 'alter ego' strikes a chord with Herbert Mead's (1934) figuration on self. According to Kaskusers, when a Kaskus member decides to dwell in the online space and to play a role s/he will act on behalf of what Kaskusers call the 'ego'. Mead (1934) labels such identity the 'I,'.[4,5,6] Solo Kaskusers view that a concentration on the 'ego' means leaving the social or society behind. Practices focusing only on the 'ego', therefore, create a misbalance or incoherency leading to a sense of guilt. This is when Kaskusers began to recognize the urge to guarantee the balance between going offline and, to cite Sodron, 'coming back' offline. *Sembada*, then, should be understood as a mechanism to control the possession and use of digital power to deal with the 'I'.

The centered notion of power has been a constant subject for scholars of Indonesia and Java, particularly in terms of nation-building within centralistic power, charismatic leaders, and hierarchy (Anderson 2007, 2006, 1991; Antlöv 2005).[7] Johar's bullying, then, shows an act of performance assessment of those in power. For Solo Kaskusers, as all have the same digital power, they have to equally participate as a collective not based on a charismatic center. Thus, the matter of power in Kaskus focuses both on impact and on validation. This understanding explains why Johar's unresponsiveness was unforgivable, as it threatened the validity of Kaskusers' courtesy of going online with their digital power.

As Kaskusers perceive digital power as the means to participate in the rich experience of online chatting and reaching out to the network of the city, the same power should also find its meaning in the general offline world. Confining digital power merely to Kaskus' online sphere is perceived to injure the ideal of having digital power. Accordingly, Johar's unresponsiveness represented a betrayal of digital power; an abuse of the initial possession of power itself and the collective imagination of what digitality and being in Kaskus means. Therefore, in Kaskusers' view, although Johar was a Regional Leader or the center, they had to confiscate Johar's power because it was a menace to the justification and validation of being digitally powerful.

Such an approach to 'digital power' evokes a consequence that in order for Solo Kaskusers to be able to recognize the power they can obtain, they need to find an object or event to exercise the power and justify its possession. Therefore, after helping Ilham, Solo Kaskusers started to regularly seek someone in need of the helping hand. Helping Ilham and participating in other social activism are events that are not simply an act of altruism but also an event to justify the power they possess.

Chapter 3 describes that Gatherings and their city promotion functions also as ritual, where fellowship is relied upon, and creativity and feedback are expected. Kaskus social activism shares the same feature. Reflecting on the aid campaign for Ilham, Prima described that the whole dynamic during and post-Ilham's advocacy was considered an 'education process' through which the group was tested as tension emerged. Cohesive cooperation and conflict will be 'decisive for the community's future', he argued: 'let it explode, and we'll see who is going to burst out [leave], and who remains and becomes established (*klop*)'.

Exercising digital power in offline events is hence a form of communication about being loyal to the community at the same time. In this sense, as rituals, the annual gatherings and social activism are not simply automated and repetitive occurrences that serve merely to reach out to the exterior, but events that maintain the community's confidence as well. They are the filter that weeds out those who underperform in terms of general expectations. It is, thus, socially punitive.

As a strategic decision, such a fellowship project is measured through feasibility as well. KRS would always first determine whether the project is possible within their range of digital power. As a ritual, there is high hope that social activism will be successful. On one hand, there is recognition of the need for solidarity with others, but on the other hand a failing social activism will crumble the community's confidence as a powerful agent. A communication ritual should feature functionalities (see Basso and Senft 2009), hence, the pragmatic decision here is in part being honest and true to both their own capabilities and the limitations of their digital power.

Events are also a visualization of how powerful the digital power is. Successful Gatherings and social activism verify that digital power is functional. Tangible power has to be regularly tested. As such, regular habitual acts present the notion of mediated solidarity. Access to digitality and dwelling in f=160, according to Solo Kaskusers, needs social justification from both Kaskusers' self-justification and by people in the offline world. Otherwise, they would simply be 'a bunch of Internet people' as Surandy described them while introducing Solo Kaskusers to Ilham's mother.[8]

The installment of *sembada* represented the establishment of a curriculum to develop social awareness not only as a method of coming back to society, but also to differentiate Kaskus Solo as an online community with other online communities or other 'bunches of Internet people'. As Amakuzalek formulated:

> After a while we just realized that everybody and any online community could hold meet-ups (*kopdar*). If we only come for meet-ups and karaoke, anyone could do (*buat*) that. But if we say, visit an orphanage and help them with what we can [then it would be different]. It was simply like that at first, but it was not a fad (*iseng*).[9] It means making something and not just being a fad. If it is a fad, then it would not have materialized (*jadi*). We have to be financially transparent also for the activity [for example]. Set an example of what it means to be online. This is positive [from these activities], the kids [fellow Solo Kaskusers], they have heart [to be social], and to be different [than other online communities].

Pursuing social activism and other offline activities is, to use Amakuzalek's term, to 'have heart'. The notion is quickly juxtaposed with a contradictory condition, of 'having no heart' or having no feelings; ignorance. With this disposition, being *sembada* becomes a moral ethic of not only of being in an online community but also of being a member of society and a human being.

### 4.1.4 The Institutionalization of Guilt

Such view on guilt and the role of the online community is also found in the everyday life chat in Kaskus. Take one example in what Okkirush posted on October 16, 2012. He wrote: 'I feel bad. It has been a while since we had an event. We should make something to make things merry again. We should not only frolic when we have speedy chat'.[10]

Regular everyday life online chat plays a great role in evoking the need to relate with the offline society outside Kaskus. Not all Solo Kaskusers' social activism started as a designated project such as the annual Gathering. An act of 'social solidarity' (*solidaritas sosial*), as Kaskusers call it, could start with a mundane conversation, as was the case with the Ilham campaign and the Iftar charity dinner. Regular everyday life online chat makes it possible to keep the awareness of coherence being unremittingly present without the need to create a special thread. The apparent 'feeling bad', to cite Okkirush, is such an example of presence. Such expression of feeling in everyday life chats is not simply a means to evoke the fear of being guilty, but also implies the effort to continually uphold the honor of being a Kaskuser if s/he could bear the consequences of being online.

Chatting becomes a public sphere when it acts as a sliding door for ethic production or a medium to remind one of the role of being a Kaskuser. Prudence and guilt in f=160 were also produced through chats as a pragmatic spontaneous decision as part of an organizational strategy. Hence, the maxims could be considered honest rather than superficially designed. Sodron explained that his action in adopting Prima's post as the forum's new banner was an immediate and spontaneous action rather than a contingency. This spontaneity reflects a genuine expression of shared feeling. It was this honest instantaneity in responding to a failure that made *sembada* an authentic expression in the first; it resulted from a common pragmatism rather than manufactured sentiment.

Digital infrastructure and gadgets have made it possible for Solo Kaskusers to capture the quintessence of such utterances in a matter of seconds; such utterances are expressive statements. In an online community, where textual presentations are the community's closest capital, semiotic presentation becomes a strategic entry into constructing a common code. *Sembada*'s visual form of presentation as a text becomes a sign of the coming presence of the new norm. Making text as a ubiquitous digital artifact serves to reinforce its presence in everyday life conversations as a prompt of what the code is trying to govern.

This pragmatic but strategic code-capturing of 'playful but prudent', which, although materialized from online chats, was actually the unintended extra-textual result of Prima's irritation with Johar's performance, is a reminder that ethics and norms are created from a strategic capacity to deal with the instantaneous dynamic of the community. It, by all chances, is a product of our fellows rather than the elite's suppressive creation. Kaskus digital technology has made it possible for the members to be expressive, and, as such, new codes can be agreed upon.

In the online sphere, a text that has been written can be quickly reproduced to attract attention. The written slogan, *Cengengesan Ning Sembada,* could be found in many forms afterwards. It frames and has become the title of the Chat Lounge thread; it heads the banners displayed in offline events; it is printed on the annual Gathering's T-shirts; it has even become the digital signature for several Kaskusers. It lives in the everyday life exchange between Solo Kaskusers and, in the visual age, it becomes omnipresent as the property of the community, which eventually signifies the community's presence.

This ubiquity of a maxim, at least written as 'feeling bad' as Okkirush expressed, limited the flexibility of being a Kaskuser. What is currently expected by the community, or Solo Kaskusers' attitude toward their online activity within the social fitting of f=160, is visually expressed through these artifacts which encircle the community's space. It is a form of visual organization and therefore it is very much in contrast with the traditional Javanese mechanism of 'feeling' (*rasa*) in the conception of social fitting, which is not formally scripted.

Although *rasa* is the cultural background for cybersense as Chap. 2 describes, Kaskusers have not followed its ambiguous regime. On the contrary, Solo Kaskusers' conduct is well-recorded in the *KaskusStatistics*. Unlike the operation of *rasa* in the offline society where guilt is set between the eloquent and ineloquent and between grace and disgrace, in Kaskus it is a set of clearly expressed expectations based on a definition of right and wrong through community regulations and transcribed ethics such as 'playful but prudent'. What is wrong—deviant conversation, lazy participation, junk post, late reply, to name a few—could be captured on the screen. In Kaskus, therefore, social fitting is no longer a subject of flexible feelings but is a matter of monitored visual assessment. Guilt is currently disciplined via collective monitoring and the assessment of chat statistics, posting rules, response speed, and of how coherent one is while possessing digital power. *KaskusStatistics* as a digital archive has made it possible to start a prosecution, as is what unfolded in the case against Johar.

As chat texts and timelines are recorded, unlike *rasa*, cybersensing could be compiled as a figuration as to whether a Kaskuser could be marked as an active participant in the community's action or a deviant. Digital tracking through all social media platforms also provides a course for a user's online activities. Johar was handed a guilty verdict not only because of the evidence collected from Kaskus' statistics, but also since Solo Kaskusers caught him being active on other social media platforms while replying late in Kaskus. All of these accusations of wrongdoing were validated with screenshots. Unless a Kaskuser goes offline, s/he is in a completely monitored position by others.

Errors are recorded on Kaskus and they remain forever as long as the server's hard disk can still be accessed. At the same time, with the detail of online regulations and manuscripts that describe the community's expectations like field reports, financial reports, chats, audiovisual documentation, transcribed aphorisms, Solo Kaskusers are expected to comply with the procedures of being an online community. These digital texts are the textures of being in Kaskus. Thus, in Kaskus, the flexibility of *rasa* is viewed as an antithesis to cybersensing and the data in the digital archives. In the archive—capable digital world—guilt is evidential and no longer a non-stable abstraction; it has become a reflexive assessment of transcribed conduct.

## 4.2 Militancy in an Ever-Changing Community

*Sembada* as a calculation of anticipation, reflects to some degree, Mead's 'terminal attitudes' (1938: 138). Mead argues while exploring pragmatic acts, 'the reality of what we see is what we can handle' (1938: 105). Although Mead relies on the selective measurement in coping with a forthcoming new experience or object, both Mead's terminal attitude and Kaskuser's notion of *prudence* deliver a course of calculation of preparation to encounter the signified objects. Manipulating the distant object marks the beginning of encountering the world that the perceiving actor anticipates, and explores the possibilities of manipulating the object beforehand (1938: 232). Hence, the human maintains the 'terminal attitude', that is, the readiness of the actors to make contact with the object 'are beginnings of the contact response that will be made to the object when the object is reached' (Mead 1938: 161).

Kaskusers' formulation of *sembada* is indeed about calculation and anticipation, but it does not necessarily lead to manipulation. As an intersubjective effort between actors, to some degree, the actor respects the foreignness of the object, thus keeping the distant object's status 'distant' despite the fact that contact is made. For Solo Kaskusers, it is an attitude of being fair to the possible consequences that are at a distance. Each Kaskuser should be alert to changes in their practices as part of their mode of Kaskus dwelling, accordingly, while continuously calculating the consequences of being online. Take the Ilham campaign as an example: Although such an event was simply unforeseen when Kaskusers started to dwell in the chatting forum, readiness to change the dwelling practice was expected only when such cases occur without making it into a regular thread on, for example, social activism alertness. The main motive of *sembada* is the readiness to accept the unforeseen; it is a submission to alertness.

### 4.2.1 Community on the Move

For Solo Kaskusers, prudence (*sembada*) was imagined as a strategy to deal with the consequences of online dwelling which are unforeseen, both in interaction with other people, or with the content of a post. Accordingly, Kaskusers are expected to embrace change as trained well-disciplined community members. In criticizing the modernist approach of captivating the exterior to understand the world on the basis of our definition, Ingold (2011) warns that life changes should not be overshadowed by the fear of uncertainty but should be connoted with a potential for capacity-building. The Ilham campaign evoked a community's reflection of how to become an ideal digital citizen as a continuation from what they had previously discovered during the organization of Gatherings. Thus, each individual should be aware of the rising commitment forthcoming in anticipating their future possible activism and paths while dwelling in Kaskus and getting used to its properties again, such as the speed.

The events, the activism, the collective action, and the empathy to those in need are evolving unpredicted events that could be considered an 'education process' to use Prima's term, or 'coming of age' to use Harya and Sondron's terminology, through which all the cyberpractices to be correct (*nggenah*) and uphold togetherness (*guyub*) are reaffirmed. In his view and the views of those who were against Johar, correction was unnecessary as each Solo Kaskuser had already become an example to each other while upholding the community's codes to their best ability. Johar was not corrected and transformed into a disciplined member of Kaskus Solo, but was simply expelled as he did not recognize the community's path of transformation. Similar to online chatting techniques in preparing a post while avoiding red-bricking, there is a sense of determinism while sensing what the community is expecting as Kaskusers' 'terminal attitude'.

Before the Ilham Case, Solo Kaskusers focused on designing their home and their own togetherness (*guyub*), which eventually shaped their ethic of being correct and in order (*nggenah*) and evoked the sense of citizenship, as part of a coming of age (*pendewasaan*). Similarly, as a continuation of the experience of online wayfaring, the path of experiencing a reattachment or reconnection to the social has followed that of a 'coming of age' (*pendewasaan*). Harya expressed his conviction on reconnection that 'coming of age' means 'limiting egoism and thinking about other people'. He described his own experience while dwelling in f=160:

> When I talk about [online] flaming, I feel that now I could do more than just flame [other people's posts]. Becoming an adult is not that we resign [being ourselves], but [is] for something bigger than us, and to be able to see a bigger and grand design.

Being coherent in accommodating the interior and the exterior is an ideal of a reality that many Javanese hope to have.[11] Kaskus' version of coherency is, however, not simply an altered copy or a simulation. It is a hope or ideal that they revealed through experiencing activism.

Online communities are often simplified as a simulation of the real world (see Balsamo 1996: 126). The other side of the argument focuses on online dwellers' creativity in establishing their own world (see Boellstorff 2008; Pearce 2009; Kobayashi 2010) that does not 'prioritize simulating or 'mirroring' reality, but assumed human creativity produced its own realities' (Boellstorff 2008: 244). The relationship between the online and offline reality is a pivotal subject in digital engagement. In Kaskusers' experiences, the perception of online/offline configuration is believed to be the basis for the recognition of reality for digital citizens. While reality has become the subject of new media studies, separating online/offline and virtual/real can be problematic because every reality has its own resource of production (Rheingold 2000; Danet 2001; Boellstorff 2008). In Kaskus, the perception of detachment has consequences for both realities and will consequently provide the path for the action taken.

In the early digital era, Rheingold (2000) argued that the online/offline separation eventually becomes less significant, as what matters to online forum members is the intimate social connection that emerged through intensive communication. Thus, any social connection that materialized is a valid reality, he argues, when, in any space including virtual spaces, users can leave their old selves and form new identities and new connections while transcending all spatial boundaries. While such an optimistic approach is challenged by more pessimistic accounts (e.g. Putnam 2000; Turkle 2012) that consider virtual intimacy to be fragile as its bonding is simply plastic, current scholars focus more on the mode and materialization of practice and engagement. These are the two elements that form the reality of a community.

Boellstorff's (2008) study on Second Life players, for example, presents a contrasting conclusion: motives are fluid as digital life has an agency of its own—both through online social relations and digital artifacts—to change the course of the users' realities. While making the distinction between the 'actual-world sociality' and the 'virtual-world sociality,' he argues that 'the sociality of virtual worlds develops on its own terms' and that Second Life is simply not a derivative of the actual world (Boellstorff 2008: 63).

It is problematic to compare these studies since they focus on different types of online communities and online individuals. Nevertheless, they offer a common understanding that online reality could be strategic and should be operable for the online community in order to help them to develop their community and norms. That is, the online realities should offer a means to find their own meaning in the context of everyday life activities. If these interpretations of online/offline relationships are taken as anything but dualism, then they could view reality as a process set in structure and dynamic in content, because there is an unceasing process of communication or revelation between actors and between realms. Such an approach to reality and intersubjectivity offers a path to view that reality in online wayfaring is changing accordingly since it is confined within the ability to perceive the spheres. In short, it depends on how the members of an online community are able to see their reality as something affecting and real.

With such understanding, it is to be expected that primary norms are changing according to how Kaskusers perceive their realities. Changing the mode of dwelling as the consequence of advocating Kaskus' norms does not reflect instability but indicates new revelations about being in Kaskus. The decade-long life in Kaskus illustrates that online life in Kaskus has been evolving with norms of 'freedom', to 'equality', to 'order', to 'togetherness', to 'citizenship', and now to 'prudence' (*sembada*) with each stage offering different realities. These findings correspond with those of scholars in the field who notes that reality is changing until actors can achieve temporary common terms (see Habermas 1998, 1992) and each reality can only be noticed when it crosses paths with another, regardless of cohesion (see Ingold 2011; Ingold and Vergunst 2008). In each step of the experience, Solo Kaskusers perceive their reality—in order to sustain their imagination of being a member of a community or society—only when their experience of being in Kaskus reveals itself as crossing paths, for instance in the case of the 2010 Gathering and the Ilham advocacy. The assessment of Kaskusers' notion of citizenship, or netizenship, should fit within these stages accordingly.

In this detail of perceiving others, or in this case the 'offline world', Tim Ingold argues that each world is comprised of actors themselves, and thus signification can only be formed when the two subjects' paths cross (2011). He further recommends that the means for scholars to 'understand "movement" through the Internet' lies in the conduct of the digital dwellers (Ingold 2011: 249). This approach gives an understanding that the relation between the online as the social and the offline as the ecological setting should evolve continually as part of a human's perceptual engagement with the constituents of their world.

The perceptual engagement of Kaskus activism and netizenship could both be traced to reflections on the course of being in an online community. The first trace emerged during the preparations of the Kaskus Solo annual Gathering in 2010, as Chap. 3 describes. At that time, Solo Kaskusers were in search of a Solonese identity to articulate the Gathering's theme. However, such activism is confined to the community's annual celebration and is singularly directed toward the city.

In 2010, shortly after the annual Gathering, the understanding of 'activism' and 'being a good citizen' was once again challenged by another social encounter through which Solo Kaskusers revealed that the notion of being a Solonese could no longer be limited to its relationship with the city; instead it had to be extended to not only the city but also to the people that call it home. As such, helping Ilham or going offline is then no longer a reconnection to the city as it was with the first 2010 annual Gathering but has, moreover, become part of the responsibility of being digital; that is, becoming a member of a society while possessing digital power.

### 4.2.2 *Reliance within Networks*

The norm of collective reliance extends Solo Kaskuser's notion of togetherness and secures the ever-changing community, where trust is seeded through successful cooperation among Kaskusers. Bruhn identifies that trust binds collectively through the 'expectation that people will interact honestly and cooperatively to benefit each other' (Bruhn 2011: 22). In Kaskus, such trust materializes through reliance on a cumulative network.

Within this recognition, Solo Kaskusers perceive togetherness as a network of unions. Involvement in a network means trust. For Kaskusers, someone without an online forum and offline community is depicted as a person without a role. Sodron describes his involvement in the network as follows:

> That is why we keep it [our online relationship as friendship is important)]. It [having friends] is not about important or unimportant (*penting atau tidak penting*), but it is rooted in ourselves. Apart from Kaskus, whether it [Kaskus] will continue to exist or not, these people [Kaskusers] have become my friends. When one calls and says that s/he needs help. I am ready [to help]. Consciously (*sadar*) or not I am ready to help.

By enlarging the KRS network, somebody might know somebody else who could become the problem solver in the future. Social security is not just measured by the quantity of friends, but also by the quality in terms of varied and plural backgrounds. Friends with different backgrounds of capital could serve Solo Kaskusers' different needs. Like Kaskus' plural network, Solo Kaskusers' offline network is also plural.

Knowing the heterogeneous background of Solo Kaskusers gives a certain comfort to begin with. It provides the imagination of being in a vast network of potential reliabilities or a neighbourhood of specialists. In the uncertain offline world, having friends is a comfort. Like Icesusujahe once assured me, 'maybe one day they could help us in real life, maybe we could do business with them. Look at Plerdisk, the Internet shop he runs is also from Kaskus [read: a joint venture with other Kaskusers]'.

It does not necessarily have to be an emergency cry for help or reciprocal inquiries that motivate the Kaskus network, as it was in the Ilham campaign. A network is more like a social investment. Therefore, Kaskusers do not recognize the social distance that distinguishes friends, colleagues and acquaintances. They are all simply friends who could become a possible actor in solving potential problems. Making friends is part of the 'terminal attitude', to use Mead's (1938) term, against the future. The formation of Kaskus therefore relies on the practice of sharing and supporting everyday life. Armin expressed that bonds between two strangers are already actually established through membership in Kaskus and through *statistics* readings. It is not a strange practice when a Kaskuser asks another Kaskuser, who is a stranger, for help just by relying on common membership in Kaskus, providing that s/he has a good reputation in the *statistics*. Armin describes the social practice as follow:

> Again, this regional forum was created for Kaskus users who have a certain bond with Solo. [But] besides that, we could always add friends (*menambah teman*). There might be a time when we need a friend's help and we will have many connections. Most importantly, it is now habitual (*kebiasaan*) for young Indonesians to find solutions to problems using Kaskus, whether it is life problems or simply required information.

Armin also explained further that intimacy in this kind of network could become platonic since friendship could be established further through private messages or off-screen communication.

In such communication, deeper trust is explored through intimate communication that shares 'life problems'. This practice leads to heart-to-heart conversations (*curahan hati*, abv. *curhat*) in Indonesia. This 'heart-to-heart conversation' does not have to be romantic; instead, as Armin expressed, it covers all the subjects associated with 'life problems'. It is not rare to find that a Solo Kaskuser will have a closer friendship with those with whom they normally have heart-to-heart conversations. Mochi was close to Fajar and Dolhpin_86, while Amakuzalek talked with Wahyu and Surandy, and Novi was close to William. This kind of fellow-listener relationship goes beyond identity boundaries. Take the Novi-William friendship as an example: Novi is a female Muslim and political activist who wears a veil (*hijab*), and is interested in the supernatural subjects of chat, while William is a Christian male of Chinese descent, a computer expert, and a gamer.

For such affinity, it is common to hear that these community members would use the intimate terms 'like brother/sister', or 'already like my own sibling' to describe the quality of the network and personal relationship. These proven reliable relationships offer some sort of comfort and security in the face of community dynamics.

### 4.2.3 *Responsiveness to Change and Militancy*

This chapter amplifies how Solo Kaskusers are exploiting the next possible normative resources, in this case the Javanese notion of prudence, to warrant its notion of citizenship. In this path, Solo Kaskusers eventually reproduced the ethic of digital prudence (*sembada*) as an accountable correctional measure to survive in both online and offline spheres. Thus 'having the heart', to echo Armin's spirit of altruism and solidarity, is an appropriation of becoming a reflexive digital being; that is, to exercise digital power.

Each new phase of Kaskus engagement—the decision to dwell in a certain forum, to participate in chats, to terminate BB17 and FC, to go offline, to promote the city, to participate in social activism, and to participate in other community engagements—is a consequence of reflexive engagement and readiness to change community practices. The changes are demanding and require further effort to what has been given. Kaskus, once an underground community that was famous for illegal digital materials, is now related to various social activism. Here, tension emerges between the effort to be disciplined and social exclusion. Cohesion has always had its own ghost of becoming.

'To be militant!' expressed Harya in explaining how Solo Kaskuser should be aware that community practices in Kaskus are always changing while embracing the unforeseen dynamic of their community's wayfaring. Here, again, the notion of militancy surfaces among Kaskusers. Before the time of offline activism, militancy was perceived as an ethic of diligence in providing quality digital information in threads as the role of a responsive chatting partner. At the previous stage, as Chap. 2 describes, militancy is a negation against becoming a *lurker* or *troll*. Currently, militancy is about enduring changes to facilitate becoming an active citizen in society and a devoted member of the community of netizens.

In social activism, Solo Kaskusers invest significant effort to become militant: submitting their time, money, energy, while suspending their own personal activities, conflicting with friends, and exploiting their immediate recourses. Militancy at this stage, in sum, is no longer about a measured submission to Kaskus, but about the consistency in becoming a netizen. It is only through this sequence of online-offline activities and engaging with the existence of others—the city in Gatherings, the society in social activism—Solo Kaskusers' level of militancy in upholding *sembada* can be recognized and measured. Measurement is a key aspect as all Solo Kaskusers' activities are recorded in the *KaskusStatistics*. Reading *KaskusStatistics* provides illustrations of how consistent a Solo Kaskuser to be responsive to the community's new challenges, norms, and ethics.

Indonesians' imagination of the relationship between community or association and the society in terms of being 'militant' could be traced to the glorious narrative of the 1928 Youth Pledge (*Sumpah Pemuda*). The event, which took place in Batavia, now Jakarta, produced the national pledge for unity by various Indonesian local and regional youth associations as a call against the Dutch colonial government. It is celebrated today as a nationalistic heroism delivered by flaming youth spirits and association (see Abdullah 2009: 46–48).

Such a background gives a socio-political setting for Kaskusers to view militancy as a materialization of an expected heroic ideal to advocate those who are weak. 'From zero to hero' becomes a saying that is popular among Solo Kaskusers to describe the notion of their militancy. Social media-based activism in this frame is not only a medium for 'talking back' against the elites in class relations, but also acts as a validation medium for social solidarity in a nationalistic frame. It is a method that confirms a Kaskuser's belonging in both society and a network.

After the fall of Suharto, scholars reporting from the conflict areas warned that local young people and students were actively becoming actors who construct local identities and contested the singular notion of nationality (Van Klinken 2007; Davidson and Henley 2007; Bräuchler 2003). Local identity is also a subject of capital close to the reorganization of power and economy, which was used to gain support from the masses in 2000–2004 for communal conflicts in Indonesia. This is not the case with Solo Kaskusers.

For Solo Kaskusers, their connection to local identity is not a matter of regionalism. Furthermore, Solo Kaskusers' militancy is not about chauvinism. Regional awareness and regional activism is taken into account simply because it is a in situ reality. It is the closest resource and location of a social unit. Although they are connected to other Kaskusers across the archipelago, to experience 'Indonesia' as a unit is too large and abstract for Solo Kaskusers. As such, the city and the surrounding society became the closest reality of responsiveness they could take hold of.

This interpretation of Kaskus experience and militancy echoes the objection against the separation between the 'social' and 'technology'. The ethic to be a militant online dweller comes from realizing the separation between online and offline activities and recognizing digital power and guilt. Kaskus activism is, hence, a consequence of going online and not purely a moral code of consciousness. Since a human has the capability to embody the mediums s/he encounters, the modern dichotomies between sociality-performative could become a misleading approach (see Van Loon 2008: 9, 104, 132), particularly in understanding the reflexive processes and the mutual agency of actors. Social engagements, or in this case Kaskusers' notions of militancy, do not necessarily lead to a firm end as it preserves the dynamic of the evolving perceptual encounters. The formation of Kaskus Regional Solo and its connectivity to the local city and society, accordingly, is also not about local reaction to 'global moral corruption', borrowing Bowen's (2003) depiction of regional cohesion. Instead, it is some sort of civil correction to the 'morally corrupt' fellow, like Johar, within the continual mediated contextuality of their local surroundings.

## Notes

1. http://archive.kaskus.co.id/thread/4814780/0#
2. http://archive.kaskus.co.id/thread/4814780/0#
3. In the previous chapter, I described that in Javanese those who are part of disorder and deny togetherness are 'insane' (*ora nggenah*).
4. George Herbert Mead differentiates 'I' and 'me' with 'I' as the 'Me' is part of the self that learns interaction with others and the environment. Social influence is internalized to this part of self, making it control the 'I'. The 'I' is the advocate of the individual since the 'I' represents an individual's response to the attitude of the community (1934: 196).
5. Linguistically, there is no distinction between the first person singular subject pronoun of 'I' and the object pronoun of 'me' in both Bahasa Indonesia and Javanese.
6. Rosenthal and Bourgeois (1991) argue that Mead (1938) and Ponty (2002) share similarities on the idea of the formation of self that rely on the relation to the external.
7. In recent years, Indonesian scholars like Antlöv and his colleagues (2005) argue that each scholar should be contextualized within their own time periods and their own ghosts. Suharto<!--Suharto-->'s authoritarian New Order politics was the ghost of scholars observing Indonesia before 1998. Geertz (1956) and Anderson's (2007) assessment about the practice of power under the Suharto regime, however, contributed to a general description of power in Java that classically, power is a tangible contingent product which should be pragmatic in control and self-gratification.
8. http://archive.kaskus.co.id/thread/4814780/0#; Post #62.
9. There are two definition categories for '*iseng*'. First, it means 'fad', 'playful', 'tease', or 'amusement'. Second, it means a productive leisure activity such as a hobby or 'getting busy'. My definition: there is a sense of arbitrariness while doing something and giving something a chance.
10. Post#1076, http://old.kaskus.co.id/showthread.php?t=16750389&page=54
11. De Grave (2011, 2007) explains that the idea of thought in central Java correlates strongly to the mental narrative of human-to-human, human-to-God, and human-to-universe relations. In the context of martial arts and natural healing, he explains that Javanese healers gather the knowledge (*aji*) for it has the conscious responsibility to others as a man that lives, although the moral consequences of having the power to heal is not imperative.

# References


Abdullah, Taufik. *Indonesia: Towards Democracy*. Singapore: Institute of Southeast Asian Studies, 2009.

Anderson, Benedict R.O'G. *Imagined Communities: Reflections on the Origin and Spread of Nationalism*. First published in 1983. Revised edition. London: Verso, 1991.

Anderson, Benedict R.O'G. *Java in a Time of Revolution: Occupation and Resistance, 1944–1946*. Jakarta: Equinox Publishing, 2006.

Anderson, Benedict R.O'G. "The Idea of Power in Javanese Culture." In *Culture and Politics in Indonesia*, edited by Claire Holt, 1–70. Singapore: Equinox Publishing, 2007.

Antlöv, Hans. "The Social Construction of Power and Authority in Java." In *The Java That Never Was: Academic Theories and Political Practices*, edited by Hans Antlöv and Jörgen Hellman, 43–66. Münster: Lit Verlag, 2005.

Balsamo, Anne Marie. *Technologies of the Gendered Body: Reading Cyborg Women*. Durham: Duke University Press, 1996.

Basso, Ellen B. and Gunter Senft. "Introduction." In *Ritual Communication*, edited by Gunter Senft and Ellen B. Basso, 1–20. Oxford: Berg, 2009.

Bell, David. *An Introduction to Cybercultures*. London: Routledge, 2001.

Boellstorff, Tom. *Coming of Age in Second Life*. New Jersey: Princeton University Press, 2008.

Bowen, John R. *Islam, Law, and Equality in Indonesia: An Anthropology of Public Reasoning*. Cambridge: Cambridge University Press, 2003.

Bräuchler, Birgit. "Cyberidentities at War: Religion, Identity, and the Internet in the Moluccan Conflict." *Indonesia* 75 (April 2003): 123–51.

Bruhn, John G. *The Sociology of Community Connections*. Second Edition. Dordrecht: Springer, 2011.

Danet, Brenda. *Cyberpl@y: Communicating Online*. Oxford: Berg, 2001.

Davidson, Jamie and David Henley. "Introduction: Radical Conservatism – The Protean Politics of Adat". In *The Revival of Tradition in Indonesian Politics: The Deployment of Adat from Colonialism to Indigenism*, edited by Jamie Davidson and David Henley, 1–49. Oxon: Routledge, 2007.

De Grave, Jean-Marc. "L'initiation Rituelle Javanaise et ses. Modes de Transmission : Opposition Entre Javanisme et Islam." *Techniques & Culture* Volume 1 No.48–49 (2007): 85–124. Accessed March 1 2014. DOI : 10.4000/tc.3032.

De Grave, Jean-Marc. "The Training of Perception in Javanese Martial Arts." In *Martial Arts As Embodied Knowledge*, edited by D. S. Farrer, 123–144. New York: SUNY Press, 2011.

Endraswara, Suwardi. *Filsafat Kejawen Dalam Aksara Jawa*. Jakarta/Yogyakarta: Gelombang Pasang, 2006.

Evers, Hans-Dieter and Rüdiger Korff. *Southeast Asian Urbanism: The Meaning and Power of Social Space*. 2.Auflage. Münster: LIT Verlag, 2003.

Geertz, Clifford. "Religious Belief and Economic Behavior in A Central Javanese Town: Some Preliminary Remarks," *Economic Development and Cultural Change* Vol. 4 No. 2 (1956), 134–158.

Geertz, Hildred. *The Javanese Family: A study of kinship and socialization*. Michigan: University of Michigan Press, 1961.

Habermas, Jürgen. *On the Pragmatics of Communication*. Cambridge: MIT Press, 1998.

Habermas, Jürgen. *Postmetaphysical Thinking*. Translated by William Mark Hohengarten. Massachusetts: MIT Press, 1992.

Humboldt, Wilhelm Freiherr von. *Über die Kawi-Sprache auf der Insel Java: nebst einer Einleitung über die Verschiedenheit des menschlichen Sprachbaues und ihren Einfluss auf die geistige Entwickelung des Menschengeschlechts, Volume 1*. Amsterdam: Druckerei der Königlichen Akademie der Wissenschaften, 1836.

Ingold, Tim and Jo Lee Vergunst. *Ways of Walking*. Surrey: Ashgate, 2008.

Ingold, Tim. *Being Alive Essays on Movement, Knowledge and Description*. Oxon: Routledge, 2011.

Kobayashi, Tetsuro. "Bridging Social Capital in Online Communities: Heterogeneity and Social. Tolerance of Online Game Players in Japan." In *Human Communication Research* 36 (2010): 546–569.

Mead, Herbert. *Mind, Self, and Society*. Chicago: University of Chicago Press, 1934.

Mead, Herbert. *The Philosophy of the Act*. Chicago: University of Chicago Press, 1938.

Merleau-Ponty, Maurice. *Phenomenology of Perception*. London: Routledge, 2002.

Newberry, Janice C. *Back Door Java: State Formation and the Domestic in Working Class Java*. Toronto: University of Toronto Press, 2006.

Pearce, Celia, and Artemesia. *Communities of Play. Emergent Cultures in Multiplayer Games and Virtual Worlds*. Massachusetts: MIT Press, 2009.

Putnam, Robert D. *Bowling alone: The Collapse and Revival of American Community*. New York: Simon and Schuster, 2000.

Ras, J. J., and S. Stuart O. Robson. *Variation, Transformation and Meaning: Studies on Indonesian Literatures in Honour of A. Teeuw. Working Papers/ Koninklijk Instituut voor Taal-, Land- en Volkenkunde Leiden Volume 144*. Leiden: KITLV Press, 1991.

Rheingold, Howard. *Virtual Community*. Revised edition. Massachusetts: MIT Press, 2000.

Rosenthal, Sandra B. and Patrick L. Bourgeois. *Mead and Merleau-Ponty: Toward a Common Vision*. New York: SUNY Press, 1991.

Sagar, Krishna Chandra. *Foreign Influence on Ancient India*. New Delhi: Northern Book Centre, 1992.

Santoso, Soewito, and Kestity Pringgoharjono. *The Centhini Story: The Javanese Journey of Life : Based on the Original Serat Centhini*. Singapore: Marshall Cavendish, 2006.

Sindhunata. *Putri Cina*. Jakarta: Gramedia Pustaka Utama, 2007.

Sutardja, M. *Dora-Sembada. Dutch East Indies. Commissie voor de Volkslectuur Serie no. 234*. Amsterdam: Indonesische Drukkerij, 1917.

Tönnies, Ferdinand. *Gemeinschaft und Gesellschaft*. Leipzig: Fues's Verlag, 1887.

Turkle, Sherry. *Alone Together: Why We Expect More from Technology and Less from Each Other*. Reprinted edition. New York: Basic Books, 2012.

Van Klinken, Gerry. *Communal Violence and Democratization in Indonesia*. Oxon: Routledge, 2007.

Van Loon, Joost. *Media Technology Critical Perspective*. Berkshire: Open University Press McGraw-Hill Education, 2008.

CHAPTER 5

# Bricked and Buried: Sanctions Against Fake News

In KRS' first decade, reflexive changes seemed to be a series of stabilizing pragmatic actions crafted into continuous enrichment to the online community's normative order. This approach to digital participation, then, while it might appear to signify ruptures or events, should not overshadow Solo Kaskusers' experience of being militant in everyday life, which is tied to endurance in the form of civil correctness and speedy feedback. This discrepancy is the focus of this chapter as it investigates the forms in which citizenship is expressed in Solo Kaskusers' everyday lives.

To assess this, Kaskusers' notion of citizenship should be investigated from the perspective of their internal discipline and external possibilities. The first part of this chapter describes Kaskus' internal dynamic, which shows how digital citizenship is a matter of attentiveness and monitoring during online dwelling to keep bad information from surfacing. For Kaskusers, to become a netizen in everyday life is to be able to carefully participate in discussions or chats about public matters, that is, to debunk hoaxes, to monitor both citizens' and the state's performance, and to investigate the subject of information, both online and offline. The eagerness to become a netizen, however, is not without influence from external possibilities. The local political dynamic encouraged by the mayor moved Solo Kaskusers to become active citizens and cancel the risk of frustration in dealing with bureaucrats and other offline realities. Furthermore, the will of participation became stronger as they could see that KRS' relationship with the state and other offline actors is reciprocal as it responds to Solo Kaskusers' 'ping' of action.



A. Seto, *Netizenship, Activism and Online Community Transformation in Indonesia*, DOI 10.1007/978-981-10-5397-9_5

## 5.1 Civil Correctness

The proliferation of new media in post-authoritarian Indonesia was envisioned as the means to access democracy and articulate civic empowerment (Wayansari 2011; Nugroho 2007; Lim 2003). The support for this notion can be found in the interpretation of the Habermasian (1991) digital space as the host public sphere. This view, however, is not without criticism of the process of new media democracy that is currently taking place because civil society dialog in Indonesia itself does not always feature a civic attitude, on the contrary, it can deliver a grim, uncertain picture.

With a window of opportunity, citizens could attempt to accrue power through conflicts augmented by digital communication. Van Klinken (2007) and Birgit Bräuchler (2003) present compelling documentations that during the unstable time post-1998, 'civil society' groups turned into clashing groups and violence was digitally mediated. Even though the online sphere was expected to uphold democratic ideas, it was in such cases not neutrally exploited. During those troubled times, the Internet became a catalyst for false news and hatred, for instance, by amplifying the sectarian Moluccan conflict (Hill and Sen 2005: 140; Van Klinken 2007: 96). Conversely, civil society elements, like bloggers, have also been prone to communal withdrawal during periods of stability. Triastuti and Rakhmani (2011), for example, exemplify how the Indonesian blogger community was at odds with its own notion of citizenship as it separated into silos, identifying themselves as either Javanese or non-Javanese.

Given such criticism, questions have been raised as to whether technology in this sense is creating a 'modern' citizen. Webster (2006), underlining the construction of reason, underscores that the basis of the information society is not the quantitative evaluation of access to the Internet but the qualitative evaluation of Internet usage in self-development as part of modernity. He (Webster 2006: 57) argues that 'post-traditional' society is expected to rely on the capacity for reflexivity in terms of the use of information. Measuring digital citizenship is therefore difficult.

In the context of Kaskus, this is further compounded as the forum has no certain political or economic agenda and the evolving notion of netizenship is dependent on the course of experience being successful in such engagement as previous chapters have described. Solo Kaskusers' experience illustrates that they were more able to relate to their agency as citizens after they participated in Kaskus' various civic engagements as part of their capacity-building. Such capacity-building can be seen in Kaskusers' everyday life chats. Harya, who was responsible for monitoring f=160 as the then Regional Leader, offered an optimistic view. He proposed that unlike oral debates, online chats serve as a transcribed dialog archive that can be read by the public.

This view provides two advantages. First, the forum is a medium to reach a wider audience on the subject matter, because, in the era of search engines, Kaskus chats are indexed for the public. Second, with such awareness, Kaskusers have attempted to build the space as a medium of training to discuss issues in a moderated way. As Chap. 3 illustrates, posts that are out-of-topic or are not evidence-based are subject to deletion.

Solo Kaskusers believe that moderated discussions on various issues could impact their roles as citizens. It is a matter of socialization and internalization. They expressed that they could be influential in society and to the state-citizen relationship in everyday life, if they could uphold civic duties: (1) when there is a certain cry for help from other citizens as Chap. 4 describes; and (2) when they actively perform civic monitoring as part of civil correctness—both against the state apparatus, as vertical monitoring, and against other Kaskusers, as horizontal monitoring—as this chapter will describe.

### *5.1.1 Fight Club Legacy: Bravery*

Kaskusers who have been members of the forum since the early days, like Armin, Amakuzalek, Sodron, Wahyu, Rheanz Icesusujahe and Harya, often credited the daring civil monitoring that occurred in Kaskus' now-obsolete Fight Club (FC) for Kaskusers' persistent vertical and horizontal monitoring. Nothing was off limits in FC. Even politically and socially incorrect topics found their way into the debates. Accordingly, Kaskus, particularly its FC, became a realm where the limits of former political taboos were broken.

It was not long before chats in FC, however, became problematic. As the forum lacked curatorial and monitoring processes at that time, the initiative to uphold a discursive debate became weak and arbitrary arguments flourished. Mockery and insults frequently appeared in the FC debates and posts were often simply just slander or defamation in text. Instead of data and arguments, derogatory remarks and explicit language filled the forum. Some Kaskusers described FC as 'chaotic', 'scary', 'politically incorrect', 'unfriendly', and 'uncontrolled'. Surandy, for example, argued that in the end many of the debates tended to be 'uneducated' (*tidak sekolahan*) and were merely altercations (*debat kusir*). He illustrated that with the exception of those who intended to join digital quarrels, FC became the least desirable space to be.

His concern, particularly as a Javanese, is contextual, as traditionally in Solo and in Java in general, being straightforward and outwardly expressing opinions is considered unrefined. Studies on Java classically describe that traditional Javanese people are trained to be reserved with eyes cast down as a sign of cultivation (Hildred Geertz 1961: 66; Siegel 1993: 184, 122, 24). This conduct is believed to be a mechanism to avoid conflict and is thus a representation of fineness (*kehalusan*). Such self-restrained attitudes have become so deeply institutionalized that they extend beyond just managing body language by also regulating how opinions are expressed. Against this historical background, FC's debates therefore were, in its time, radical.

Besides these grim depictions of FC, the forum also gained recognition for its role in creating a new cyberculture of blatant expression. Lisa Siregar, a blogger and senior news media journalist, explained to me that in the Indonesian online sphere, Kaskusers, while they are indeed well-known for their harsh statements and are considered to some degree 'uncultured' (*urakan*), they are respected for being bold and blatant in expressing their opinions. Some thread administrators like Armin, Amakuzalek, Sodron and Harya believed that, accordingly, FC's permissive chatting environment helped Kaskusers train themselves to be politically expressive.

Harya, who was a well-known flamer in FC, defended FC's 'chatting chaos' as not being for nothing; instead, it served to 'train' Kaskusers who are mainly simple Internet users to be 'democratic', by first overcoming shyness (*malu*) and, second, learning how to be 'brave' (*berani*) citizens. Kaskus is interpreted as a space that allows shielded-identity citizens to express their opinions or report an event without fear of being scolded inappropriately or subjected to capital punishment. This depiction of FC should be set in a context where such activities were difficult under Suharto's state surveillance (see Crouch 2010). As Wahyu explained, the blatant and sensitive subjects discussed in FC left a legacy of 'bravery' among Kaskusers as they seek out opportunities 'to be involved with subjects that they would have previously been reluctant to talk about'. This bravery has trickled into monitoring the performance of the state apparatus, even inspiring the creation of a dedicated thread on the Kaskus forum: 'Report Police Misconduct Here'.[1]

The forum in f=160 provides direct evidence of Wahyu's notion of citizen monitoring. *@laliaku* was motivated to start the thread after seeing a banner from the Solo Police Department encouraging citizens to report any police misconduct.[2] Taking a picture of the banner, he created the thread as a pool for reports. Within three hours the thread grew large enough to become a trending topic on f=160's front page. Solo Kaskusers were not only highlighting the existence of the thread with the 'bump-up post',[3] they also started to report their personal experiences with the police. *@Superpekok* suggested further that Kaskusers should not only report any issue but also in their everyday lives as citizens use their audiovisual gadgets to monitor the police. Although it is no longer currently listed on the front page, the thread was active until the end of this research in 2015 and has become an infinite archive for citizens' experiences with the police department in Solo.

That thread is not a singular phenomenon. In the general Kaskus forum, outside the regional forum, there is also another thread dedicated to reporting police misconduct and violence.[4] The thread gathers reports nationally for any form of misconduct, which are later relayed to the national police department call center. All cases reported are updated regularly.

Some Solo Kaskusers believe that such responses to civil monitoring were only possible because Kaskus, as an online forum, had become a possible location and a training ground for Kaskusers to be critical, a practice that they had once feared because of political and cultural pressure. Harya stressed: 'Here in Kaskus, you are protected'. Kaskus' shielded-identity has made it possible for online dwellers to express their concerns about a subject against the state or public misconduct without having to fear the risk of reprimand.

### 5.1.2 *Support and Bullying Mechanism*

To be 'brave' also means to generate civil correction. Amakuzalek and Armin explained that the bullying in FC is not simply a dark play, but also works as a control mechanism. It is a form of collective monitoring that counters derogatory remarks and weak arguments in the discussions. Especially after FC was closed down in 2008, its 'alumni' continue to proliferate the spirit of the debate forum in other threads, such as in those in f=160, only with stronger moderation. The thread 'Family Registration and National ID (*Kartu Tanda Penduduk*) Application in Solo is Full of

Corruption' is an example.[5] The thread was created on February 4, 2010 by *@wargapendatang*, with a post complaining about the slow service at Banjarsari district office. *@wargapendatang* shared his experience in processing his national ID application, complaining that the procedure was complicated but a district officer had offered to speed up the process for a fee. The thread soon became popular and attracted continuous discussion for five consecutive days, with time distance between replies averaging an hour and peaking to minutes after office hours.

*@Wawunk* replied to the first post, conveying his best wishes to *@wargapendatang* for a strong resolution. *@Manciek_banget* replied, stating that *@wargapendatang* should be aware of his role as a citizen and should refuse to bribe the district officer. He added a campaign asking other Solo Kaskusers to reflect on their roles in corruption and argued that corruption exists largely because of citizen's conformist attitude toward bribery. *@angs* posted a harsh reply: 'The reality is, civil servants perceive that corruption is a culture, so fuck the government!' The next post from *@Diablos* in reply to *@angs* criticized the latter's position, using more friendly language:

> If you say it has become a culture of corruption, then, we have to investigate, where this culture is rooted. What are your comments, people?
>
> If this has become a tradition, why are we keeping such a bad tradition? Anyway, if I were you, I would wait for the process and would not pay more than what has been regulated. :handshake-emoticon.

The chat about how to stop the corruption culture continued for a week. On February 10, 2010, six days after the first post, *@wargapendatang* reported back to the thread that district officials had visited him at his residence to explain the matter. The official visited him after he was informed by a Solo Kaskuser that the case had emerged on f=160. *@wargapendatang* then explained to his fellow Kaskusers in the thread that the official was able to present the necessary documents, and no bribery had taken place. Monitoring the state in Kaskus also brings offline consequences. It is possible that a Kaskus thread becomes a starting place to start offline mediation.

As the matter was resolved, the thread was closed without any further discussion on the subject about the corruption of civil bureaucracy or citizens. Unlike the permanent thread dedicated to monitoring the police, civil monitoring of both the state and its civil servants is only started when a case surfaces. Here, f=160 as a space for reportage is more of a pragmatic tool of protest or social-political pressure but still able to create an omnipresent public sphere that continuously monitors civil servants' conduct and the state's best practices. Reflecting on the case, Icesusujahe, one of the discussants in *@wargapendatang's* thread, expressed, however, that through such threads on f=160, KRS' citizenship potential is to become a watchdog. As with the case with *@wargapendatang*, he continued, KRS's function was to demand transparency from the government and good conduct from his fellow citizens, both online and offline.

Solo Kaskusers also added that the most important aspect of this discussion is that online conversation leads to 'action'. Therefore, successful qualitative measurement of citizenship is to be viewed from how cases like those of *@wargapendatang* could be solved through such action—the thread has proven the forum's ability to urge a Kaskuser with bureaucratic influence to relay the complaint to the related public official and demand clarity. Such offline action would not have materialized without the thread, as the latter preceded the first. This notion of active monitoring as part of continual attentiveness therefore differentiates Kaskus from other social media platforms. Whereby the latter tend to seek to change an outcome. Kaskus' weight is on transformative monitoring of the process that led to it in the first place. Solo Kaskusers consider each case and thread reports to be a lesson learned.

This could be seen in what resulted over a year later when *@wargapendatang* created another thread which brought about a different result. This time the thread, 'A Letter to Joko Widodo', was addressed to the then mayor of Solo. *@wargapendatang*, again, was complaining that the bureaucrats of Solo are corrupt and explained that his frustration stemmed from the difficulties he had encountered while getting a birth certificate for his newborn baby. He offered a reward to those who could help solve the matter [Post #4]. Instead of receiving support from his fellow Kaskusers, the thread attracted a backlash against @wargapendatang's intention to pursue 'unprocedural' action. He was bullied because of his intention to bribe the related officials. He got bricked and lost his greenbadges. The thread was eventually locked five days later without ever resolving @wargapendatang's problem.

Harya formulated that f=160 as a monitoring medium works not only toward other institutions, but importantly against their fellow citizens as well. He saw that Solo as a small networked city could be subjected to selfmonitoring to uphold civil discipline. In contrast to the use of red-bricks in the Kaskus forum, this could not yet be defined as civil correction, but it seems possible that the public sphere here could result in public monitoring and sanctioning, at least digitally.

In this view, *@wargapendatang's* desire to bribe officials betrayed the constructed home of Solo and the militancy value of f=160. Solo Kaskusers preserve such optimism in defining the good conduct of citizenship because they, as the previous chapters describe, have seen before that it is possible to have a space of order. Hence, for Solo Kaskusers, creating a digital city is not a matter of digital infrastructure like Solo's city hotspot, but a collective self-disciplining as they have learned from the virtue of being in Kaskus.

The monitoring against their own fellows also takes place even when it means that the other would be given a difficult punishment. For example, when three football fans were accosted by hooligans in Jakarta in June 2012, a Kaskuser, *@Heartbreakkingz*, revealed that one of his Facebook friends had been involved in the brutal beating. @Heartbreakkingz gathered *@Irwan*'s Facebook status and photos to provide evidence for his post. Online media portals such as *Kompas Online* took the post as a source, and the matter later attracted the attention of the police who were eventually able to solve the case with the help of the evidence provided by the forum posts.[6]

### *5.1.3 Collective Validation*

In some cases, Kaskusers will only ignore a post so that the thread will not be indexed. Thereby, Kaskusers refuse the attention the poster was likely seeking to receive and to surface. Kaskusers are trained to deny recognition and legitimacy in the public sphere to those who are considered to deviate from participation that supports the common good. With this collective practice in refused engagement, Kaskusers were about a decade ahead of the debates that would break out about the importance of preventing the circulation of bad information, fake news, and hoaxes, for example, in the post-Brexit and Trump worlds (see Pickard 2016; Seaton 2016).

Take the thread, 'Somebody Condemn the Albino Water Buffalo (*Kebo Bule*)'[7] as an example. The thread was started by *@Andhikasukma*, who at that time already had over 10,999 posts, on November 27, 2011. He wrote:

> Good morning bosses, especially [those] in Solo and Yogyakarta Regional. I am sorry if I write this in the wrong room [read: forum], or am providing misinformation. I just want to share my response to a thread that is badly judging the *Kebo Bule* parade tradition around the Solo Palace. I have tried my best to deliver my opinion, but the TS insisted that the tradition is unimportant.

He then provided the link to the mentioned thread and continued with a final remark, 'I think the parade as a tradition on the night of the Islamic New Year celebration should be taken as part of our heritage, not mocked'.[8] He ended his remark with the angry face emoticon.

At the end of his post he provided a linked citation to a thread written by *@Sejarah* in another thread. The citation says:

> In the parade there is a procession, namely the *Kebo Bule* Parade, in which the buffaloes lead the parade. The buffaloes are called 'white' because they differ from the usual black Buffalo, these ones are pink. Let me first explain the history of the Ki Slamet White Buffalo that I compiled from some stories. In the Surakarta Palace, there is a group of buffaloes that are believed to be sacred, namely Ki Slamet. These are not just buffaloes but one of the Palace's heirlooms. In the book of Babad Solo (The History of Solo) written by Raden Mas Said, the ancestors of these buffaloes are those that were the beloved pets of King Pakubuwono II.

Although he did not explicitly mention it, *@Andhikasukma's* post echoed the dispute between conservative Muslims and traditionalist Javanese regarding the interpretation of tradition and Islam, with the first accusing the ritual as a form of shirk, idolatry or polytheism.[9] On the other hand, the traditionalist Javanese, objecting to such opinion, considered the interpretation from the religious group as an attack on their tradition while arguing that the understanding of the religious group about the parade is a simplification of Javanese symbolism.[10]

The thread attracted a great amount of attention with 160 comments within the first twenty-four hours. Most of the replies posted on the thread tended to be neutral and stated that the public should make a distinction between religion and 'cultural events'. It was *@Ciu* (Post #9), forty minutes after the initial post, who commented with the following reply: 'every person has their own perception of culture, it is common. It is best not to burden each other's part'.

By writing 'each other's part', *@Ciu*'s was the first commentator to bring the subject of the two clashing groups to the thread readers. Even though Ciu's comment supported neither the traditionalist Javanese nor the conservative Muslims, Ciu's avatar is an Irish Leprechaun with a glass of beer, not to mention that 'Ciu' itself is a name of a local Solonese alcohol brewing art. As such, the avatar implies that the post should be interpreted as a comment from a rather secular online persona.

Andhikasukma replied to the first nine posts, particularly to those of Ciu's: 'Why were you all so surprised? ☺ Yes, this is buffalo, Boss. Not camel. ☺ Surprised or confused?' (Post #10). Andhikakusuma's semantic play is more blatant: 'Camel' symbolizes the typical animal for transportation in Arab countries, and thus alludes to conservatives Muslims.

*@Hoshigami* replied to Andhikasukma in Post #11, 'Wow, why did you say c*mel [sic]? Careful there, somebody might get upset'.

*@Amakuzalek*, who has a royal Solonese title and is related to the reigning Prince of Solo, did not bother to advocate the traditionalist and only posted: 'whatever' (Post #19).

After some replies, *@Rheeanz* brought the discussion back to the issues of 'religion' and 'shirk'. He stated: 'Shirk or not, it depends on personal beliefs. I am not interested in talking about religion', (Post #40). He added, 'what are you aiming at by starting such a thread? Are you trying to initiate a [horizontal] conflict?' (Post #42).

*@iki_sure*, who has been described by Armin as a Kaskuser that comes from traditional Javanese peasantry, asked the traditionalist Solo Kaskuser not to be enraged by the post. He wrote in Post #44, 'even though it is a culture that needs to be kept, but, in reality it is only an animal, a water buffalo. So, if somebody is saying that the tradition is odd and stupid, well, [let us] just be patient'.

Amakuzalek (Post #72) took into account that Andhikasukma actually did not dwell in f=160, suspecting that an outsider might be intending to incite conflicts among the local Solo Kaskusers: 'Are you trying to muddy the water (*adu domba*, lit. sheep fighting, to fight against each other)?' This post was supported by *@Harya*, who was at that time still the Regional Leader, who complained that Andhikasukma's post and comment were hardly a discussion about tradition and religious practices, instead, relations, but their tone was tendentious to mock the conservative Muslim groups (Post #123).

*@areMean*, who had spent six years in an Islamic boarding school, posted: 'Culture and *adat* (customary rituals and laws) are better to be taken as part of the richness of our cultural heritage, but when it comes to belief, only God knows. ☺' (Post #130). Similarly, *@Dolphin.86*, whose avatar is her own picture showing her face wearing a *hijab* stated in Post #148: 'Let the person who objects [to the parade] express his/her opinions, this is a free Internet [space]. I don't come from Solo, but I respect this tradition. We all have our rights'.

After two weeks, the thread went cold, was bumped from the first page, and closed by Harya. Harya told me that had Andhikakusuma objected to the closing of his thread, he would have been bricked by Kaskusers for inciting a discussion that slandered others. The thread did not shift into hefty or bashful debates about Quranic verses versus Javanese letters, or philosophical or historical justification of the *Kebo Bule* procession because Solo Kaskusers thought that such issues could not, at least to their knowledge, be resolved by any arguments. Andhikasukma, on the other hand, was scolded by several Solo Kaskusers because of his opinion. Harya, who had the authority to lock the thread, stated that Kaskusers were eventually 'trained' to restrain themselves from reacting to 'provocative' messages because there is a collective desire to keep the forums enjoyable as demonstrated in the thread.

Moderated chat is one of the features that Kaskusers are proud of. Compared to other social media platforms, to use Sodron's account, Kaskus is not a 'hit-and-run' (*tabrak lari*) social media sphere. Instead, dwellers should be answerable for their posts, otherwise they could be bricked and lose their online dwelling privilege. Sodron said,

> In Twitter, you could post a *junk* and keep your handle afterwards regardless of the bullying you receive. Do that in Kaskus, we will make sure that your ID will be deleted and you will be bricked again if you come back. It is a one-time opportunity, so be correct (*nggenah*).

Kaskus forums rely, therefore, on what I call collective validation; and validation takes place every day. The validation not only works against the information presented, but also against other Kaskusers. As such, these efforts create a set of references for those who are looking into the matter. Wahyu, who once moderated a chat lounge, reminded me that unlike the mainstream social media platforms that only pursue headlines, Kaskus threads as forums offer a continuous discussion on a subject and it was the responsibility of Kaskusers to report matters relevant to public life or public interests.

The threads taken as examples in this chapter exemplify how monitoring civic behaviors and attitude among the non-activists in Kaskus takes place in their everyday lives. By providing a space for public chats, Kaskus offers opportunities for citizens to exchange monitoring of the state's performance and other citizens' attitude toward politics, bureaucracy, and civil obedience. This relies on the durable experience that stems from the long training of becoming orderly Kaskusers through digital dwelling. Digital citizenship did not materialize overnight; it was only through the continuous reorganization of threads that Kaskus threads as part of the public sphere became a space for discussions and monitoring. It was the training in digital dwelling that allowed Solo Kaskusers to become netizens.

There are at least two legacies or historical functions of the FC debates that crafted Kaskusers' notion of citizenship. First, it is, borrowing form Brenda Danet (2001: 331), a form of 'radical destabilization'. Her work illustrates how new computer typography provides possibilities for 'a radical destabilization of norms, perceptions, and behavior' that serve a class struggle opposing the solemn traditional fonts (ibid.).[11] In the case of Kaskus and the FC forum, it is not the fonts that destabilized society, but, to use Harya's term, the bravery of Kaskusers to express their opinions, address public matters, and monitor the texts of posts and messages; a bravery that was catalyzed in the early FC threads. As a radical destabilizing, outsiders might consider what Solo Kaskusers are doing to be chaotic, but for Solo Kaskusers there was a processual control mechanism that emerged from the forum.

Bullying provocateurs in Kaskus forums seems to work as conflict management. It, however, only materialized after Kaskusers were trained to dwell as netizens and thereby began to care about building an identity and understand the importance of home. Presenting an arbitrary hoax or provocative post poses the risk that the caring Kaskus ID will be bricked. On the other hand, such posts from an ID without reputation will be ignored.

Such risks underscore the second function of FC's cyberculture: Provocative messages can only be posted if they can be validated by the collective in the thread. During the reorganization of language presentation in Kaskus general forums and Kaskus regional forums, Kaskusers started initiated an 'anti-rotten comments' (*anti komentar busuk*) campaign to combat slander and hoaxes. 'Of course one will be bullied, and bashed, if his/her opinion was not carefully expressed without data and with weak argumentation. We are on the Internet, so speak with data', Harya said.

## 5.2 Speedy Feedback and Intimacy

In addition to internal socialization and training, Solo Kaskusers also admitted that their evolving civic participation was very much externally influenced by the feedback they received from the city government. They consider the city government to be cooperative, for example, during the experience in organizing the 2010 Gathering, Ilham campaign, and the advocacy for @wargapendatang's National ID application. Furthermore, Solo Kaskusers' awareness of becoming a citizen seems to have been encouraged by the mayor's popular political leadership. As Prima put it, 'it was the mayor's ability to communicate with the citizens'.

The close relationship between KRS and Mayor Jokowi began with a thread in August 2010 during a charity event that Solo Kaskusers organized. The project started with a thread written by a Kaskuser to report about a public school building that was in urgent need of renovations. As August that year was Ramadan month, when charity events are commonly held, Solo Kaskusers began to discuss a fundraising strategy. It was also only several weeks after the 2010 Gathering; the spirit to organize an offline event was high.

One night that week, Prima coincidentally noticed that the mayor's Facebook Messenger account had gone live. He buzzed Jokowi, introduced himself, and informed him about the event. The mayor directly replied to his message and invited him to a meeting at city hall. Armin recalled the visit:

> At first, we just wanted to get his opinion and maybe some suggestions on what we should do since it is actually a public school [note: they were afraid of infringing on the Department of Education's authority], but instead, he even helped us further by supplying the rice and financial help for the students. On the charity day, he came to the school also. We just also learned that day to our surprise that he is one of us! He is a Kaskuser!

When asked whether Jokowi had helped KRS with the event as 'Jokowi-the-Mayor' or 'Jokowi-the-Kaskuser', everyone seemed to be surprised by the question since they did not make a distinction between the two. When the same question was asked to Jokowi, he only answered shortly: 'Well, I help what I can'; without responding to the distinction whether he had joined initially participated as s Kaskuser or as the mayor.

Furthermore, besides being known for his active digital activity, Jokowi seems to be keen to engage with digital technology as well. He told me that he has high hopes for the new media space and believes that a crucial part of good governance is a communicative cooperation between the state and its citizens. Through this communication and public feedback, 'government officials could correct themselves', he said. In explaining his motivation for installing free hotspots across the city,[12] he explained:

> I want them (read: citizens) to be well informed (*tahu*), so that they could educate themselves about anything. When the city is dealing with an educated citizen, it would be easier to govern, [resulting] in a smooth cooperation. […] I am active [on social media] because I want their [people in social media] voices to be heard. The government should facilitate this process [by providing Internet access].

His hopes are not rhetoric. In his early months as the new mayor of Solo, he supported a website called 'Solokotakita' on www.solokotakita.org. The pilot project was started in March 2009 with students from the Architecture Department from the Sebelas Maret University. The website describes its objective[13]:

> Solo Kota Kita has been developing tools for neighbourhood advocacy and citizen planning in Surakarta (Solo), Central Java, Indonesia since 2009. The goal of Solo Kota Kita is to increase awareness of urban issues so residents can strengthen their voice in participatory budgeting […] This early effort gained the support of then Mayor Joko Widodo—now Governor of Jakarta—to survey and map all 51 neighbourhoods in Solo. [...] The tools could be used to understand urban problems that challenge citizens, like education, poverty, health, and other indicators.

*@pLinThenG*, who worked as a data collector for the project started an initiative to create a thread on f=160 to side-mine citizen's independent report and data. He titled the thread, similar to the city's website, 'Solo Our City: Unofficial web supported fully by the Surakarta City Government',[14] and wrote an introductory remark:

> All this long it has been difficult to obtain information about the region because of the complicated bureaucracy, especially when it is a piece of information regarding the data of a district (*kelurahan*). In addition, the authority will try to cover it up.

In the chat, he added that at first the city's website was intended to become a tool and pool for administrative data collection on the district level, but Jokowi was further interested in developing the project into a collaborative site involving more massive citizen reports [Post #4]. *@pLinThenG* continued, on Post #8, that the collaborative data input would cover citizens' reports as a strategy to counter the false data presented by district officials. He was hoping that Solo Kaskusers could participate as netizens.

From 73 posts in the thread, the tone was positive and Solo Kaskusers did not consider themselves to be victims of the state's incapability of supplying demographic data. Conversely, they felt that the initiative was a gesture of how the state will eventually see citizens as equal participating agents to create, as the thread's title implies: 'our city'.

This fetching of good governance for 'our city' or 'home' is an action of preserving the mutual belonging between the dwellers and their environment. Examining users of the Usenet newsgroups, Jones concludes that there is an inversion of power and belonging through which members of the online groups sense the feeling that 'no longer do we, as members of the group, belong to the community, rather the community belongs to us' (Jones 2002: 16). Following such understanding, Solo Kaskusers' participation as netizens in their everyday lives could be viewed as an enlargement of the home they have created in f=160 to the offline environments, a further offlining of the online. As they have previously successfully occupied their first home, f=160, now the society and the city belong to Kaskusers too.

Solo Kaskusers have learned the discipline of togetherness, data patching, and monitoring as part of the creation of community and space while successfully building f=160. These principles are currently being transferred and exercised in the offline to reproduce their notion of a 'common home'. This was only made possible by their assessment that they had established cooperation with the state. As such, this imagination of being citizens has become a perceptual experience, as they began to view the state actors as partners.

Solo Kaskusers hardly use the term 'citizen' (*warga*), but chose the local phrase '*wong Solo*' (Solonese or people of Solo). By using this term, all city actors—Kaskusers, the state apparatus, the elites, the mayor, the zookeeper, members of the Transportation Board, journalists, and other fellow citizens among others—are equal as the Solonese.

### *5.2.1 Speed and Digital Intimacy*

Speed has been identified as the decisive power of digital media technology (e.g. Van Loon 2008; Bell 2001). With this technological change, Van Loon (2008: 146) argues that 'immediacy is the new form of transparency'. In Kaskusers' experience, speed plays a great role in building intimacy between state actors and citizens. In KRS, the communication feedback as a capacity to respond is not merely assessed through replies, but also in terms of how fast a response can be transferred. Also in the case of Kaskus, Kaskusers highly value the ability to provide speedy responses as the events in the Ilham campaign in the previous chapter illustrate. This is what I refer to as the importance of 'pinging ability'.[15]

When state actors simultaneously have an online identity and become digital inhabitants, like Jokowi, their immediate responses to fellow members of the digital community would be considered an obligation. Consequently, failing to honor this expectation could reflect a lack of attention to, if not ignorance of, maintaining the online relationship or intimacy. In such online culture, civil servants will be assessed by the digital public based on their speedy and unbureaucratic feedback.

Since the fall of Suharto's New Order, transparency, accountability, and bureaucratic reform have been major issues for reforming the state (Bünte and Ufen 2009). While investigating democratization and Islam in Indonesia, Robert Hefner once wrote that the current challenge for the civil society movement in Indonesia is to 'find democratic partners in the state' (2005: 298). Today's digital spaces like Kaskus present a new possibility where civil and state actors could meet and engage in colloquial communication. Sometimes, they, like Jokowi, are even fellow digital inhabitants long before the state actor becomes a public official.

Jokowi's influence on KRS is visible in Fig. 5.1. Even though he never posted any messages in f=160 as his offline self and he has yet to reveal the online ID he uses to chat in Kaskus, his presence at offline events and as a public figure have made him a popular actor who is often mentioned during online conversations in Solo Kaskusers' threads. Fig. 5.1 illustrates how often Jokowi was mentioned throughout 2011, his last year in office before entering the campaign in 2012 to become the Governor of Jakarta.

This network analysis of references to Jokowi in 2011 also shows that those who often mentioned 'Jokowi' in their chats in f=160 are those who apparently also played great roles in navigating the development of the community through uncertain times: Prima, Amakuzalek, Armin, Harya, Surandy, Icesusujahe and Hoshy. Three of them were RLs of KRS (Armin Harya, Surandy), three had attended the offline picnic meeting that led to the decision to reorganize f=160 (Prima, Harya, and Armin), two were the founders of the Jakarta Chapter (Icesusujahe and Amakuzalek), Prima is the person who initiated f=160 and created the 'Playful but Prudent' maxim, and Hoshy is the owner of the Internet cafe-turned-office for KRS.

While he does not directly impact the online community's organizational policy, his mentioned node shows how Solo Kaskusers depict him as

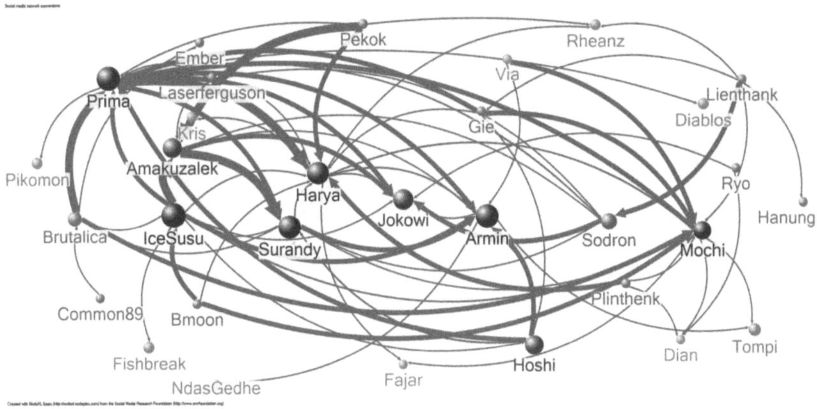


**Fig. 5.1** Network analysis of references to Mayor in Kaskus Regional Solo, 2011 (*Edge size represents the sum of counts when the node is being mentioned by others; **Vertex size represents the Eigenvector centrality)

an inspirational state actor who is able to move Solo Kaskusers to go offline and participate in the city's activities. Assessing why Jokowi plays a role as an 'inspiring figure', Prima expressed: 'coincidently (*kebetulan*) he is a mayor who is the easiest to meet, the most comfortable person to have a chat with, and has the heart to say hi first'. To recall Amakuzalek's description of the digital intimate distance from the previous chapter, mutual chat has made Jokowi one of the 'friends-in-the-pocket'. Because of his down-to-earth communication style in the online sphere, Solo Kaskusers perceive Jokowi to be a charismatic leader.

The new possibility of direct communication between Jokowi and Solo Kaskusers has raised a sense of belonging and created the perception that political elites are no longer beyond reach. Accordingly, Solo Kaskusers' view that such relationships create a window of opportunity to empower the state apparatus and to repair the decoupled relationship between citizens and the state in the post-1998 era. 'Worthy to be supported (*mumpung bisa didukung*),' as said Prima boldly.

Through the habitual chat and the possibility of red-bricking, it is not hierarchy that Kaskusers identified as the relation of power structure between actors, but cooperative ability. This symmetric social media communication behavior is expected for any relationship that transpires, for example, between Kaskusers themselves or between Kaskusers and public officials. In f=160, chat is organized as a co-routine system where the flow of information is no longer dependent on actors but collective accomplishment to secure the flow of chats and projects. A broken node marks users who have a failed pinging ability.

If Javanese stratification is a matter of hierarchy as Anderson argues (2006), then, the practice of online dwelling in Kaskus has formed something different: a combination of equal communication and solicited participation. Solo Kaskusers view that any elite actors, as long as they step foot in the digital realm, are no longer considered to be dominant subjects. Everybody has a chance of getting bullied as this is responsive digital engagement. Indonesian online community members, like Solo Kaskusers, are fond of public figures that are digitally engaged. They support the latter, while considering them to be fellow digital inhabitants. Such a relationship contests Javanese political hierarchy as it deconstructs the social boundaries in terms of how the common can reach the elite.

As Chap. 2 discusses, seniority in Kaskus is signified by green-badges, which represent the quality and quantity of individual participation in collective activities. It symbolizes that a person is reliable and can be a patch for others' efforts. Such recognition of a standard ability for tangible action or pinging digresses from the traditional Javanese expectation of the Just King (*ratu adil*),[16] which depicts the coming of a figure that is an amalgamation of the ruler and the people or the servant (Laksono 1986; Moertono 2009) who would be at the helm of the direction the nation would take. The people, therefore, are expected to patiently await his arrival. In this top-down disposition, citizens do not possess the power to create a leader on their own; instead, they must wait for a God-sent figure.

The imaginary Just King stands in direct contrast to the Kaskus idea of citizenship and cyberculture. Presumably it is why the term Just King has never emerged on Kaskus. In Kaskus' vocabulary, an 'elite' is a person who eagerly participates in the community's activities. Kaskus' notion of leadership sends a signal of collective participatory and fellowship, and thus, to recall Prima, a community leader is a person that 'could be supported'. The term 'could' in the narrative connotes the decisive role that Kaskusers possess to select their patron. If the supported person fails to achieve tangible accomplishments, his/her support will be rescinded or subjected to pressure through bullying as was the case of the second RL as Chap. 4 describes.

In Solo, a city with a strong legacy of kingship, traditional aristocratic social background, and layers of postcolonial and post-authoritarianism bureaucracy, this interpersonal digital media communication contests the traditional estranged public relationship between actors. In Solo where citizens are culturally categorized, and the citizens categorize themselves as '*wong cilik*' (lit. small man; read: powerless) while the state apparatus is the '*penggede*' (lit. the big man; read: the rulers) (Eklof 2004: 119–120), this practice is revolutionary.

### 5.2.2 *Fandom*

The support for political meritocracy, however, becomes problematic when it turns into fandom. The proliferation of social media and online communities also enables such Indonesian charismatic leaders to strengthen their grip on the public. A very good example of this is a thread written by *@inacatering* in February 2, 2011 with the title 'Vote for Jokowi'.[17] The TS intended the thread to become a digital campaign calling for Kaskusers to drive Jokowi to run as a presidential candidate in 2014. The thread starts with a banner 'Indonesia needs a leader like this' succeeds with a picture of Mahmoud Ahmadinejad, the former Iranian President. Under the picture, it was written 'Iran is free of western influence [sic]'. The next line is 'Fernando Lugo: A president (ex-Bishop) who doesn't take a salary'. The thread continues with a banner 'Uphold Religious Pluralism' and ends with a sentence 'Never engaged in corruption but participates in eradicating corruption'.

The thread's body compiles articles from various online news to argue that Jokowi is not a corrupt politician. The second article is news on Jokowi's decision not to take his salary as a mayor. Enclosing the post, Inacatering wrote 'therefore this is my choice' followed by pictures of Joko Widodo wearing traditional Javanese clothes in a parade, talking with street vendors, and riding his bicycle. At the bottom of the post, there was a web page link to a Kaskus thread and another web page link to a Facebook page quoted as the 'source' of the posted materials. The thread managed to float on the first page of f=160 for a week, accompanied by posts from Kaskusers who expressed their support for Jokowi. The last post in the thread, before it was locked after going inactive, was on July 19, 2012, after attracting 109 replies and comments.

There was no critical comment against the campaign. No Kaskusers objected to the comparison between Jokowi and Mahmoud Ahmadinejad and discussing the democratic condition in Iran.[18] Similarly, there is no critical account of how Fernando Lugo's populism and leftist ideology is comparable to Jokowi's.[19] Because of its careless assessment of Jokowi's political ideology, Inacaterings's thread could be viewed as political fandom. This finding contrasts Harya's belief that in the online forums, Kaskusers could only 'speak with data'. Speaking with 'data' becomes problematic when is mashed from various sources without careful studious crafting as the thread exemplifies.

Inacatering's thread echoes similar concerns about the optimistic linear relation between online discussions and democracy-building. In the Indonesian context, Hill and Sen (2005) contend that online discussions in Indonesia are not enough to be considered discursive democracy because it had yet, at the time of their study, to demonstrate the 'skills of reading and writing, the elegance of arguments and intellectual sophistry' (Hill and Sen 2005: 146). Barendregt (2008) unapologetically argues that unlike Habermas' (1991) European bourgeois middle class, the Southeast Asian new rich, including Indonesians, and their media encounters, 'do not necessarily display the features of the middle class in the West: e.g. rationality, democracy, individualization, and secularism' (Barendregt 2008: 161).

While these claims are obvious in Inacatering's thread, it should also be noted that at least the Kaskusers tried to be discursive. They did so, however, in a rather experimental way. It is therefore also necessary to consider Kaskusers' educational environments. One reason why international politics did not unfold as a subject of discussion can be found in the limited education that most Indonesians receive in terms of global history and international politics in the general Indonesian school curriculum.[20] The assessment of digital capacity should be therefore proportionate to a digital inhabitant's competence to participate in the discussion they are having. To be able to avoid arbitrary information circulation, the participation of those in the know is required. As it is with the 'inaccurate' depiction of culture in the annual Gatherings, KRS and other Kaskus forums, and any other space for the 'commons', sometimes sophisticated expert contributions about the subject being discussed are lacking.

To this point, Laura Gurak's (1999) concern about the risk resulting from the speedy circulation of inaccurate information in the online forums comes to mind. She argues that online mobilization in organizing protests is 'double-edged'; on one hand, it makes the mobilization of individuals simpler, while on the other the accuracy of information might be weakened.

She proposes that in evaluating the development of democracy, discussion forums should be viewed through the features of rhetorical activities, such as speeches and debates that reflect the ethos and delivery.[21] Ethically, Solo Kaskusers are very open to discussions and the language regulations have made it certain that in Kaskus, people can have chats and discussions respectfully while keeping in mind the goal to not bring disorder to their online 'home'. Discussions and opinions exchange nested in Kaskus has also proven to be effective in delivery, as it reaches out to a wider audience, at least in f=160 with the case of monitoring threads.

Gurak's approach is compelling to justify Kaskusers' activities since, regardless of the inaccuracy of 'culture' in the Gatherings and the fandom in the 'Vote for Jokowi' thread, Kaskusers still manage to convey the intended message: the need for a closer relationship with the offline world, the society, the state, and city through tangible participation. Therefore, it is not enough to simply consider the level of education which Kaskusers have, but attention must be given to the quality of information they give, even with its faults.

In Solo, providing infrastructures for free and ubiquitous Internet access seems to be a popular public service. This can be seen in the city's existence as a literal hotspot. The Solonese are quite proud of the program, and by 2010, I had heard the story repeated time and time again that when an individual rides a *becak* (rickshaw) through the city center, instead of observing the panoramic city landscape s/he would go online with Internet access from one hotspot to another. When asked in 2011 how he came up with the idea for the innovative project and public service, Joko Widodo, the then mayor of Solo, explained that the goal was 'to open minds (*melek*)'. He also looked at me questioningly, wondering why I had not quickly related technology with education. He added in a confident tone: 'Well yes, as they [citizen] access information freely, they could do a lot. It is a basis for a better development (*berkembang lebih baik*). Everything is there [on the Internet]'.

'Opening minds', to cite Jokowi again, is a procedural effort. It needs, as the previous chapters explain, thread administrators and chatting regulations to ensure order. It also requires that capable experts and curators are also involved in this chatting realm. This finding is a reminder that the responsibilities for providing accurate information and discursive democratic education to the public are still largely influenced by the hands of the capable. If accuracy of information is supposed to be discursive and non-experimental as in Kaskus, the educated, the experts, or those in the know need to substantiate this democratic and educational space by joining the commons' online forums.

In the context of netizenship, without the participation of these experts, citizen chats in KRS, however, appear to be ambivalent: on one hand, Solo Kaskusers actively monitor the public service and fellow citizen's behavior, which seems to produce democratic participation; on the other hand, their fondness for leaders like Jokowi presents the risk of becoming a cult and being influential in the making of a charismatic leader and devolving into political fandom as *@inacatering*'s thread exemplifies.

Until this chapter, I have described the journey of how Solo Kaskusers revealed their own notion of netizenship. That account of becoming citizen, nevertheless, is a series of eventful and livable experiences, through which goals are set within the realm of the achievable. These series of struggles and success give Kaskusers the hope and confidence that it is possible to become a citizen. Such hope brings with it an attitude of patience and durability in revealing the further challenge to be in Kaskus. Citizenship for Kaskusers is therefore a matter of becoming a netizen, with durable discipline, in self-restrained, horizontal and vertical monitoring, and reaching out to others or the external for universal rights and common order. Such effort to accrue the awareness of citizenship, however, becomes uncertain if their knowledge resources are stagnant. This dilemma is the focus of the next chapter.

## Notes

1. http://kask.us/9220766
2. http://archive.kaskus.co.id/thread//9220766
3. To post a very short message, just to keep the thread afloat in the register or on the main page.
4. https://www.kaskus.co.id/thread/000000000000000008044604/divpropam-laporan-kritik-saran-dan-pertanyaan-seputar-forpol/
5. http://old.kaskus.co.id/showthread.php?t=3298195
6. Sabrina Asril, "Provokasi di Facebook<!--Facebook-->, Perusuh di GBK Diamankan." *Kompas*, (June 1, 2012). Accessed June 6, http://megapolitan.kompas.com/read/2012/06/01/14523461/Provokasi.di.Facebook..Perusuh.di.GBK.Diamankon June 1st, 2012.
7. http://archive.kaskus.co.id/thread/11675204/
8. In Solo, the Keraton's albino water buffaloes become an attraction in the parade on the night of the Islamic New Year celebration. According to Babad Solo written by Raden Mas Said, the original water buffaloes always

followed the Sultan Pakubuwono X during the parade. Since then the water buffaloes have become the symbol of people's loyalty and wealth (see: Sumarno 2013).

9. Taufiqurrohman. *64 Ritual Syirik Nusantara* (Jogyakarta: Pusat Ilmu, 2015).
10. Nurshodiq, 'Tradisi Suran Dalam Masyarakat Jawa (Studi Perbandingan Antara Wilayah Surakarta Dengan Wonosobo),' *Journal of Educational Social Studies*, Vol. 1, No. 1, June (2012): 55–59.
11. Danet (2001) argues that at the turn of twentieth century, while the traditional font style like Times New Roman and Arial were perceived to be classic, young typographers started to create new fonts especially those resembling graffiti or street art calligraphy that disobeys the normative font-designing. Some of the fonts were associated with a subculture and a rebellion against the common norms of font management.
12. HAW, "Solo Bakal Miliki Jalur Akses Internet Terpanjang Di Indonesia." *Solopos*, (October 11, 2011). Accessed October 11, 2011. http://www.solopos.com/2011/10/11/solo-bakal-miliki-jalur-akses-internet-terpanjang-di-indonesia-119241
13. http://solokotakita.org/en/about/history/
14. http://archive.kaskus.co.id/thread/5625670/0#
15. The term 'ping' is taken from an Internet signaling technical term meaning a measurement of reachability. It is used here to refer to Kaskusers and their round-trip feedback time, or response and success rate.
16. The Just King (*Ratu Adil*) is a messianic figure in Indonesian Folklore that will bring justice and peace.
17. http://archive.kaskus.co.id/thread/6935097/0#1
18. For democracy in Iran under Mahmoud Ahmadinejad, see: Nader Hashemi, "Religious Disputation and Democratic Constitutionalism: The Enduring Legacy of the Constitutional Revolution on the Struggle for Democracy in Iran," *Constellation*. Volume 17 Issue 1 (March 2010), 50–60.
19. For Fernando Lugo political ideology in Paraguay, see: Mitchell Seligson, "The Rise of Populism and the Left in Latin America," *Journal of Democracy*, Volume 18 Number 3 (July 2007) 81–95.
20. For citizenship and history education in Indonesia, see Mary Fearnley-Sanderand, Ella Yulaelawati, "Citizenship Discourse in the Context of Decentralization: The Case of Indonesia," in *Citizenship Curriculum in Asia and the Pacific*, edited by David L. Grossman, Wing On Lee, Kerry J. Kennedy. (Hong Kong: Comparative Education Research Center and Springer Media, 2008).
21. Gurak (1999) highlights ethos as group quality, such as the cultural and moral tone of a community. She identifies *delivery* as having several features, such as speed, durability of messages, and the outreach of the message.

## References

Anderson, Benedict R.O'G. *Java in a Time of Revolution: Occupation and Resistance, 1944–1946*. Jakarta: Equinox Publishing, 2006.

Barendregt, Bart. "Sex, Cannibals, and the Language of Cool: Indonesian Tales of the Phone and Modernity". *The Information Society: An International Journal* Volume 24 Issue 3 (May 2008): 160–170.

Bell, David. *An Introduction to Cybercultures*. London: Routledge, 2001.

Bräuchler, Birgit. "Cyberidentities at War: Religion, Identity, and the Internet in the Moluccan Conflict." *Indonesia* 75 (April 2003): 123–51.

Bünte, Marco, Andreas Ufen. "The new order and its legacy: reflections on democratization in Indonesia" in *Democratization in Post-Soeharto Indonesia*, edited by Marco Bünte and Andreas Ufen, 3–29. New York: Routledge, 2009.

Crouch, Harold A. *Political Reform in Indonesia After Soeharto*. Singapore: Institute of Southeast Asian Studies, 2010.

Danet, Brenda. *Cyberpl@y: Communicating Online*. Oxford: Berg, 2001.

Eklof, Stefan. *Power and Political Culture in Suharto's Indonesia: The Indonesian Democratic Party (PDI) and Decline of the New Order (1986–98)*. Copenhagen: NIAS Press, 2004.

Fearnley-Sander, Mary, and Ella Yulaelawati. "Citizenship Discourse in the Context of Decentralization: The Case of Indonesia". In *Citizenship Curriculum in Asia and the Pacific*, edited by David L. Grossman, Wing On Lee, and Kerry J. Kennedy, 111–126. Hong Kong: Comparative Education Research Center and Springer Media, 2008.

Geertz, Hildred. *The Javanese Family: A study of kinship and socialization*. Michigan: University of Michigan Press, 1961.

Gurak, Laura. "The Promise and Peril of Social Action in Cyberspace." In *Communities in* Cyberspace, edited by Marc A. Smith and Peter Kollock, 241–262. London: Routledge, 1999.

Habermas, Jürgen. *The Structural Transformation of the Public Sphere*. Translated by Thomas Burger. First publication in 1989. Massachusetts: MIT Press, 1991.

Hashemi, Nader. "Religious Disputation and Democratic Constitutionalism: The Enduring Legacy of the Constitutional Revolution on the Struggle for Democracy in Iran." *Constellation* Volume 17 Issue 1 (March 2010): 50–60.

Hefner, Robert W. "Introduction: Modernity and the Remaking of Muslim Politics." In *Remaking Muslim Politics: Pluralism, Contestation, & Democratization*, edited by Robert W. Hefner, 1–36. New Jersey: Princeton University Press, 2005.

Hill, David T. and Krishna Sen. *The Internet in Indonesia's New Democracy*. Oxon: Routledge, 2005.

Jones, Steven G. "The Internet and Its Social Landscape". In *Virtual Culture: Identity and Communication in Cybersociety*, edited by Steven G. Jones, 7–35. First publication in 1997. London: Sage, 2002.

Laksono, Paschalis Maria. *Tradition in Javanese Social Structure: Kingdom and Countryside: Changes in the Javanese Conceptual Model*. London: Coronet Books Incorporated, 1986.

Lim, Merlyna. "From Real to Virtual (and Back again): Civil Society, Public Sphere, and Internet in Indonesia." In *Asia.com: Asia encounters the Internet*, edited by Kong-Chong Ho, Randy Kluver and Kenneth C. C. Yang, 113–128. London: Routledge, 2003.

Moertono, Soemarsaid. *State and Statecraft in Old Java: A Study of the Later Mataram Period, 16th and 19th Century*. Singapore: Equinox Publishing, 2009.

Nugroho, Yanuar. *Does The Internet Transform Civil Society? The Case pf Civil Society Organizations in Indonesia*. Dissertation. Manchester: The University of Manchester, 2007.

Nurshodiq. "Tradisi Suran Dalam Masyarakat Jawa: Studi Perbandingan Antara Wilayah Surakarta dengan Wonosobo". In *Journal Of Educational Social Studies*, Vol. 1, No. 1, June 2012: 55–59.

Pickard, Victor. "Media Failures in the Age of Trump" *The Political Economy of Communication* 4(2) 2016: 118–122.

Seaton, Jean. "Brexit and the Media" *The Political Quarterly* Volume 87, Issue 3, 2016: 333–33. DOI: 10.1111/1467-923X.12296

Seligson, Mitchell. "The Rise of Populism and the Left in Latin America." *Journal of Democracy* Volume 18 Number 3 (July 2007): 81–95.

Siegel, James T. *Solo in the New Order: Language and Hierarchy in an Indonesian City*. New Jersey: Princeton University Press, 1993.

Sumarno. "Upacara Tradisi Wilujengan Negari Mahesa Lawung Kraton Surakarta Di Krendhawahana". In *Jantra* Vol. 8 No. 2 (Desember 2013): 189–200.

Taufiqurrohman. *64 Ritual Syirik Nusantara*. Yogyakarta: Pusat Ilmu, 2015.

Triastuti, Endah and Inaya Rakhmani. "Cyber Taman Mini Indonesia Indah: Ethnicity and Imagi-Nation in Blogging Culture". *Internetworking Indonesia Journal* Vol. 3/No. 2 (2011): 5–11. Jakarta, 2011.

Van Klinken, Gerry. *Communal Violence and Democratization in Indonesia*. Oxon: Routledge, 2007.

Van Loon, Joost. *Media Technology Critical Perspective*. Berkshire: Open University Press McGraw-Hill Education, 2008.

Wayansari, Agustina. "The Internet and the Public Sphere in Indonesia's New Democracy: a Study of Politikana.com." In *Internetworking Indonesia Journal* Vol. 3/No. 2 (2011): 23–33. Jakarta, 2011.

Webster, Frank. *Theories of the Information Society*. Third Edition. Oxon: Routledge, 2006.

## News and Online Sources

Asril, Sabrina. "Provokasi di Facebook, Perusuh di GBK Diamankan." Kompas, June 1, 2012. Accessed June 6, 2012. http://megapolitan.kompas.com/read/2012/06/01/14523461/Provokasi.di.Facebook..Perusuh.di.GBK.Diamankon June 1st, 2012.

HAW. "Solo Bakal Miliki Jalur Akses Internet Terpanjang Di Indonesia," *Solopos,* October 11, 2011. Accessed October 11, 2011. http://www.solopos.com/2011/10/11/solo-bakal-miliki-jalur-akses-internet-terpanjang-di-indonesia-119241

CHAPTER 6

# The Unsettled Online Community

The previous three chapters describe how Solo Kaskusers became a community through various experiences. Everyday chat offers possibilities for the community to transform while strengthening their identity. Community transformation should be understood here as an ability to change the mode of dwelling and the action of the community with sophistication where new codes of conducts and practices, which are serviceable as resource of stabilization, are emerging from criticism of past weaknesses through sequential reflexive actions. As a result, some previous code and practices are left behind, while those practical for the strengthening of community presence are further proliferated. These complex changes that Solo Kaskusers experience are based on a continual reflection on the past, and as their everyday struggle as online community members, and none of the Solo Kaskusers are yet able to offer any suggestions as to how their community might look in the future. Their narrative of going to Kaskus implies only continual change—from junk posting, to chatting, to online dwelling, to forum organization, and to offline activities. Sodron and Kris use the term 'journey' (*perjalanan*), and Harya, Sodron, and Armin use the term 'process' (*proses*) to denote their dwelling activity in Kaskus. Both words were used to mark the sequences drawn from being part of the Kaskus experience or sequence of revelations while establishing the importance of their environment.

Regardless of the troubles in coordinating and keeping the community, Solo Kaskusers tend to situate their digital life sequences in their



A. Seto, *Netizenship, Activism and Online Community Transformation in Indonesia*, DOI 10.1007/978-981-10-5397-9_6

community-building while embracing unforeseen challenges, or *proses*, like their experience in enlarging their activities from the online to the offline. On one hand, this appears to be a skillful method for dealing with the liquidity of online community, while, on the other, outsiders might consider this an uncertain expansion of activities. Is letting the path of online dwelling to follow uncertain goals and future too fluid? Should experiences produce a method of stability? This chapter addresses these questions by investigating Kaskusers' responsivity in becoming netizens, which is rendered between the notion of transformation, intimacy, the ghost of play, and the stock of wonder.

## 6.1 Tempering Certainty and Being Organic

According to Ingold (2011), the readiness to embrace changes and unforeseen events is not a form of uncertainty. Instead, it is a readiness to accept life's possibilities, which, as his concept of wayfaring underscores, allows us to preserve our capacity as organisms to cope with our environment and challenges. He emphasizes that 'the forms of organisms are not genetically preconfigured but continually emerge as developmental outcomes within matrices comprised of mutually conditioning relations' (Ingold 2011: 9).

While he unapologetically criticizes the modernistic certainty of institutionalization and social construction, Ingold (2011) argues that actions could not be juxtaposed simply to the dichotomy of production and consumption since the dwelling approach stresses the route and practice. Accordingly, Solo Kaskusers identify their needs by letting, as Ingold (2011) stresses, the path of becoming take place as part of their skillful wayfaring, namely the '*perjalanan*' (journey) or '*proses*' (process) as Kaskusers stated. In the Kaskus context, Solo Kaskusers perceived the dynamics of digital communication not as a symptom of misdirection but as the enrichment of the subject of online communication. Change itself is imminent as each digital media user could alter or challenge the direction of communication. Similarly, Van Loon (2008) formulates media engagement as transduction:

> mediation as a 'coming-in-between' is thus not a 'passing' of content from 'point one' to 'point two' but instead the constitution of specific orientations and sensibilities that order (enframe and reveal) how we make sense in terms of perception, thought and communication. (Van Loon 2008: 132)

Ingold (2011) and Van Loon's (2008) approaches provide access to understand Solo Kaskusers' realist approach on the subject of future in their activities and community meaning-making. With this approach,

Kaskusers' experience and activities, which are the result of a correspondence with the newly-revealed circumstances and environments, should be viewed as evolving, but unstable, skill of production. Each Kaskus experience (*ngaskus*) is a revelation that sets a new path for another course of becoming in sequential relevance to the forum, the city, and the offline world. Experiencing Kaskus as a dynamic dwelling therefore cannot be compiled into a sum of motives because it is an evolving path characterized by the 'revelation of being online', to echo Sodron's account.

For dwellers in f=160, being a citizen of Solo is a bottom-up course or path because the online dwelling journey of 'orientations and sensibilities', to echo Van Loon (2008), has led them to realize the need to become citizens of Solo. The sequences of thread dwelling, forum dwelling, offline meet-ups, the Gathering, and activism were not anticipated when Prima and his colleagues established f=160 in 2006. These sequences of life consequences could only be revealed through the mastery of cyber practices and reflexivity of being-in-Kaskus as described in previous chapters. Each change—how Solo Kaskusers developed order in f=160, how they organized the annual Gathering, how '*sembada*' was set as the new norm—provide a narrative of struggle and community navigation in revealing their role as Kaskusers.

Significant for these revelations is the evolving views on the relation of Kaskusers to their social and online environments. The main question becomes whether a community can endure without imagining a certain objective or intent of becoming. As such, the decision about what to become as a Kaskuser depends on the perceptual experience and the revelation of each online journey according to their current perception of their environment(s).

Therefore, any technological determinism that argues that the presence of digital media is to be taken as—to name some expectations—greater agency, or democratization, or social cohesion, or community organization, should be revisited in terms of each community's online experience and perception of the environment. On the other hand, communication and, in this case, community becomes a form of mediated citizenship. Rather than reflecting the community's instability, such a path of being digital is, thus, unsettled and organic.

### *6.1.1 Organic Community*

At the dawn of the proliferation of digital gadgets, Beniger (1987) had pessimistically warned that a virtual community is a 'pseudo-community'. In Beniger's view, a computer-mediated community is superficial as it could not replace the warmth and trust associated with the 'organic community—based on interpersonal relationships' (Beniger 1987: 369).

Beniger's concern about the pseudo-community's problem of emotion was tackled by the early history of f=160's warm connection. From playful, rich, and intensive communication, Solo Kaskusers gained the feeling of warm and trustworthy connections as the intense communication wrapped with gadgetry interaction linked both bodily and mental interactions. The materialization of trust and solidarity can be viewed from the willingness of online forum members to go offline and reveal their online identity. Furthermore, for Solo Kaskusers, the rich experience and intensive communication are as impactful as any civil community. The results are tangible: space, order, extension to other communities, social activism, and Kaskusers' developing notion of citizenship.

A few years after Beniger's work, Jan van Dijk (2006) echoed such concern about the fluidity of virtual communities. While Beniger relies on the irreplaceable traditional human emotion of face-to-face meetings, Van Dijk (2006) points to physical proximity as an important feature of the old community. Van Dijk also brings the subject of 'organic' to the discussion:

> An organic or physical community (in a neighbourhood, quarter, extended family or workplace) is a relatively stable unit with many short and overlapping communication lines and joint activities [...]. Virtual communities, on the other hand, are loose affiliations of people that can fall apart at any moment. (Van Dijk 2006: 166)

For him, the contrast between an organic and an online community is the ease by which a member can leave without drawing the attention of other members. While online communities comprise groups of people that use a medium of communication that allows them to come together regardless of location or time for specific interests or activity, organic communities depend on the physical rather than the interests that draw together like-minded people in online—or even more simply put—communities of interest (Van Dijk 2006).

Both Beniger's pseudo-community and Van Dijk's stability of physical community denote the term 'organic' as a part of the physical. By contrast, Rheingold (2000) and Jones (2002) define the term as a form of growth of a virtual or online community like the nature of the organism itself. Rheingold describes online communities as 'colonies of microorganisms that grow in petri dishes' (Rheingold [1993] 2000: 6). He calls for a reassessment of the meaning of community for the online community while arguing that the term is not a matter of geography but is, instead, emerging connections. The importance is, thus, to observe what it means to be in the community. Jones (2002) directs the discussion of organism further to the matter of change, as organic matter develops in its arrangement complexities. He calls for a redefinition of community that does not weigh the term down with a physical proximity. Rheingold and Jones' call to observe the online community as a growing unit is still less discussed.

Kaskusers' experiences actually echo Rheingold (2000) and Jones' (2002) notion of organic and change. The experience of f=160 dwellers is what I would call an organic community. It is a bottom-up group that is engaging in a process of informally organized self-discovery characterized by a dispersed community navigation as it has no formal leadership or objectives. Accordingly, there are several consequences emerging from this form of community.

*First*, it has no certain medium or long-term goals. Thus, members are dependent on the experience of revealing their path in the making, along with the course of their developing skills in community organization while navigating its delivery of presence. At the same time, they are trying to find new skills to create new goals, such as organizing the annual Gathering and social activism in Kaskus. The notion of presence becomes important as it does not exist in an empty space without preceding experiences. Therefore, *second*, the possible surrounding environments will become the community's main resource for normative vocabularies, such as Solo Kaskusers notion of togetherness (*guyub*) and prudence (*sembada*). *Third*, because of these external resources and the resulting community-building, the community will intersubjectively assess what it means to dwell in the online as a purposeful meaning, which is also a means to mobilize member participation while embracing uncertainty.

Because of these consequences, being organic is less pragmatic in the sense that decisions are based on the sum of practices and sequential revelations of online dwelling. The organic aspects of the community are marked by pivotal decisions, based on considerations made by members to ensure the community's survival in moments of uncertainty. In Kaskusers' experience, differing from Ingold's (2011) optimism about wayfaring along the lines of experiences, being organic is rather unsettling because they always have to quickly produce new norms and regulations to justify what it means to be online as the previous four chapters describe. In such moments of uncertainty, casualties can emerge, such as the outcasting of Johar and Mochi's delay in finishing her study.

Indeed, members might come and go, but the space and the organization of the current union are evolving. Kaskusers' experience therefore calls for revisiting the comparison between 'organic community' and media-based community by reinvigorating the first's definition, that is, the subject of being 'organic'. The story of Solo Kaskusers described throughout the previous four chapters is a temporary sum of how digital inhabitants grow organically by understanding a space, its digital practices, and its environment. In this account, instead of abandoning the offline realm, society, the city, and offline norms have become the properties and resources of the digital practice.

The narrative of participating in Kaskus (ngaskus) shows that online dwelling and its activism are a collective project of endlessly questioning what it means to live in a digital space while repositioning their roles against the pre-existing offline environment. The shifts from ghost reader to dweller, from *junker* to chatter, from online to offline participant, from leisure chat to activism, from being a member of an online community to becoming a member of society were ingrained in f=160's early digital practices, in the retrospective question of how to explore the possibility of what being online could offer. Being an organic community for Solo Kaskusers, then, is not instability, but struggle-driven consequences.

Keeping up with the Kaskusers is about maintaining all the possibilities unfastened for the community's future provides further resourcefulness and freedom of reflectivity for members to shape the community. At the same time, such freedom and embracing the open-endedness is not by definition, neutral; instead, in f=160, it is interpreted within the discourse of being Kaskusers, being Solonese, and their location in Kaskus, the Regional Forum, in f=160, and in the city. In short, Solo Kaskusers' becoming is a wayfaring of juxtaposing themselves in continuously self-revealing environments.

Ingold (2000) also emphasizes that one's path to the future or becoming is rather in the contextual part of the relational others. He eventually formulates that a 'person-organism' is an approach that draws attention to 'undergoing growth and development in an environment furnished by the work and presence of others' (Ingold 2000: 4). Unlike Mead (1938) and Habermas (1992), Ingold's subject-object or subject-subject relations are not guaranteed to cease with a significant formation of cohesion as each individual has his/her own path. To translate Mead into Ingold's idea, the latter's 'me' is related not only to society but to the environment as a whole including the technicalities that Kaskusers are facing. Ingold further formulates that this person-organism comes not only through perceptual experience to confirm with the generalized others, but the skill of living with the others as a continual evolving property that adheres to changes in the revelation of becoming. Human-environment relations are the modus operandi for the use of skill and the dwelling perspective in which the skill is created based on practices (Ingold 2000: 5).

For Solo Kaskusers, this openness to the path of the journey or on the subject of future is a pragmatic approach to the yet-undefined responsibility of the community. This journey of 'having the heart,' to recall Amakuzalek's description about understanding others, is not materialized through a preconfigured community program, but rather defines itself in the frame against the assessment of how to establish the importance of the larger environment or the external.

Harya explained that the community is based on one's relationship to other members and unlike formal organization, the steady engagement could only rely on 'feelings' like emotional gratification and fellowship solidarity. As Harya problematized the matter:

> This is not like a (political) party that gives [social status] recognition, or student associations that offer an education program for learning skills. Here, it is [a social] education [to become a society member] if we understood it that way. At least if we are active [in the city, in the kampong], it is because we need [to create] a comfortable (*nyaman*) community. With us [in f=160], it depends on the feeling, whether we feel the need to [join and be a part of the KRS community]. All we could do is to create social events, to build the [public] consciousness, that 'oh... there is such community and we could do something'.

The pragmatic choice of a flexible future is not a matter of uncertainty, but a chance for Kaskusers to have options for how they can participate in crafting the community's future. Therefore, the development of KRS and f=160 depends on Solo Kaskusers' continuous wayfaring experience within larger social units, that is, the city, and the offline society.

Embracing the current ideal of being prudent depends on how Solo Kaskusers perceive the coming experiences ahead of them. Kris, who is the account manager for Kaskus Solo offline events, in an optimistic tone stated that it is also foreseeable that the community might develop into a professional organization such as an NGO, or even a political party. Harya expressed in Arabic, '*lillahi ta'ala* (lit. trans. God Almighty) knows what we do and what our sincere intentions are' and further explained that going offline and doing deeds could not be predicted; it is only meant to produce goodness.

Such unsettling optimism makes being on the path of wayfaring and 'becoming' risky. Armin and Harya, both of whom had the experience of becoming an RL, admitted that keeping the group's integrity is a challenge since the nature of the activities and community is voluntary. While comparisons to other civil organizations such as political parties and religious organizations might seem attractive here, it is important to remember that Kaskus' initial formation was as a leisure group.

At the same time, Solo Kaskusers' notion of journey and dwelling differs from the traditional Javanese concept of path, which sees wayfaring (*laku*) as the process between birth and death. Magnis-Suseno (2005) describes this as 'the beginning' and 'the end', two bookends of a continuous quest to gain the knowledge needed to return an individual's union with the divine. This path, he (ibid.) underscores, is traditionally interpreted as a certainty of the path of faith (*nasib*), as life has been written (*takdir*) by God and therefore cannot be rewritten. As individuals are one with the divine in the beginning, life is therefore a path back to God and society, the achievement of which marks the end.

While such a classical interpretation of life's course might be popular among the older Javanese who regularly listen to traditional music, watch the philosophical *Wayang* theater, and consume other traditional cultural products, younger Javanese people contest this submissive way of life. The young Solo Kaskusers as the products of urbanization, have a relatively different demography from those observed by Magnis-Suseno (2005). It is therefore not surprising that the bookend version of a path with both a beginning and an end never surfaced in any threads on f=160, in any conversation, or in any of the community's acts. Unlike the traditional deterministic Javanese view of a life path, Solo Kaskusers' account of becoming is an open-end. In KRS, such personal and collective change is what Sodron and Harya described as, again, '*proses*' (Eng. process). Solo Kaskusers deny the submissive Javanese belief of life as a transition with a predefined end, and instead, perceived the change of their community from 2008 to 2012 as digital wayfaring that would continue to provide new revelations; unlike faith (*nasib*), community is not predestined.

Indeed, Javanese norms—'being correct', 'togetherness', and 'prudent/fair'—have been used to facilitate these changes, but these tend to become the pragmatic resources for the reproduced moral language needed to generate common terms rather than being pre-existing normative orders that strictly direct their lives along 'the beginning' and 'the end' conceptualization. While these younger Javanese people are surrounded by Javanese everyday life, they are not strictly confined to it. They go online and visit non-Javanese websites. Kaskus' disclaimer, for example, which offers an interpretation of 'freedom' that enriches Solo Kaskusers' normative vocabulary (see Chap. 2), was adopted from global online norms. To conclude, although Solo Kaskusers have been using Javanese vocabulary to organize KRS and f=160, it would be a simplification to argue that Solo Kaskusers experience the same normative experience as the previous generation.

As participants in an open-ended activity, Solo Kaskusers have denied that their end is simply becoming a member of f=160, or citizenship, or a member of society, as parts of the definite classic faith. To them, it is a sequence to reach the exterior. In the future, it may be a political ideal or a democratic civil society, as Kris who has been a member of f=160 since day one proposed. Therefore, as we see from this approach, 'Solonese' as a term used by Solo Kaskusers is neither a form of ethnocentrism revival nor a pseudo-tradition. Instead, it is a growing resource and identity that helps Kaskusers to make sense of their online chats and to create the identity of being a Kaskuser. It is not the subject of Javanese or global digitality, but rather, the mediated online intersubjective chat that becomes the actual foundation for reflection. They never use terms like 'being Javanese', 'being a Muslim' or 'being Indonesian'; instead, they are 'being Solo Kaskusers' as a designation for being an actor in the location they dwell, both in f=160 or in the offline city. The path of online dwelling is neither uncertain nor a determinist submission to the End or to God; it is a project to create a home—thread, f=160, Solo, and a *process* of 'coming of age' (*pendewasaan*).

The second feature of the organic online community is that the community is resilient and cannot be confined to a single platform. Its resilience can be found in its ability to move from platform to platform or to utilize various digital platforms simultaneously. Although Kaskus management, as the owner of the digital space, owns f=160's webspace, they do not own KRS or Solo Kaskusers' digital life. Surandy assured me with a confident tone that,

> [W]e believe what we do is good here. We are not confined to [digital] space anymore. If Kaskus dissolves, we would meet somewhere else. Technically, all we need is a server and free webhosting. The most important, however, is our will.

Here, the growth of the organic KRS also points to the creativity of survival and enlargement. All Solo Kaskusers echoed Surandy and expressed that the existence of their community transcends its digital location, platform changes, policy changes, and gadgets. As such, the online organic community is resilient to technological change. They exist by exploiting different platforms and digital spaces, not to mention Fusion Net and the city food stall as their main offline locations, with Mochi's house terrace as the second.

There is a sense of militancy in adding new spaces. Their artifacts have multiplied from digital space to T-shirts, banners, and flyers. Their networks have developed to include other forums in Kaskus, other CSOs in Solo, the city government, the Red Cross, the Health Department, shops, the local zoo, the national RRI radio, to name a few. In short, KRS and Solo Kaskusers are not—as they insist—confined to f=160 and have the ability to occupy new spaces.

The confidence to manage both these intentions and the space, however, is challenged by some problem, namely Kaskusers' tendency in being organic. First, as a forum with rich communication, the network and relationship among members relies heavily on emotional solidarity and intimacy. Second, the role of emotion plays heavily in the mobilization of participation. Third, the initial formation of Kaskus as a location of leisure chat and play continues to preserve the ghost of play. Fourth, and finally, while Solo Kaskusers have no certain innovative goal to achieve, their image of a good citizen always comes back to the ideas with which they are already acquainted, which seems to deny the creativity of being organic. Each of these issues will be explored more fully in the following sections.

## 6.2 Personal Communication and Intimate Mobilization

The 'success story' of KRS expansion across both online and offline spheres and moving toward social engagement owes a great deal to an informal small group coordination model where members and the network are managed through personal and sentimental relationships. Sodron expressed that he felt that being underground while facing the challenges associated with defining their identity has 'brought them together' (*guyub*) and thereby transformed the community into a brotherhood.

Members like Sodron and Amakuzalek have expressed that members of the community were concerned that the sense of 'brotherhood' would be missing as f=160 is currently experiencing a growth in membership. They expressed their concerns that personal affinity is influencing how the organization is managed, especially when the size of the community is growing. As the backbone of the network, personal communication influences how f=160 directs itself and organizes the group's solidarity. Sodron warned,

> I don't know when we are getting larger [in membership size] whether we still could be active like this, since, frankly speaking, we are active [in social engagement/activism] is because our we-feeling [emotional attachment]. When it is not exclusive, we are going to lose the bond. What I meant by 'exclusive' is when we feel that we are underground, (it is) just us [circle of friends].

Aside from the challenge of maintaining the personal communication and the affectionate network, new and greater memberships require a further effort to speed up the process of bonding. For Solo Kaskusers who have been in f=160 for a decade, having the experience of becoming a visitor, then a dweller, to a community member, a citizen, and a member of a society is a path of wayfaring where at each point new solidarity and meaning was revealed together with fellow Kaskusers; for new Kaskusers, these stories of wayfaring are a legend to follow. For senior Kaskusers, the past hard times of the online journey have become the source of their collective memory of the community's struggle and solidarity; for new Kaskusers, the journey has just begun. The meaning-making of bearing the community activities' load might be different. Thus, Sodron was concerned about the quality of militancy of the new Kaskusers as they did not reveal the path to citizenship as did his generation of Kaskusers.

Intensive communication offers a speed-up process of this intersubjective bonding since Solo Kaskusers could be in touch anytime and in any place. Experience compression is possible but it cannot be skipped. Everyone needs to have the ability to emotionally adjust, for example, if s/he needs to encounter such threads like those examples in Chap. 2. Most newbies would avoid sentimental threads since they do not yet have the connection with the person to whom the thread is dedicated or because they have not shared the experience of a rich online/offline experience described by Mochi as 'working together'. Here, not even emotional confusion has the right to exist since having the time for rich perception competes with giving speedy feedback. This fear rests on a perceived superficiality of bonding.

On one side, Solo Kaskusers had hoped that they could recruit more members so that they could reach their goal of campaigning for citizens' awareness of social problems in order to gain more support from the network when they engage in offline activism. Yet, on the other hand, they recognize that their current cohesion molds—and is molded by—the group's solidarity through two foundations: in-group solidarity, which started as underground online groups navigated by senior Kaskusers; and sentimentally-based solidarity of emotional attachment and mobilization formed through intensive communication and shared experiences stretched over half a decade.

### 6.2.1 *Personal Communication and Senior Kaskusers*

Personal communication secured the group's cohesion during the reorganization of f=160 when the digital space shifted from a 'free space' into a 'regulated space' as Chaps. 3 and 4 describe. The period of establishing the foundation of 'order' (*keteraturan*) in f=160 was perceived by Solo Kaskusers as a success, as the shift was supported collectively and was largely secured because of the role the community's elite took on when they seamlessly initiated the off-page back-channel communication with their chatting partners. Indeed, as the previous chapters describe, the Javanese normative notion of togetherness (*guyub*) and properness (*nggenah*) helped to bundle and justify the community's change, but the senior members' collective support of the new wave or changes was pivotal in bringing the new order to the mainstream on f=160's threads.

After the offline *wedhangan* meet-up was held to prepare for the picnic, to recall what has been described in Chap. 3, the five Solo Kaskusers who attended the meeting at that time contacted their personal network and lobbied them to prepare a common narrative to be presented on f=160. These senior members are essential for navigating other community members' wayfaring as they are linked to other senior members and online dwellers to pool the actors that would support mainstreaming certain narrative changes in the community. Furthermore, as senior members they not only had the capital to bully or brick those who did not support the transformation, but they also, more importantly, had the digital charisma needed to motivate and reassure their fellows that change was necessary.[1]

These elites are charismatic in the sense that their *KaskusStatistics* were often perceived to reflect their high degree of engagement in chat subjects, and this perception made them well-respected by other community members. Thus, a nonconformist act against these elites carries the risk of losing a strategic chatting partner. As such, when Armin started the thread that outlined the new online rules and campaigned for f=160's reorganization, the general dwellers more or less agreed to support the proposed changes.

Such stories about behind the screen (*dibalik layar*) close circle communication by the community's elites appear persistently in f=160's history of online interactions and have become a mode to mobilize opinions. As KRS transformed into a community, Solo Kaskusers consciously incorporated off-page personal communication to prepare, or even to shape, a single, or stronger narrative to be presented on the f=160 web page. The goal was to streamline and organize public opinion in order to minimize conflicts and to strengthen the common justification. Such method is, more or less, antithetical to those who were found in Kaskus during the freedom of speech era in the early 2000s when all communication took place on the main screen. Kaskus' senior members are buzzers that craft the arrangements in the off-page location.

However egalitarian it may seem on the screen, the organization of the community as well as the movement or the organic development, is heavily dependent upon its senior dwellers or elite actors. Here, the role of key actors as 'motivator' (*penggerak*)—to use Amakuzalek's term—like Surandy, Prima,

Harya, Amakuzalek, Armin, and Mochi, is decisive. They have their own personal networks of closest chatting partners who could be approached as they are the regulars on f=160 and communicate intensively. Their chatting partners are, too, usually other members who dwell in the forum to the same degree. As much as they try to keep the predominant dynamic on f=160's main screen, how KRS operates is actually very politically organized. These senior members not only have the capital associated with hard power like green-badges and clone IDs, but they are also able to use soft power like their organizational experience and skills. Prior to their online dwelling experience, some (Harya, Mochi, Amakuzalek, Armin, Prima, Surandy) already had experience in organizing a community—either at school or as part of religious groups, civil society organizations, or their own local neighborhood. Furthermore, usually they also have wide social networks and could bring sponsorship to Kaskus' event. In sum, senior members direct the community's wayfaring because they have the capital to offer to the community.

Figure 6.1 visualizes relatedness in f=160, which was knit through significant nodes.[2] Despite the fact that there is no singular center, as the figure shows, these significant nodes are actors who had a decisive impact—if

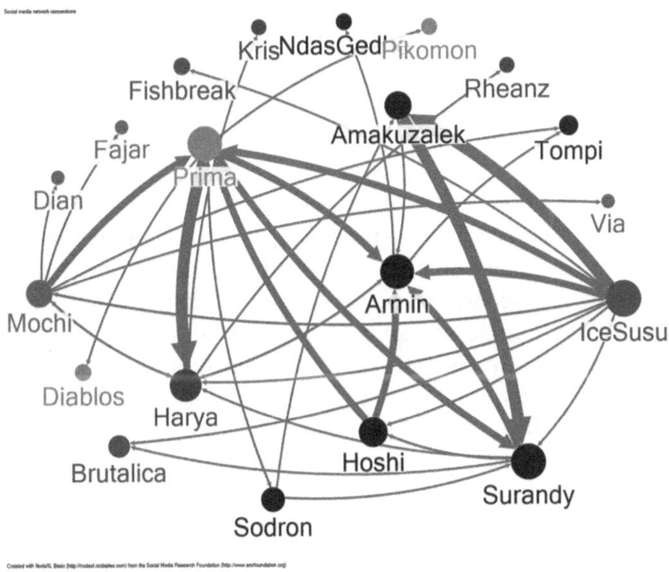


**Fig. 6.1** Kaskus regional solo network
(*Edge size represents the sum of counts when the node is being mentioned by others; **Vertex size represents the Eigenvector centrality)

not actually directing—KRS's wayfaring and dynamics. These actors include Prima, Armin, Harya, Surandy, and Icesusujahe.

Because of his initiative in 2006 to start a thread to cater for those who were interested in Solo, Prima could be referred to as the founder of what later developed into f=160. He also promoted the first offline picnic in 2009. A meeting held to prepare for it led to the establishment of a pact to regulate the online forum. A year later, he was the first to mention the term '*sembada*', which was eventually set by Sodron as a thread title and soon became the community's maxim.

Armin is one of the very few participants left from the early offline *wedhangan* period, an event he later criticized when he was campaigning for the need to regulate f=160 and its offline activities. He was also, consequently, elected as KRS' first Regional Leader. It is also worth noting that Armin was also one of the five Solo Kaskusers, along with Prima, who participated in the picnic meeting that later resulted in the agreement to reorganize f=160 and the establishment of the chat rules.

After being known as a flamer, Harya rose to prominence in 2010 when he challenged the community to become 'Solenese' in its identity. This later materialized into the game-changing 2010 Gathering, which has since become a substantial annual event that serves to support and reconnect to the city. He too played a major role in flaming Johar's posts after the Ilham advocacy movement, which led to the RL's resignation. Subsequently, he won the popular vote to replace Johar and become the forum's next RL.

Two other nodes who are part of this elite are Surandy and Icesusujahe. Both were regarded as senior Kaskusers who could pull all the strings of KRS' network to become the social anchor of the community and bridge differences between community members. In 2014, Surandy became the fourth Regional Leader, while Icesusujahe is a chat administrator.

At the level of a second layer in Fig. 6.1, Mochi, Amakuzalek, Hoshi and Sodron, for example, sustained the agenda and subjects that the first group tried to mainstream on f=160. Mochi, the promoter of language control, is personally close to Prima and Icesusujahe. Prima was also Mochi's backer—if not patron—when she campaigned for language change in f=160. Amakuzalek, the coordinator of the KRS' Jakarta Chapter, is very close to Icesusujahe, Surandy, Sodron, and their families in their offline interactions. Surandy, for instance, stays with Amakuzalek when he visits Jakarta. Hoshi, the TS of KRS' Buy-and-Sell thread, allows KRS to use his Internet game center as KRS's offline base, where he also lives next door to Armin. It became clear while approaching Solo Kaskusers off-screen that personal relationships and intimacy seem to be significant for shaping one's further role in KRS.

The operation of personal communication and network actually implies that KRS, as an organic community, is not free from the bias of social engineering in ordering its everyday life dynamics. The transformation of f=160 from a space into a community resonates with Bauman's thesis on community as a domineering form of social organization (Bauman 2001). He warns that community is not a stable world and that it is our imagination of 'lost paradise' (2001: 3) that depicts community as a warm connection that offers security. Community is a result of 'social engineering' (ibid.: 37), which relies on the dynamic, or struggle, of shared agreement. Agreement in a community, he argues, is a realm of enforcement, which

> make[s] sure that people would act in a certain way rather than in other ways, to taper the range of their options, to manipulate the probabilities; to make them do what they otherwise would probably not do [...]. (Bauman 1997: 191)

This can be seen in KRS's offline activity organization. Offline engagement is not only morally normative, it also conveys a hidden agenda for the community's sustainability. Internally, activism presents a window for recruitment, '*kaderisasi*' (trans. training; regeneration; lit. 'cadreization'), and appropriating social networks. Recruitment and regeneration are urgent since KRS is a voluntary community in which there is no certainty that Solo Kaskusers will continuously dwell in f=160 and actively participate in community activities. This evokes the question of integrity and the intentions that drive voluntary activity: Are social activities intended for the common good? Or are they part of a greater organizational purpose, both as a moral justification or as a mechanism to cohesion?

Taking the Iftar of 2011 as an example, the event was actually put at risk when Mochi was the elected coordinator although she was reluctant to take on the role. While she had indeed been elected democratically, the voters had been approached by some senior Kaskusers to ensure they would vote for her. During an offline meet-up I learned that even though she was hesitant to take on the role, replacing Mochi was not considered an option as several senior Kaskusers had agreed on the given organizational 'career strategy' discussed internally among them. While the Iftar as social activism was textually the primary concern, expectations about Mochi's leadership training as an extra-textual message of the event was certainly not less important. Although Mochi complained that taking on the role of event coordinator would delay the completion of her academic program, the off-screen political nuance was certain: Mochi was set to be part of the next generation of seniors. Such practice runs the risk of placing offline activities simply as the reification of online dynamics.

Ultimately this example shows that personal communication and networks are not simply organizational mechanisms but also, conversely, present the potential for elitism and collusion. To this point, the flow of information, organization management, and solidarity are assured through the friend-of-a-friend network instead of simply open communication. This contrasts the spirit of equality or transparency in the context of participative citizenship, all while its own internal network relies on personal lobbying.

Off-page communication became prevalent after the imposition of orders in f=160 as a means to create, as Solo Kaskusers stated, a 'comfortable space for all' (see Chap. 3). This had significant consequences for Solo Kaskusers as it reminded them that they had to behave in the online as if they were in a harmonious home. Subsequently, chats indicated by chat admin of having potential conflicts were shoved to off-page personal communication in order not to bring disorder into their f=160 home.

Since the forum had evolved to become a 'family,' and the digital space was reconstructed to become a 'home', any chat or text such as harsh criticism has also been diminished and conflicts between Kaskusers toned down and kept away from the public presentation of f=160. Sharp differences are expected to be first discussed through private channels and this leads to hush-hush conditions and gossip tailing the forum's actuality. This growing tendency eventually abandons the spirit of Fight Club from the initial years of Kaskus.

Personal communication through private channels has actually also betrayed the ideal of 'Freedom of Speech,' which—to use Goffman's terminology (1959)—was able to dismiss the duality of the front stage and back stage dramaturgy. Conflicts and disagreement slowly started to shift away from the main page to private messages, off-page communications, or to off-screen events, which was apparent for example, during the Iftar event preparation.

Therefore, Mochi's objection to her assignment as event coordinator never emerged on the main page or even off-page online communication, although Solo Kaskusers had a special chat thread to talk about all the preparations and challenges. It became a subject of discussion among Solo Kaskusers only when the offline meet-up took place. Congruently, Harya and Armin's account on community succession, which initiated Mochi's appointment, never went public at all.

Mochi never extended her protests to f=160 and, similarly, Harya and Prima did not investigate her initial lack of leadership in the designated online thread. The realities on the main page with the offline coordination were not simply the same. Harya and Prima did not eventually know how Mochi perceived the whole event, and vice versa.

I know their sides of the story since I had personal communication with them and discussed the case with all three Kaskusers who were involved in the dispute. In short, Solo Kaskusers' formula for perceiving each chat in each space does not go along with how they actually perceive the reality of the situation. Personal communication and network, eventually, has unexpectedly formed an online-offline or main-page-off-page discrepancy.

Icesusujahe and Surandy, to voice some others, complained that in some cases in order to maintain harmony, they could no longer be transparent. Icesusujahe provided an example:

> There is a friend who has now withdrawn from the forum. When I asked why, expressively he said that he feels uncomfortable with the way one of the fellow member talks [read: post]. He said that the other friend somehow has changed [note: he told me that the 'other friend' becomes boastful]. I just see it that both [parties] are just different in character, [...] I wanted to try, to mediate between them, but it is difficult and it is awkward to bring both parties to discuss the matter. So, that was it.

Unlike during the early years of Kaskus when Solo Kaskusers could explicitly express their language presentation, today, self-restraint plays a greater role in chats. Those who could not adapt to the new mechanism, like those in Icesusujahe's story, would experience a disconnection from the community.

Indeed, while some conflicts have gone public on f=160, like Prima's resignation from one of KRS' events,[3] conflict resolution nevertheless takes place mainly off-page. Prima went back to the public f=160 page simply to announce the matter had been resolved and to close the thread, and later he told me that Adhy had contacted him personally off-page to encourage him to stay with KRS.

Although conflicts nowadays, in contrast to what would have happened prior to 2008, go beyond the main pages of f=160, there is now a calculated risk as part of being prudent (*sembada*) to avoid crossing the convenience of friendships. This attitude is problematic when conflicts in events and dramas are treated as a filter to membership. Some Kaskusers, like

Harya during the 2010 Gathering preparation meeting, and Prima during the conflict against Johar, actually also understand that harsh debates and conflicts à la FC are necessary, as they serve as formative dramatic rituals for community-building. As Chap. 4 describes, Prima believes that arguments on matters of the community should be materialized into conflicts so that members can be tested to see who will give the best performance, and to identify those who have the capacity to be admitted to the community as it was in his disagreement with Johar.

Some Solo Kaskusers like Harya, Prima, Amakuzalek, Sodron, Superpekok, and Surandy sometimes even act as online flamers—similar to what Harya did when he interrogated Mochi's competence to coordinate the *Iftar*, or prompted Johar's underperformance after the Ilham Case (see Chap. 4). As the Regional Leader who had to monitor and control the chats, Harya stated that he would allow flaming posts to surface to some degree as a means to instigate debates and make the forum a training ground for plurality. However, as damage control, he would contact the related Kaskusers via direct message if he considered that the conflict might get out of hand. Those who ignored Harya's scolding would run the risk of being banned from the thread. In the end, personal relationships and private message communication have made f=160 into a forum for relatively like-minded Kaskusers.

### 6.2.2 *Mobilization and Intimacy*

Personal communication and personal approach also played a major role in mobilizing community participation in f=160. Collective participation is characterized by friendship and solidarity, which relies on warmth and emotional bonds. Most Solo Kaskusers admitted that the interpersonal communication that transpires in and from Kaskus will be multiplied through communication taking place on other digital platforms. Friends are not only connected in Kaskus, but also in other online media platforms. This underscores Amakuzalek's statement that 'we know our friends since we follow them 24/7,' which implied that he checks his friends' social media updates regularly. Exchange takes place continually as each Kaskuser shows their presence in the form of social media statuses, pictures, videos, and notes.

Everyday life communication, both online and/or offline, is a routine through which a Solo Kaskuser affirms the emotional bond one feels with other members of the community and the community itself. The gadgets and chats are the property of everyday life. The network has expanded via the use of any possible communication methods or platforms. While online chats and threads are certainly the center of the information traffic, personal relationships and where the discourse of community is being reproduced, Solo Kaskusers continue to reconnect with each other through personal communication and private channels, commonly referred to as the 'private network' (*jaringan pribadi*, abv. *japri*).

Through this intensive communication between followers—'a friend followed' in Twitter terminology—there is a sense of knowing each other by learning the other counterparts in their everyday life. This eventually raises shared emotion. Each member knows what the other friend is doing in their life, on a daily basis. Through his Facebook status, I knew when Prima's wife had her morning sickness even though we are thousands of miles apart in 2014. The next day, I learned that the sickness was a false alarm for the newlyweds. Through her Twitter account, we read that Mochi was preparing for her exam and was about to enter the classroom. Soon, her timeline was filled with best wishes from Solo Kaskusers. Beyond Kaskus' chat threads, the relationship between Solo Kaskusers has become increasingly personal.

In addition to online communication, Solo Kaskusers also assert that offline meetings have strengthened their bonds (Mochi, Armin, Harya and Surandy). Mochi expressed that offline experiences like organizing events and conversing in the regular meet-ups, have made her feel 'close' to the other f=160 fellows as they know each other's competencies and work style. These events are the means by which Kaskusers are able to experience 'working together', as Mochi stressed. During such 'opportunities', she explained, a member could reveal his/her 'true characters.' As such, she felt she was able to 'learn how they need each other.' Offline events are therefore another medium for intersubjective communication.

Eventually, interpersonal affection and the potential personal approach were converted into capital and a strategic method for mobilizing this network of emotion. Mochi illustrated how the personal approach has played a great role in creating a regular offline meet-up for women Kaskusers. It was Mochi who gathered the female users to come more often to the meet-ups as she recruited her own Kaskus friends to come with her. She admitted that at the first offline meet-ups, six female Kaskusers managed to come to the city's local park, but then the numbers slowly decreased when she herself started skipping some meet-ups. She acknowledges that most female Kaskusers had participated in the early meet-ups simply because of her personal call, not because they felt that such events were needed.

She also expressed her dilemma when she had to extend her study for another semester in order to have more time to be involved in KRS as she 'felt bad' for leaving her friends 'struggling with organizing some Kaskus activities'. Amakuzalek provided a similar account of 'feeling bad', when he recounted how he and Wahyu had to collect donations for the Ilham campaign around the city after office hours battling against Jakarta's heavy traffic jams. These examples illustrate that in addition to social awareness, their militancy was encouraged by the knowledge that their fellow f=160 dwellers in Solo were also giving their best so that the community's activities would be successful. In short, this network of emotion as a motivation for participation can be expressed in a straightforward formula: 'I participate because my chatting partner is doing it'. In social media communities, collective activity is expanding not only because of the notion of participation in a sense of 'I know therefore I join', but also for friendship solidarity.

Steven Jones once asserted that in online communities, emotional solidarity is greater than ever and makes 'the community belongs to us' (1995: 16) a compelling change of the classic perception that 'we belong to the community'. As the digital connection in Kaskus is also very personal, the online community becomes personally tangible. Community is identified in the detailed membership of friends and their everyday life experiences and eventually the collective participation.

The interwoven personal relationship as a base of solidarity is intrinsic to the practice of 'looking for friends' and extending one's network—as Chaps. 2 and 5 describe—for it is a lucrative experience of staying in f=160. Failing to participate in the community's event, would likely result in a loss of friends as Johar had experienced.

Like any network, this role of private network risks the emergence of elitism and collusion. As a chat-based social media forum, Kaskus offers an open-end space of possibilities, and, therefore, in addition to an affectionate relationship in which showing and having solidarity with our friends is imperative for maintaining the network's potential.

Accordingly, text and other visual communication codes on f=160, sympathy to the social offline world, and the desire to reconnect with the city do not simply mobilize community participation. While a common identity might work as capital for increasing solidarity (see Castells 2010), solidarity itself would only be certain through the personal bonds of friendship. This means any social activism does not necessarily, and directly, represent democratic, ideological or citizenship ideals. The mobilization and large participation, sometimes, are just about in-group solidarity and maintaining friendship.

## 6.3 The Ghost of Play: The Myth of Real and 'Real'

What is *ngaskus* actually? If I only read [browsed] around, that is also *ngaskus*, if I come here [to the weekly *wedhangan*] it is also (considered *ngaskus*). Also, when we do social activism. [Sodron]

Reflecting on the annual Gatherings, Harya expressed that 'to play a role (*kebermanfaatan*) for the greater good' is part of the new identity of being a Solo Kaskuser; the search for identity eventually led KRS to voluntarism and activism, both online and offline. Sodron chimed that community events serve as reminders to Solo Kaskusers of what being Solonese means and signifies the online community's existence in the larger society. Icesusujahe even stated a further deterministic view, that it is 'useless to introduce ourselves to the public if we do not have any positive activities [for them]'.

At the same time, he also expressed his concern that with the escalation of such deeper participation and engagement in Kaskus, there is a growing tendency that some Solo Kaskusers have withdrawn themselves from the community's activities. These less active dwellers of f=160, he suspected, had to 'take care of their real-life family'. Illustrating his own conflicted experience, Icesusujahe described that there is always a tension between choosing to spend his free time with his family or 'with his smartphone and Kaskus'. Icesusujahe's statement underscores the opposition between 'the online community' and 'the offline family'.

### *6.3.1 Can Leisure Be Real?*

Stemming from leisurely chat, Kaskus activity is still ordered by Solo Kaskusers as secondary to their offline routine. Icesusujahe, who felt the competing demands of Kaskus activities and non-Kaskus activities, was not alone. Mochi, for instance, expressed that she faced a dilemma when she had to extend her studies for another semester so that she could engage more deeply with KRS' social activism. She felt guilty that if she left she would 'leave her friends all alone with their duties'. Recollecting these experiences, she stated: 'At some point I have to get back to my real life and finish my studies'.

As most Kaskusers feel that the decision about whether they will remain in KRS and participate in both online and offline activities is a matter of personal choice, the distinction of online-offline activities hardly materialized into an online discussion on f=160 or during offline meet-ups and Solo Kaskusers never expressed the dilemma openly. Nevertheless, it was one of the popular topics of discussion when I spent some time with Solo Kaskusers in the offline personal time conversations—or what they called 'heart-to-heart' (*curhat*). They expressed that living in two realms is a dilemma with which they have to contend, particularly in terms of the consequences and direction of action.

The most publicly known occurrence of when a Kaskuser had to make such a personal choice is when Armin resigned temporarily from f=160. Like Mochi, Armin experienced a similar dilemma when he 'had to choose' between 'his life' and 'KRS'. In 2010, he resigned as Regional Leader so that he could 'concentrate on his real life'. He wrote on his resignation thread titled '[Sorry and Thank You] A Love Letter from @areMean' [sic] on July 12th, 2010[4]:

> Beloved fellows of Regional Solo Kaskusers,
>
> Sigh….
>
> It seems that it has been a while since I have created a thread.
>
> First of all, I would like to thank all fellows (*rekan-rekan*) of Solo Regional, who have entrusted me with the Regional Leader tag to be set under my ID.
>
> Further, I would also like to apologize for any mishaps that I might have made, both as a [online] moderator and during offline encounters.
>
> As you may have noticed lately, I have been rarely going online on Kaskus, my threads or the posts I have to moderate have been left unmaintained, and it is also the case that I am hardly able to participate in offline meetings lately, may that be in *wedhangan*, playing futsal; I even skipped several meetings to prepare for the Gathering. For all of these absences, I apologize to you.
>
> The cause of these all is that I have many things and problems in my Real [sic] life that I have to fix.
>
> Therefore, I would like to ask your permission to resign as Solo Regional Leader.
>
> Besides the already mentioned matters, it is also no less important that my resignation could make way for *Regenerasi* [sic,] [Eng. new recruits].

He explained to me that mid-2010 had been a difficult time for him in his personal offline life, or, to use his writing style above, in his 'Real life'; he had moved from place to place, lost his job, and then had to find a new job. He expressed that 'at that time I could not even manage my own Real life, how could I have managed Kaskus?' Armin's resignation signified the current loose ends that are associated with being in f=160: the distinction between the online and offline, of real and unreal, and the matters of regeneration, fellowship, and presence/participation-absence/resigning.

These dilemmas are rooted in the condition that their perception about Kaskus and KRS has never been transformed into a non-virtual phenomenon. Solo Kaskusers view that the real life is located outside the KRS network. Armin's above transcription of 'Real life' with a capital 'R' could be compared with Anderson's (2006: 150–151) illustration of the Javanese 'Real' as the grand truth of reality, and the 'real,' the pragmatic reality.[5]

The dilemma is the initial motivation for dwelling: simply to have leisurely chat. This is the ghost of chatting. The depiction of chatting as a leisure activity means that it is currently perceived to be part of consumption, instead of a potential act of production. When Solo Kaskusers started to dwell in f=160, their initial motive or interest was simply for playful and informal chat. This means any results stemming from involvement in Kaskus are connotatively associated with being a novelty.

Most Solo Kaskusers admitted that the very initial reason they signed up for Kaskus was simply for leisure (*iseng*) and to chat; further participation in forums was unintended. Therefore, even though dwelling in Kaskus could become a productive activity, discussing a certain subject, reading books, establishing social networks, and learning photography or how to fish, among others, would largely be described as consumptive leisure by Solo Kaskusers.

Such a view of realms distinguishes the unmerging events of 'online' and 'offline,' between 'Kaskus-related' and 'Real-life-related,' between 'playing' and 'working', between 'leisurely chatting' and 'coming back to society'. As long as the activities are Kaskus-related, they will not be perceived as part of the 'Real life', despite the fact that the effort required to materialize the activities is genuine. Solo Kaskusers tirelessly show their integrity in terms of achieving the community's goal and take some events into the offline space.

As something that stemmed from novelty and leisure, for some Solo Kaskusers—like what Icesusujahe, Mochi, and Armin described before—Kaskus' derivative activities are secondary to their lives, although they are loyal participants in KRS' activities and considered by many as key actors as Fig. 6.1 illustrates. Assessing their statements, the following can be ascertained: for Icesusujahe, Real life is spending time with his family, although hanging out in Kaskus might lead to social activism; for Mochi, the Real life is to become an accomplished student; for Armin, the Real life is to find a job and a home instead of being a member of a community and monitoring the threads. This ordering shows that Solo Kaskusers were ambivalent in playing their multiple identities as Kaskusers and offline members of a society.

Such perceptions of Kaskus raise the view of online forums as a 'virtual'. The online-offline entity is perceived as a shifting binary instead of a sequence; as virtuality refers to those in the online world, then, the offline world represents anything that is not online. Consequently, the offline life is where there are no alter egos, no play, and where the *Real* and *tangible (nyata)* life are. Thus, even though Solo Kaskusers have experienced the community engagement and emotional satisfaction that comes from social activism, these activities are still considered as derivatives and are yet to be considered the property of Real life—regardless of how tangible Kaskus offline activity might be—like the Iftar with a group of orphans, promoting the city, rebuilding a school.

When asked through a questionnaire to identify their priorities, Solo Kaskusers distinguished the subjects of their Kaskus activities with terms from their offline-roots as Fig. 6.2 shows. This research finds that some activities are indeed considered to be important for Solo Kaskusers, yet they found it less Real (Fig. 6.2, Point 2 to Point 5). Despite the fact that Kaskus activities are not perceived as the Real, they are not necessarily perceived as 'unreal' as a Solo Kaskuser could experience the weight of engagement. 'Organizing annual Gatherings' (Fig. 6.2, Point 3) and 'discussion' (Fig. 6.2, Point 7), as examples, are two activities that could represent an equal perception of importance and reality in Kaskusers' everyday life. Kaskusers tend to perceive Kaskus activities as not 'unreal' since they correspond the activities with prudence (*sembada*) making it normatively toned. Converting 'chatting' into monitored and subjected 'discussion', for example, brings the former to its relevance for the offline world.

The hesitation to define online-based activities as 'Real'—regardless of their laborious activities—shows that Solo Kaskusers are hesitant to include Kaskus' activity as being a real part of their Real life activities. By contrast, all offline-based activities (Fig. 6.2, Point 9 to Point 14) are considered less important, but are assigned a higher degree of reality. Except 'random online chat', Kaskusers perceive online-based activity numbers one to seven as important, but they are secondary. On the other hand, offline activities eight to fourteen are considered to be less important but rather compulsory to complete. Accordingly, although currently Solo Kaskusers believe that Kaskus' offline activism is not simply a play or game since they

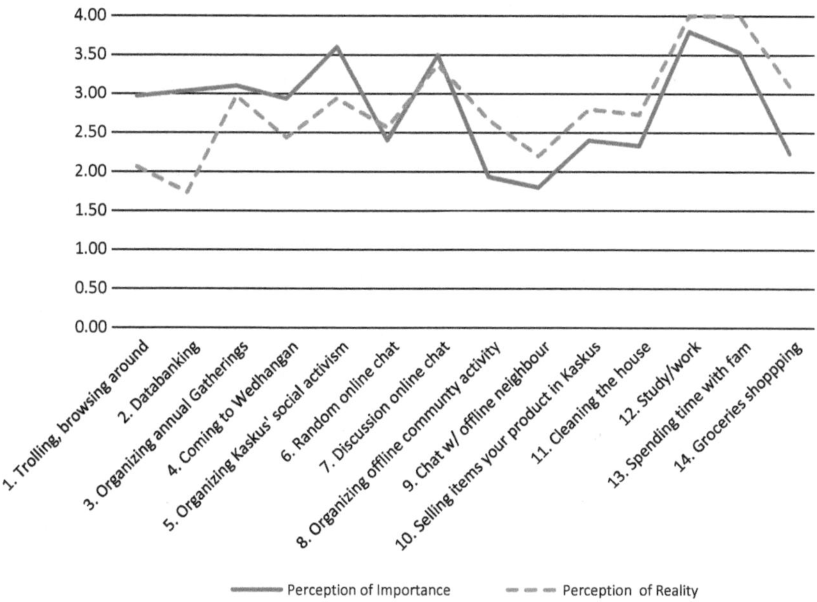


**Fig. 6.2** Priority given as semantic comparison between importance and *Real* according to Solo Kaskusers

are part of creating the common good, some Solo Kaskusers, nevertheless, consider these activities not to be their primary property of life. This could be seen from the weighting against 'organizing social activism' which gains high consideration as important, but not realized as a primary in Kaskusers' everyday life (see Fig. 6.2, Point 5).

Although both 'organizing annual Gathering' and 'organizing social activism' are public outreach activities, they do not necessarily convey the same reality, with the latter considered to be far less 'Real'. Such differences may arise because of the degree of avoidance. While the latter relies on the self-appraisal of guilt and prudence, the first is rather difficult to avoid because a Kaskuser will have to face the same request for community participation annually. Regularly failing to comply with these requests could lead to exclusion because annual Gatherings are events representing a state of the union; every member should already be able to foresee the regularity of the event, thus the compulsory participation.

This perception of involvement in Kaskus can present a risk as Kaskusers who share the view might only contribute to KRS, both in f=160 and in offline activities, with less discipline than other fellows in Kaskus might expect. Or even, as it was with Armin, such disparity and the fear of being militant in each compartment of reality might lead some Kaskusers to withdraw themselves from f=160, while choosing to make the other reality their primary concern.

Such juxtaposition of 'real' and 'Real' could only lead to uncertainty. Although the online community and its activities have been established in both the online and offline spaces, without its inclusion in Solo Kaskusers' perception primacy, KRS and its offline properties would remain 'virtual'. If so, KRS would always be in an existential crisis as members' participations would become secondary, making it unsustainable.

To use Mochi's dilemma as an example, unless being a society member through Kaskus activism is equally important as being a student, then the primacy of the 'Real life' is still assigned to the completion of her studies. In Kaskus' Trade Forum, she was also selling her own handmade soaps. Her online trading activity was, nevertheless, Real for her. In sum, in her view, all of her activities that directly affect her personal basic need—education and income—are primary. Different activities, although housed in Kaskus, could result in a different perception of reality.

Having both realities is actually what Van Dijk (2006) calls the 'total experience', a holistic human experience that is contingent upon physical presence. For him, interaction with the environment, senses and conceptual modes lead people to understand their reality. That is, a person's total experience must be understood through the lens of 'perception, interpretation and interaction in continually changing contexts' (ibid.: 221). The procedure of total experience or 'holistic' is therefore interplayed (Van Dijk 2006: 5). Following this approach, it is possible to understand that the relationship between the online and offline, or the avatar and the body, or Kaskus and 'the Real world' (*dunia nyata*) is not a matter of dissociating, but is instead merely a pragmatic identity operation in everyday life. Separating the two identities is a complex procedure that is ineffective for self-presentation, thus the person who is operating the two identities is imprinted on them both.

To interpret this insight in the lives of Solo Kaskusers, one could view that the online persona also lives in the body-operant and having the online persona has become a part of the offline self. Again, from an outsider's view this is not a dualism, but an integrated expectation of experiencing both realities; an enrichment of the online and offline by each other.

Each body represents the online persona and offline character. The body-operant has become a reminder of f=160 and vice versa. When I see *@areMean*, I remember the offline Armin who is wise, and when I see

Armin in the offline encounter, I remember *@areMean* who is humorous in f=160. Another example of a crossover act was provided in Chap. 1—when Wahyu mimicked the movement of running away with a scooter similar to the.gif emoticon. The total experience is therefore an integrative experience of both going online and offline. Nevertheless, the appropriation of both online and offline worlds could only exist when the transfer from sphere to sphere was considered to be something that was needed, integrated and not decoupled. These complexities that Van Dijk (2006) suggested are however not yet distinguished by Solo Kaskusers, thus the 'Real' and 'real' distinction.

### *6.3.2 The Four Perplexities*

Kaskus' perception of a conscious uncoupling of the two realities shows too that there is also a sense of perplexity, or confusion among Kaskusers in the online and offline distinctions. There are four perplexities in the separation of the online and offline world, the first of which is the ordering of primacy as described above. The second perplexity is found in the confusion that could easily be noticed regarding the identity play and the personal affect. Although there has been a conscious effort to integrate the online and offline world, there is a dissonance between what belongs to the online and what to the offline. For example, the use of '*ngaskus*', which once was a verb to denote the activity of online chatting only, today also signifies offline activities as Sodron expressed in the beginning of this section. On the other hand, Harya expressed that no matter what, 'online conflict between Solo Kaskusers should always be resolved only on the screen of f=160'.

At the same time, Solo Kaskusers do not make a clear-cut distinction between one's role in the online and the offline world. As such, a Kaskuser might eventually act both as an online persona and as an offline character, especially when the person behind the screen has been widely known for his/her offline identity. As examples: Amakuzalek is the person a Kaskuser will seek out when someone needs help with Cantonese translation even though he never uses the language in f=160; Prima is the hub of the city government although in Kaskus his online persona plays a computer geek rather than an activist; and although religion is never talked about in f=160, Harya was occasionally invited to give Islamic sermons in Kaskus' offline activities. When cases regarding citizen's inquiries or collective engagement emerge, Solo Kaskusers who work as civil servants in their real life, like the mayor of Solo, are expected to respond to the matter in both their capacities as the online persona and as a civil servant. In the

Kaskus environment, this multiple identity is sometimes shifted continuously between sequences of online and offline participation, but also sometimes takes place simultaneously.

In the offline sphere, some Kaskusers are even called by their online persona's name by some while others refer to them with their offline, 'real' names. When the online persona is more memorable than the offline name, the subject would be called by his/her Kaskus ID accordingly, and the same is true vice versa. Harya is called *meneer*, Dyah is *Mochi*, and Surandy is *Mbah_Sur*. On the other hand, other Kaskusers refer to Armin, Wahyu, Sodron, Heru, and me using our offline names. Harya and Mochi admitted that they sometimes felt that there is public expectation that they will be *meneer* and *Mochi* during the offline meetings, even though their offline reality is different from that of their online persona. Armin would always be known as the first Regional Leader that hosted the weekly *wedhangan* and as a graduate of an Islamic boarding school; regardless of how menacing he can be, for instance with his sensual innuendos in the online sphere, in the offline meetings he is respected as the senior or older brother who is socially expected to provide the community with strategic suggestions since he worked as an event organizer, and thus possesses the knowledge. Both the online persona and the offline character within the contextual Kaskus environment, both socially and virtually, have become, to use Holden's term (2006: 15–16), '(a) mediated identity'.[6]

In cases where the online identity is adopted to the real world identity, it is also common that a Kaskuser would introduce him/herself with a Kaskus ID or add the word 'Kaskus' as his/her family name. Most of my Solo Kaskuser friends also use their Kaskus names on Facebook and Twitter. This does not mean that they are taking the online persona to the offline or carrying the online persona to other web platforms, but is instead a mark of affiliation between the online persona and the 'Real' person.

Third, confusion is related to the recognition of Kaskus dwelling against one's personal emotional well-being, which is often considered to be 'Real'. Although the activity comes from the real world, the feeling or the impact is 'Real'. For example, Icesusujahe also once told me that his main motivation for looking for new friends on f=160 was to find potential friends that might help him in his 'Real life' in the future. For him, although these friends are part of the virtual f=160 world, they become 'Real' when they transform into a safety or support net.

Having the experience of organizing several collective actions also evokes a real feeling of spiritual and emotional satisfaction (Harya, Mochi, Surandy), or as Sodron described the feeling, 'the reward [of participating in activism] is indeed invisible [unlike obtaining green-badges], but we definitely could feel it'. Novi explained her joy with happy facial expressions when she told me a story from two years ago about how she participated in the reconstruction of a school that KRS was helping to rebuild.

Here again, I would again recall the occasion when Prima expressed his disappointment with Johar, as he deliberately raised his tone while expressing his frustration. The conflict between Prima and Johar presents an example that while both parties had a longer period of knowing each other in the online realm, shifting the same bond to the offline is not as speedy as a login or logoff. Johar's underwhelming performance destroyed any emotional bonds he had built online in f=160. A failure in transforming the online norms to the offline reality therefore can result in disappointment and disbelief in cyberculture. It is not a matter of adaptation and change, but of how Kaskusers in their discipline, recognize the time-compression, or delay, that simultaneously occurs online and offline. Each time we log in, we have to be ready to engage with various experiences of emotions. Once we dwell in a thread or forum, we have to be ready to emotionally engage whenever we meet our friends. In the end, an online community, once a leisurely getaway, has become as emotionally complex as any other community.

Several days after his wife's passing, Surandy read the thread Prima had created as a dedication to Surandy's late wife, and he wrote as a response that he could not stop crying when he was reading the messages of condolence. For him, the messages were all personal, coming from friends with whom he has daily digital encounters, and friends to the degree that he could imagine their mimics, voices, other physical expressions, and their sincerity to the expressions and friendship. Here, when it comes to 'feeling', KRS becomes 'Real', being in the online community is always 'Real' when it is part of an emotional engagement.

The fourth perplexity relates to a condition where the reproduction of norms stemming from the offline world—the 'Real life'—in the online circulation and community does not necessarily result in online realities that are parts of the offline world. Although offline norms have been reproduced in the online world, the latter is still perceived as part of the world that is mainly reserved destined for leisure and consumption. Take the reproduction of the Javanese notion of togetherness (*guyub*) as KRS' cyber norm as an example. When Solo Kaskusers were in search of certain members' participation, they employed the term *guyub*, which stems from the offline world, through chatting and titles of threads. The term is used to advocate the urge to form mutual trust, which understanding is taken from the ethic in 'Real life'. Here again, Harya's illustrations provide a good example,

> a Kaskuser could have a strong online ID with a formidable reputation, a significant number of cendol, and an old join date, but it is all virtual. [...] It means that Kaskus has become only their alter-ego. Me myself, I am proud of becoming a part of a community that is active in the region. Posts can be deleted, but togetherness (*guyu*b) is difficult to find, and we could bring it anywhere.

Online chat also represents togetherness, but coming offline is perceived to meet the expectation of its Javanese *guyub* term. To make certain the *guyub* and to correlate the online and offline worlds, Solo Kaskusers interpreted the procedural act through another Javanese norm, prudence (*sembada*). To this point, the presence of the offline life in online-related matters in the context of Solo Kaskusers is evident but the converse condition is not apparent.

Indeed, some Kaskusers have remained diligent in upholding such prudence in their everyday lives: Prima has integrated his activism into social entrepreneurship; Amakuzalek does the same while becoming a political publicist; and Mochi was also the president of the student senate. Yet, they perceive KRS's activities not as 'Real life' activities, as in the case with Mochi and Armin exemplify. What is still lacking is the awareness to change the perception of these online norms so that they are viewed as independent reality and not a derivative of the chatting environment as part of consumption.

Appadurai (1996) warns that consciously recognizing a practice as 'consumption' risks terminating its legitimate purposefulness or agency. This is what he calls 'methodological traps', which are the legacy of the 'Veblen effect' (Appadurai 1996: 65), the fallacy of seeing consumption, or 'play' in this context of research, as the end of the production cycle while keeping away its potential role in social reproduction.[7] While arguing 'where there is consumption there is pleasure, and where there is pleasure there is agency' (1996: 7), he notes that consumption could be a potential procedure for production. It is the routine rites of passage that could lead to a whole new form of social organization and create meaningful time (1996).

Media scholars have been presenting how digital consumption is a location and a source of production and reproduction (Miller and Slater 2001; Boellstorff 2008; Pearce 2009; Kobayashi 2010). Kobayashi (2010) even exemplifies individualistic online gaming environments, where individual skill is required to overcome the environment, as indeed a creative community through which they reproduce the social connection to induce gaming cooperation and partnerships to win the challenges. In this arena, online gamers learn social skills and develop social connections (Kobayashi 2010).

Accordingly, Ingold (2010, 2011: 211) argues that each product delivers its own narrative to explain the process and the contextual social life of the artifact. Therefore, to see the productivity of KRS, one could observe its production of artifacts and the actors' struggle to manifest them. KRS and f=160 as products of online chatting, represent a decade of digital experience and the texture of struggles. The consumption of online chatting, being in a community, f=160, of spiritual gratification, and participating in wider social units serves to cultivate Kaskus' Freedom of Speech, the green-badge merit system, statistics, cybersense, public debates, speedy feedback, equal partnerships, cooperative reliability, and online norms, to name just a few products that have been formed from f=160. Consequently, the latter also influence the former; that is, the products also influence the productions. This mutual development of consumption and the reproduction of community values is the spirit of the network which serves to carve a path for Solo Kaskusers from their trolling baby steps with thread dwelling in the early 2000s to social activism in 2012.

Nevertheless, narrative alone is not justification. Solo Kaskusers do indeed seem to be open when they narrate their story of f=160 and they are proud of where they were in their path of online wayfaring. Yet, the ghost of Veblen's (1994) dichotomy between production and consumption seems to be more irrefutable than ever in KRS as all these productions are yet to be perceived as 'Real', as illustrated above.

Instead of viewing the two worlds as parallel realities or as an entirety of reality, Solo Kaskusers were trapped in the fallacy of online-offline dichotomy, of leisure and non-leisure. A disciplined separation between the two digital distinctions would only lead Solo Kaskusers to an inaccurate perception of life in Kaskus. There is always hesitation to justify KRS' activity by its own term, that is to admit that it has become part of Solo Kaskuser's life and not simply isolated within the f=160. This treatment of online activity and offline activity as online consequences creates a risk of a false pseudo-compartment between each world, thereby reducing the online-offline ordering and their entity as interconnected activity, and leisure or consumption as a productive engagement.

When asked about the dilemma between leisure chat and activism, Surandy was certain that taking part in social activism could also be 'fun', and formulated, 'simply to find the most fun for you and do it with joy'. His formula implies when 'fun' exists within community engagement, KRS activities could then be collectively perceived as primacy. This brings us to the subject of 'fun' as socially engaging as a prerequisite to become 'Real'.

Surandy's perception implies that having 'fun' does not mean that production or reproduction is absent, rather, it denotes the character of KRS public engagement. It recalls what has been illustrated in Chaps. 2 and 3, that to chat, a Kaskuser requires a wide potential repository of chat-ready users and extensive social networks. Discussion about public service and citizen monitoring could also start as part of small talk as it is a common conversation-starter in Kaskus. At the same time, productive activity could be fun, even if it is unintended like the Gatherings, or monitoring police conduct on the street (see Chap. 4).

It is troublesome that while some Kaskusers felt that KRS playfulness would only lead to disorganization, some others expressed that they felt that f=160 ought to maintain its playfulness while objecting to formality, depicting the first as a betrayal to the initial equality and merriness of the birth nature of the space itself. Icesusujahe voiced several concerns about his fellows,

> I don't want to be serious with this [activism] I went to Kaskus to run away from the stress in my real life and just to discuss things that have nothing to with my life. But [we also realize] it (the obligation to voluntary activity) is all for the common good (*kebaikan bersama*).

These cravings, however, are considered to be taboo or inappropriate to express in public. The current convention among Solo Kaskusers asserts that since the new ideal of contribution represents the goal of a greater good, bringing back the recognition of 'fun' as it was with the mundane chat of the old days would be a setback. Any intention to misbehave is perceived to be a degradation of the notion of responsible citizen and Solo Kaskusers as members of a society.

The problematic fondness of Kaskusers for the language of mockery as a preferred style of communication style is an example. Erick's argument implies that however wrong the blatant and adult language may seem, it could, at the same time, also enrich the community's solidarity and identity, thus becoming a productive feature of being in a community. Similar to Surandy, he was convinced that maintaining humor and, accordingly, Kaskus as a frolic arena for chat and alter ego is what differentiates between f=160 as a community and as an organization. He described: 'frolic chat and mockery should always take place, otherwise, let's just directly make an organization [instead of a community]'.

According to him, mockery should be made certain as it is the practice and field of play that dismissed the authoritative and formal structure of elders and newbies. Otherwise, KRS would no longer be 'fun'. Mockery and blatant language are signifiers of Kaskus, making it a unique space for the commons. They are reminders of being in a space of equality where all presupposed social status has to be canceled. Thus, according to this observation, it is appropriate to suggest that instead of detaching it in the online compartment or terminating the practice, mockery and frolic chat should be perceived as Real and acknowledged as part of the further offline experience as well as a part of Kaskusers' identity.

In this complexity, instead of accommodating those who object to intensive community engagement and opted for playful chat, Solo Kaskusers collectively decided that community engagement could be employed to test their fellow's prudence. To recall Prima's philosophy of why he and his colleagues flamed Johar and his supporters, the purpose was to create test cases to filter out those who did not want to stay in the forum and adhere to the new online rules. Such tests assess Solo Kaskuser's commitment in terms of participating in events, including how one fulfills the seniors' expectation as in the case of Mochi's appointment for coordinating the Iftar. In this arrangement, the existence of f=160 relies on the very best individual potential to establish the highest possible collectivity. Such an approach to community engagement leads Solo Kaskusers to a dilemma, like Icesusujahe expressed: 'Social activities are always good, but my 'Real life' is to cater to my family'.

Avoiding or leaving Kaskus by those who are facing the Real-real dilemma is also not a solution. Participating in the community is inevitable since it is a manifestation of being coherent and prudent (*sembada*), which is the moral of going online. Accordingly, these days in KRS, community engagement is not just to justify the activity of having a chat in f=160, but currently it has become part of a moral obligation to society and the common good, as Solo Kaskusers possess digital power. The choice is, therefore, either to become present and participate in KRS' activities or to withdraw from the community and leave Kaskus entirely as Armin did in 2010. In this ordering, leaving Kaskus means leaving KRS' activism and, according to the current KRS norm, it is a sign of neglecting society, which is a moral consequence that Solo Kaskusers are not willing to take.

'What we do here is leisurely serious!' said Icesusujahe. It has to be 'serious' since seriousness distinguishes between prudence (*sembada*) and guilty feelings. Going online, once considered an egocentric activity, has in its current state become a social activity. Conversely, going completely offline and leaving f=160 are perceived to be an egocentric choice. As Kaskus has become an inherent part of their everyday lives, members leaving Kaskus could be socially perceived as abandoning friendships and society. Furthermore, failing to participate in the proper manner could be considered a sign of a Kaskuser's dwindling moral understanding and his/her movement toward incoherence as online dwellers and, at the same time, as participants in the offline public. The 'voluntary' factor is therefore no longer voluntary and problematic since it is situated between the spectrum of 'being concerned' (*kepedulian*) and 'ignorance'. This strick establishment of prudence to create a coherent state of the Real and the 'real' might have eventually transformed the forum into a regime.

## 6.4 The Stock of Wonder and the Remnants of the Past

The potential for new media technologies to provide access to knowledge has been strongly viewed as a pathway to new knowledge and an entry to the subject of the future. Nicholas Negroponte, the Chairman Emeritus of Massachusetts Institute of Technology's Media Lab, even launched a program, 'one child, one computer,' and declared that computer and computer literacy is a way to provide people with knowledge-access and globally-integrated interactions. As Chap. 1 describes, this modern approach is also popular in Indonesia and Solo. The state's technocrats are keen to facilitate technological advancements as they believe that the installment of new media technology in Indonesia represents a method to create an information society (*masyarakat informasi*).

Solo Kaskusers' experience as an organic online community, however, shows that, in the context of the depiction of a better life, infrastructure and discussion alone do not guarantee innovative pursuit of the future. How a community places itself within the course of an achievement correlates to the way in which the community imagines its formative becoming or future. Although believed to have facilitated online dwellers to become better citizens, the presence of digital technology does not necessarily propel a new way for imagining a better life. One of the reasons for this is because Solo Kaskusers are confined within their traditional prescriptions of a better society, thus limiting the stock of wonder.

### 6.4.1 *Moral Vocabularies and Practice*

Although Solo Kaskusers are not traditionalists, Javanese terms have, to date, acted as the main resource to safeguard order and expectation in the community. Javanese vocabulary is reserved, with codes that dictate everyday life manners as the closest resource for proper conduct. As much as Kaskus is characterized by the anonymity, the spirit of freedom of speech, the merit system of participation, and access to global culture, Solo Kaskusers use Javanese culture to formulate their norms and ethics because it is their closest vocabulary resource of norms as part of the modalities of becoming a community.

David Bell argues that since space contains—for those who had previously been socialized in other cultural practices—social interactions, any cyberspace would contain interaction between cultural attitudes making it inseparable from its cultural contexts (Bell 2001: 8). This is not to say that f=160 is simply a 'Javanistic' space for that would deny the other cultural experiences—like freedom of speech and cybersense—but it is to say that Javanese culture as a sociocultural offline ecosystem plays a great role in forming Solo Kaskusers. Such assertions of Javanese values represent, on the one hand, Solo Kaskusers' everyday life reality; it is therefore a matter of pragmatic effort to resource their virtue from their existing environment. On the other hand, it limits expansion by definition. The challenge that Solo Kaskusers have to overcome in the future—or in the next phases of digital wayfaring—is, therefore, to create a certain method of wayfaring that keeps reproducing their creativity by taking advantage of other cultural resources and not simply to return to, or resurrect, the imagined traditional Javanese community (see Florida 1995).

To date, instead of creating another alternative to the already existing norms of the offline world, they followed the popular repertoire of 'being Solonese'. This affects how Solo Kaskusers have imagined their digital space. The imagination of f=160 as a 'free space' has now been transformed into a greater Solo area comprised not only of a geographical imagination but also of a political and social network that offers unity in the offline world.

This was rather obvious in the case when Solo Kaskusers objected to the development of a new web page for those living in Klaten, the neighboring regency of Solo. In late September 2011, several Solo Kaskusers who live in Klaten submitted a proposal to the Kaskus management requesting a separate digital web page that would be independent from Kaskus Regional Solo. The request sparked a debate among Solo Kaskusers. Support was found among those who felt that such a separation could enhance the online dwelling experience of those who have an interest in the actualities in Klaten, together with their own online threads, meet-ups, Gatherings, and social activism. Those who opposed this movement largely viewed the proposal to be an act of separatism from the 'greater Solo area'. The independence proposal, according to Kaskusers like Rheanz, represented an 'uprising'. Some Solo Kaskusers feared that as their fellow users moved away from f=160, the home that they had sought to build online would begin to disintegrate.

Throughout the debate, three issues came to the fore. First, some Solo Kaskusers were skeptical that their fellows from Klaten would be able to create their own community and if they failed KRS would get a bad reputation. Second, some Solo Kaskusers worried that the offshoot would mark the disintegration of Jokowi's geopolitical program, despite the fact that Solo and Klaten were never really integrative under a bureaucratic administration to begin with. Third, some Solo Kaskusers felt that the proposed split had not adhered to the Javanese manner as the Klaten Kaskusers had gone behind the Solo Kaskusers' backs directly to Kaskus management.

Rather than revealing the creative project of online being, the risk of exploiting Javanese symbolism and power structures (see Anderson 2007) can lead Kaskusers to resurrect the remnants of the past. This example could be taken as an early sign of the Solo Kaskusers' traditional reaction to contestation (see Anderson 2007). When each perceptual experience needs to be justified with norms stemming from their cultural context, it could be suspected that Solo Kaskusers have met their openness to possibilities. This horizon of imagining social organization is nevertheless a contrasting reality to f=160 dwellers' hope that the Internet will bring with it a new hierarchy-free attitude.

To date, although KRS is still far from being ethnocentric, its relationship with the offline environment of 'Solo' through weak investigations pose a risk that the online community might form an expectation of pseudo-Solo. Without further efforts from the online community to study their understanding on the subject of 'Solo' and its history and culture—for example, with the case of the 'Klaten uprising' and the hybrid culture presented in the Gatherings described in Chap. 4—Solo Kaskusers could be pulled into the arbitrary revival of traditions or pseudo-traditions. Without a careful approach, this advocacy of tradition, the city, or Solonese could turn into revivalism that risks materializing as a cult.

This research found that Solo Kaskusers are currently on a problematic path to both. On one hand, they have reproduced Javanese norms according to their experience of wayfaring, while on the other hand—a distinct point of astuteness—they have failed to move on from their Solonese normative surroundings. This is ironic, considering that the spirit of Kaskus' freedom of speech as a legacy of Fight Club is actually about the skill of investigation and critical thinking. On the contrary, if we look at Solo Kaskusers notion of order (*keteraturan*), which relocates harsh debates to off-page communications, there is a new potential condition that it could become the antithesis of the online freedom that Kaskusers believe in and become simply a homogeneous space of discussion similar to the old constructed Javanese harmony.[8]

Here, there is a contradiction between Solo Kaskusers' ideal of the democratic digital world and the participation ethic on one side, and on the other side, the traditional Javanese understanding of social order above individual critics. The creation of home has toned down the openness of the network; protest and indifference are reserved for forums off the main page. The order of non-offensive language use, the excommunication of Johar, the disregard of Kaskusers' protest against the language rules, and how Solo Kaskusers handled the Klaten uprising underscore the determinism of the *kampong*'s collective decision against individual choice or against the expressions of the minorities.

In f=160, regulations are not only boundaries, they are also expectations and imaginations of how a Kaskuser participates in the chat. The online norms taken from Javanese norms might not be intended to become a duplicate, but if the practice is still within the offline original's imagination, Solo Kaskusers would hardly see new innovations in creating new norms.

### 6.4.2 *The Gadget of the 'Future'*

As this chapter explains, although the tools may have changed, the rationale behind its application has remained relatively the same. The gadget of the future, therefore, continues to fight the battles of the past. Despite the 'new' in 'new media technology,' older practices still hold a strong place in the Javanese space of Solo Kaskusers in both the language of the community as well as in its practices.

In Javanese literature, besides power, the use of a weapon, tool or a gadget (*aji*) is pivotal to win the course of change, or a battle in the Wayang stories. Besides spiritual power, sophisticated engineered tools like arrows, textiles, and spears are pivotal gadgets on the battlefield. That being said, the smartphone, the computer, the Internet and other digital gadgets are sometimes treated just like arrows and spears. As such, the human-gadget relation does not necessarily incite innovative application.

In chats, the association between new media technology and old practices is still present. For example, at the beginning of the Ilham solidarity act, when Surandy wrote to his fellow conversants to ignite the conversation by saying, 'light up (turn on) your Yahoo!Messenger first!' Then we could talk about how we are going to do this,' he used the term '*sumet*' (light up) instead of 'log in'. Lighting the fire up (*sumet*) in the context of Solonese colloquial communication not only refers to turning on the stove, but also fire the benzoin (*kemenyan*)—a main component in the traditional setting of Javanese rituals, especially during times when an individual wants to mediate and communicate with spirits to engage in telekinetic communication. Surandy treated the login process as if he was handling a traditional magical tool.[9]

Being a prominent member of KRS is to have a capable gadget as a tool; a tool that keeps him/her within digital reach; a tool that is connected to the Internet network; a tool that serves all possible online interactions; a tool that could capture visual documents, open links, emoticons, pictures, and any greater data. The challenge is whether the new media gadgets will become another form of 'supernatural gadget' to help reach a better future when they can only reconstruct the past.

Although the tool is pivotal for keeping the community's presence, Surandy's story at the beginning of this chapter is a fitting reminder to assess the intimacy between the gadget and the user. Surandy's story illustrates that the network of *kampong* was once wired through lines of intercom in the 1990s. Such networks are gone today, but the offline meet-up (*kopdar*) tradition remains. Scholars have documented how the Internet, computers, Internet shops, and mailing lists became the backbone for political materials during the dawn of *Reformasi* (Lim 2003a, b; Hill and Sen 2005; Bell 2006). Today, all of those are memories of the past and have not transformed into any new political medium. However, the tradition of public discussions and debates is still commonly found (Wayansari 2011; Nugroho 2011). These stories give some retrospective that the organic growth of the gadget-user relationship is hardly about the gadget, but is about how the users survived the technological change. Although the traffic to f=160 is slowing down in 2016, Solo Kaskusers have managed to keep the community chat lit up through other social media platforms and their offline meet-ups.

## Notes

1. As a legacy from the play of identity deception and junk posting, senior members usually have more than one ID, which are called 'clones' (*klonengan*). Clone Avatar IDs are intended to post junk and to supply green-badges to the prime ID, and this keeps the Kaskusers' primary ID and his/her online persona intact and clean. As Chap. 2 describes, most Kaskus members are aware of this trick. Having senior members comply with the new regulation means a decrease in junk posting and a collective agreement on sanctioning: those who do not comply with the new regulations are sanctioned with red-bricks by members. The last resort of bricking as an oppressive mechanism worked only when the potential oppressor or bully themselves and the senior members agreed to the terms of engagement.
2. The network graph is derived from the interview sessions I conducted with Solo Kaskusers. In between transcribing the ethnographic data, I had one particular offline formal interview session with each Solo Kaskuser. These one-to-one interviews, which were limited to two hours, acted as reconfirmation of the online/offline ethnographic observation and were valuable in uncovering Solo Kaskuser's particular or popular memories or information about a particular actor, event, challenge, etc. They were asked again to narrate their view on the 'importance' of KRS and its members. For example, during his session, Regional Leader Harya mentioned many Solo Kaskusers and referred to the various—if not all—activities that KRS had been associated with; during the Internet session, however, he only mentioned six names (see Fig. 6.1) and narrated the Gatherings and civic participation more frequently than any other past occurrences although the *Iftar* events and the Klaten detachment were two of the most popular subjects at that time.
3. http://old.kaskus.co.id/showthread.php?t=6938532; http://archive.kaskus.co.id/thread/6969505/0#
4. http://kask.us/4672713
5. Solo Kaskusers also used the English word 'real'. See Armin's post as an example.
6. T.J.M. Holden defines 'mediated identity' as 'significations, conveyed through representations of sameness and difference, by media, and brought into relief by references to socially constructed group based traits and the depiction of relationships between individuals or groups' (2006: 15–16).
7. For conspicuous consumption see: Thorstein Veblen. *The Theory of Leisure Class*. New York: Dover, 1994.
8. See Headley (2004) for the comparison of Javanese harmony and the notion of home in Java.
9. In Solo, a powerful and functional gadget (*aji*) would become a magical heirloom (*pusaka*) and therefore symbolism. This symbolic heirloom can be kept from the public and only used from time to time.

## References

Anderson, Benedict R.O'G. *Language and Power: Exploring Political Cultures in Indonesia.* Jakarta: Equinox Publishing, 2006.

Anderson, Benedict R.O'G. "The Idea of Power in Javanese Culture." In *Culture and Politics in Indonesia,* edited by Claire Holt, 1–70. Singapore: Equinox Publishing, 2007.

Appadurai, Arjun. *Modernity At Large: Cultural Dimensions of Globalization.* Minneapolis: University of Minnesota, 1996.

Bauman, Zygmunt. *Postmodernity and its Discontents.* Cambridge: Polity, 1997.

Bauman, Zygmunt. *Community: Seeking Safety in an Insecure World.* Cambridge: Polity, 2001.

Bell, David. *An Introduction to Cybercultures.* London: Routledge, 2001.

Bell, Genevieve. "Satu Keluarga, Satu Komputer [One Home, One Computer]: Cultural Accounts of ICTs in South and Southeast Asia." *Design Issues* Volume 22 Number (2006): 35–55.

Beniger, James R. "Personalization of Mass Media and the Growth of Pseudo-community." *Communication Research* Vol. 14 No.3 (1987): 352–371, accessed March 1, 2014. DOI: 10.1177/009365087014003005.

Boellstorff, Tom. *Coming of Age in Second Life.* New Jersey: Princeton University Press, 2008.

Castells, Manuel. *The Power of Identity: The Information Age: Economy, Society and Culture, Volume II of The Information Age.* 2nd Edition with new Preface. West Sussex: Willey-Blackwell, 2010.

Florida, Nancy. *Writing the Past, Inscribing the Future: History as Prophecy in Colonial Java.* Durham: Duke University Press, 1995.

Goffman, Erving. *The Presentation of Self in Everyday Life.* New York: Anchor, 1959.

Habermas, Jürgen. *Postmetaphysical Thinking.* Translated by William Mark Hohengarten. Massachusetts: MIT Press, 1992.

Headley, Stephen Cavanna. *Durga's Mosque: Cosmology, Conversion and Community in Central Javanese Islam.* Singapore: ISEAS, 2004.

Hill, David T. and Krishna Sen. *The Internet in Indonesia's New Democracy.* Oxon: Routledge, 2005.

Holden, Todd Joseph Miles. "Theorizing Media in Asia Today." In *Medi@sia: Global Media/tion In and Out of Context*, edited by Holden, Todd Joseph Miles and Timothy J. Scrase, 1–22. Oxon: Routledge, 2006.

Ingold, Tim. *The Perception of the Environment: Essays on Livelihood, Dwelling & Skill.* London: Routledge, 2000.

Ingold, Tim. *Being Alive Essays on Movement, Knowledge and Description*. Oxon: Routledge, 2011.

Ingold, Tim. "The Textility of Making". *Cambridge Journal of Economics* 2010/34 (1) (2010): 91–102. Accessed March 1, 2014. doi:10.1093/cje/bep042.

Jones, Steven G. *Cybersociety: Computer-Mediated Communication and Community*. Thousand Oaks: Sage, 1995.

Jones, Steven G. "The Internet and Its Social Landscape". In *Virtual Culture: Identity and Communication in Cybersociety*, edited by Steven G. Jones, 7–35. First publication in 1997. London: Sage, 2002.

Kobayashi, Tetsuro. "Bridging Social Capital in Online Communities: Heterogeneity and Social. Tolerance of Online Game Players in Japan." In *Human Communication Research* 36 (2010): 546–569.

Lim, Merlyna. "The Internet, Social Networks, and Reform in Indonesia." In *Contesting Media Power: Alternative Media in a Networked World*, edited by Nick Couldry and James Curran, 273–88. Maryland: Rowman & Littlefield, 2003a.

Lim, Merlyna. "From Real to Virtual (and Back again): Civil Society, Public Sphere, and Internet in Indonesia." In *Asia.com: Asia encounters the Internet*, edited by Kong-Chong Ho, Randy Kluver and Kenneth C. C. Yang, 113–128. London: Routledge, 2003b.

Magnis-Suseno, Franz. *Pijar-pijar filsafat: dari Gatholoco ke filsafat perempuan, dari Adam Müller ke Postmodernisme*. Yogyakarta: Penerbit Kanisius, 2005.

Mead, Herbert. *The Philosophy of the Act*. Chicago: University of Chicago Press, 1938.

Miller, Daniel, and Don Slater. *The Internet: an Ethnographic Approach*. Reprinted edition. Oxford: Berg, 2001.

Nugroho, Yanuar. *Citizens in @ction*. Manchester: Manchester Institute of Innovation Research, 2011.

Pearce, Celia, and Artemesia. *Communities of Play. Emergent Cultures in Multiplayer Games and Virtual Worlds*. Massachusetts: MIT Press, 2009.

Rheingold, Howard. *Virtual Community*. Revised edition. Massachusetts: MIT Press, 2000.

Van Dijk, Jan A.G.M. *The Network Society: Social Aspects of New Media*. First publication in English in 1999. Second edition. London: SAGE Publications, 2006.

Van Loon, Joost. *Media Technology Critical Perspective*. Berkshire: Open University Press McGraw-Hill Education, 2008.

Veblen, Thorstein. *The Theory of Leisure Class*. New York: Dover, 1994.

Wayansari, Agustina. "The Internet and the Public Sphere in Indonesia's New Democracy: a Study of Politikana.com." In *Internetworking Indonesia Journal* Vol. 3/No. 2 (2011): 23–33. Jakarta, 2011.

CHAPTER 7

# Conclusion: We Need More Red Bricks

In December 2016, in response to the election of Donald Trump as President of the United States, Michael Moore called for greater civic participation to enlarge progressive democracy in the face of what he considered to be complacency among, in particular, progressive citizens. 'Let's get to work!' he wrote on his Facebook wall. He proposed five actions, two of which specifically focused on making the presence of the liberals more established and ensuring that civil society members equip themselves with their own 'rapid response team'.[1] In his remedy for how to cope with growing populism, Moore is calling for—while not using the term—what this book describes as civil militancy: engagement and activism that not only goes online but also organizes itself in the offline world, while being responsive. Halfway across the world, Solo Kaskusers' experience exemplifies Moore's hope of becoming militant netizens as a requirement for being members of a democratic society, along with discipline and self-restrained ethic.

The experience of Kaskusers shows that the rise of an underground community in an ethical civic organization is based on a habitual organic online community practice of being a 'militant', guided by prudence (*sembada*) incited by guilt, and a growing sense of responsibility triggered by their self-questioning identity. These reasons are not simply morally toned; instead they reflect the sequence of struggle that resulted from a justified strategic act to make online chatting meaningful. Today, such ethic has become procedural as the result of reflective discussions of what it means to be a



A. Seto, *Netizenship, Activism and Online Community Transformation in Indonesia*, DOI 10.1007/978-981-10-5397-9_7

Kaskuser, particularly on an annual basis in advance of each year's Gathering. The Solo Kaskusers' experience is interesting because of its civil militancy, which has taken the form of a non-political association and relaying KRS' own bottom-up efforts, vocabularies and knowledge production to reveal the meaning of becoming a netizen and eventually a citizen.

Since f=160 itself was created to gather stories and chats about the city, an outsider could view that the online-offline reconnection between Solo Kaskusers in f=160 with the offline world seems expected. Not to mention that the traditional Javanese notion of reaching out to the exterior—the community, the city, the nation, the spirits, the universe, or God—is still very much alive in the everyday life narratives of Solonese citizens. Investigating the Solo Kaskusers' struggle in online dwelling, however, emphasizes that this online-offline civic participation transformation is neither linear, straightforward, nor predetermined.

In the time of social media, this book investigates the role of netizen in civic participation while trying to understand how it came to be involved in civil society at large in the first place and the course of its becoming. Such investigations are currently crucial as recent studies have flagged the risk that because of its popular engagement possibilities, online movements could become superficial click-activism (Lim 2013; Lewis et al. 2014) and call for civil society's capacity-building in online communication (Nugroho and Syarief 2012). In particular, studies observing the relation between digital technology and civic participation in Indonesia have been characterized by what Nugroho (2011) expresses as 'in action'. These approaches, however, focus rather heavily on the evaluation of success and a particular event while assessing digital technology simply as an instrument. By contrast, Solo Kaskusers' experiences show that digital participation should be understood as embedded practices that are both processual and procedural becoming, while making 'actions', 'participation', 'movements', 'cases', or 'events' an unsettling series according to how they perceive their environment(s).

Such wayfaring could, at the same time, however, materialize because it was a series of disciplining regimes. Deviant Kaskusers were digitally bricked and buried. Digital media technology, for Solo Kaskusers, is not only a tool but also a mediated forum through which they shape their perception of the online and offline worlds through practices within everyday life activity as a locus for civic participation.

There are five conditions that made it possible for Solo Kaskusers to endure the struggle to establish their art of netizenship, each of which is procedural. First, it is the online practice in Kaskus that disciplined Solo

Kaskusers into becoming reliable community members through participatory chats. Here they learned how to dwell: be communicatively engaged, feed the chat flow, ensure databanking, build a reputation, and fight trolls and hoaxes by building the green-badge reputation system. This basic habitual practice is crucial for differentiating the behaviors of online forum netizens with those using other social media platforms.

Google's first class pre-assessment in its Digital Literacy and Citizenship Curriculum proposes eleven basic questions to identify quality information.[2] The last question is to weigh the author or the source of information. Kaskusers' method, as Chaps. 2 and 3 explain, tackles this question immediately: those unknown to the forum will not be considered as a true source of information and will be neglected. Such a mechanism minimizes the circulation of hoaxes and bad information. Kaskus and its collective validation is a curated information arena of circulation because those giving false information will be bullied, bricked, and the thread deleted by the administrator. To dwell in Kaskus with all the discipline and consequences is itself a practice of citizenship.

Rather than becoming an independent rupture, Solo Kaskusers' sequence of experiences exemplifies that civic participation, or 'social activism' to use their term, could find a nest and continually evolve in their mundane everyday chats. Starting simply with a leisurely chat, this rise of an underground community to take the role of netizen exemplifies that digital media consumption is not nullified by the urge for consumption. In an organic online community like Kaskus, consumption is the precursor of guilt, which leads us to the second condition of digital citizenship: guilt and prudence as a counterbalance to detachment from the offline. This is an everyday assessment of the fairness of becoming an online dweller. This emotional layer of having a leisurely chat in Kaskus triggered Solo Kaskusers' questioning of their role in society. Without the feeling of detachment, Solo Kaskusers would not have begun to continually interrogate what it means to have online power.

The 'reconnections', to use Solo Kaskusers' view, only took place after Solo Kaskusers endured sequences of experiences while reflexively correcting the agreement about the importance of being online dwellers. The organic progression of digital citizenship is thus not necessarily a civic urge, since the origin of community connection comes from previous perceptions of how Kaskusers saw themselves in the world. In KRS' case, the longing for connection appeared after the categorization and location of f=160 as a space detached from society. Here, reconnection is a consequence of the perception of detachment; feeling detached from the offline Solo society has created an urge to become citizen.

This is different from the first generation of digital activism in Indonesia because these bottom-up netizens are not the 'elites'. While digital technology was introduced in Indonesia in the 1980s as part of the government's technological advancement and education programs, its proliferation excelled a decade later with a boom in Internet cafés and mobile telephony that coincided with the fall of Suharto's 30-year authoritarian regime. This momentous background shines a spotlight on how students, activist, and political figures engaged in democratization, citizenship, and nation-building (Hill and Sen 2005; Lim 2003a, b; Nugroho 2007, 2011).

A decade later, digital tools and media were technologically developed to become more personal, with the online sphere offering further possibilities for individuals to come together and form bonds as communities (Dyah and Theresa 2010). This second phase of the proliferation of digital gadgets and connectivity in Indonesia extended the use of the technology, embedding it in nearly every possible everyday life activity. Thus, the Solo Kaskus case compels us not to make the generalization when we see mass protests on the streets or online-based social activism that these actors are necessarily activists. Kaskusers themselves even proclaimed that they are the 'commoners'.

Third, Solo Kaskusers have been fortunate that they were able to identify sufficient immediate cultural resources and a practice to justify their new citizenship activities. Furthermore, they became citizens because of their pre-existing community practices: *bakti sosial* (see Chap. 4). This voluntarism is a ritual of alignment. It signals a period where community members raise the sentiment to help others outside their community, feeling good about themselves, meaning that being in a community is not just about fun but about caring for others, reaching out to the exterior, testing solidarity and teamwork, and that the community has moral and altruistic social meanings. This, however, relies on the presence of some influential members of the community.

Fourth, Solo Kaskusers could endure the change in their activities and community because they could see that what they were doing was working. It means that any bottom-up digital citizenship should give hope and emotional joy to the actors as their efforts are fruitful. The enlargement of the online community in offline space itself could only be materialized after seeing the successful effort of creating a digital home as part of the precursor experience.

Such valuation is, however, risky because any digital activism is prone to a condition where the project is abandoned by the common masses if it fails. It also makes digital activism prone to becoming popular activism. Successful offline activity, therefore, needs to be organized to affirm their perception of impacting the community; social activism is conducted to materialize and give tangible visual evidence that the online community could create an impact, in this case, being present within the offline world as Kaskusers exemplify. Eventually, activism and participation are organized for functional reasons, and rely on short-term engagement in order to make it simpler to achieve success.

Fifth, Solo Kaskusers' notion of operational digital citizenship is influenced by a responsive state apparatus: The responsive city hall official and public transportation officer in supporting the 2010 Gathering (Chap. 3); the helpful National Department of Health during the Ilham campaign (Chap. 4); Jokowi's speedy feedback (Chap. 5); and the willing-come-to-the house district bureaucrat who explained the process of applying for a birth certificate (Chap. 5), are all examples of how Solo Kaskusers' citizenship projects were smooth because it did not meet the state's brick wall. A supportive state apparatus has therefore saved Solo Kaskusers from frustration with bureaucracy. It is difficult to imagine that such citizen's initiatives would continue if they were to face larger difficulties. To recall the fourth condition, failing to succeed with the project could lead to disappointment and disillusionment, which creates the risk of community abandonment.

These five conditions of organic community-based digital citizenship are methodologically influential. As online communities change over time, whether that be because of the presence of the new social media application or because of the dissolving community, any conclusions drawn from a single particular event would only lead to a fallacy. Investigations of online-based civic participation, therefore, should not only be conducted through an event or numbers of supporters, but most importantly to view the ethic that is established throughout the series of activity that changes the netizens' practices. Solo Kaskusers' ethical and procedural practice of wayfaring is clear: militancy and prudence.

Recent big data analysis to assess civic participation is, therefore, misleading, because it focuses more on quantitative coverage, results and not the enduring militancy. Investigation of digital citizenship should go beyond the screen by looking at the development of digital citizenship by the related actors. As much as the ethos of 'freedom of speech' and the green-badge merit system, threads and chats are still public arenas which do not represent the whole dynamic of the community. The details of social relationships among Solo Kaskusers, interpersonal intimacy, the lobbies, and the creation of networks, the production of norms behind the screen, that is, community organization, will only be transparent if off-page communications, both offline and through other online platforms, are included. It is therefore important to consider online posts alongside the information circulation among key actors and their circle of friends. Big data analysis does help a lot in understanding the width of circulation, but still fails in describing the back-stage offline communication.

Moreover, although researchers could go on to observe the meticulous details of digital citizenship in the making, it is yet unclear how to measure the impacts since an organic community has its own criteria for success. The measurement of achievement is always internal; whether their participation could actually have an impact on policies, bureaucratic change, and, above all, progressive democracy leaves much to be discovered. What Solo Kaskusers are doing right now is mainstreaming partnerships, both horizontal and vertical. However, since they do not have a certain agenda, it is still difficult to measure whether these partnerships could eventually change the state and society at large. For the struggles that the online organic community has endured throughout the troubled times, it is actually fair that a measurement of impact should be drawn.

Then, if an achievement is measurable, there is the problem with the matter of comparing these sequences of activism as each takes different forms. Can everyday police monitoring be compared with, for example, the Gatherings and imply that both are parts of the same phenomenon of Kaskusers' netizenship? Solo Kaskusers view that each revelation to the notion of citizenship itself is a matter of self-development, hence the use of terms such as 'process' and 'coming of age'. In the course of wayfaring, innovativeness, such as the notion of prudence evoked as a required resolution to the matter of guilt, is spontaneous and some sort of an order of contingency. These bottom-up activities are problematic because it makes it difficult to secure the endurance of community membership and to measure the success of the project. For Solo Kaskusers, the challenge will always be how to institutionalize and formalize guilt in order to preserve the activism.

The method of institutionalization also relies on the available technology. The collective pressure to uphold prudence in the everyday life of Solo Kaskusers takes place through horizontal monitoring, such as with the case against Johar's performance. Such monitoring was impossible during Kaskus' infancy in the early 2000s as Internet mobile communication was not yet popular. Today the monitoring and chats are located not only in f=160, but are more pronounced through their Twitter handles and WhatsApp groups.

Another problematic feature of organic community-based citizenship is with regard to the distinction made by Solo Kaskusers between 'activist' and the 'commons'. It sounds humble, but indecisive. On one hand, they want to separate themselves from the goal-oriented activist, which they perceive to be an unnatural citizen driven only by a certain political interest. On the other hand, Kaskusers' non-agenda setting for the future provides no basis for evaluation and no means for the measurement of trajectory.

In the context of measuring impact, the form and organic community's mode of dwelling is weak because the political system under a state still requires the traditional channel of citizenship, where structural change can only be pursued through politics and the machineries of democracy, such as political parties or civic associations. It could be more straightforward from an organizational perspective if such an online community transformed itself into a civic association. By doing so, KRS would have a certain agenda to pursue and project its movement.

Having a certain agenda of movement would, however, change the community into a project-based group instead of embracing the maturity of the wayfaring experience. It could also, nonetheless, help Solo Kaskusers in planning community activities in the long term, thus disciplining the community. Without the projection of becoming, Solo Kaskusers' activities seem random and arbitrary. They hinder the further care of innovation because what they are doing currently is patching the state's weaknesses: The Gatherings patch the state's weakness in promoting the city; the Ilham campaign was a patch on the state's monitoring of the equity of public health; the reconstruction of the school is a patch on the state's budgeting for education; the police misconduct reporting thread patches the state's control of its apparatus, to name just a few examples provided in this book.

Transforming the community into such an association could open the possibility to include knowledgeable actors. Here, referential knowledge is important and knowledgeable actors could help Solo Kaskusers to further establish their goals and resources. As much as the possibility of wayfaring and its notion of self-correction can shape life skills, learning in unsettling methods poses the risk of becoming unproductive when it takes place in this manner.

If no one controls the veracity of information, the risk is that an organic community is wayfaring on falsehoods. Without the participation of credible actors, communication in an organic community could face being drawn away from accurate information, especially when f=160 dwellers never position themselves as the authority of knowledge. Although Kaskus assigns the honorary attribute of 'elderly' to those in the know, presenting a digital elite in the realm might be problematic since there is no formal designated authority on particular information.

Lastly, reflecting on their ups and downs, Kaskusers expressed that the greatest challenge of wayfaring and becoming is time compression. Digital infrastructure may technically ease limitations in terms of communication and the compressed sequence of emotional experiences, but not the procedure of becoming. Kaskusers have learned instead that in processional 'coming-of-age' (*pendewasaan*), power-play is more strategic and effective to form a community, to stabilize the regime of normative terms, and to organize digital activism. In sum, if we are to arbitrarily take Kaskusers' reflective appraisal on their one and a half decade of digital experience in dwelling and wayfaring, it seems that today's popular digital protests have betrayed the intersubjective struggle of becoming a netizen, for the sake of an instantaneous project.

## Notes

1. https://www.facebook.com/mmflint/posts/10154046637756857
2. http://archive.ikeepsafe.org/educators_old/more/google/

## References

Hill, David T. and Krishna Sen. *The Internet in Indonesia's New Democracy*. Oxon: Routledge, 2005.

Lewis, Kevin, Kurt Gray, and Jens Meierhenrich. "The Structure of Online Activism". *Sociological Science* Vol.1 (February 2014): 1–9. Accessed March 1, 2014. DOI 10.15195/v1.a1.

Lim, Merlyna. "From Real to Virtual (and Back again): Civil Society, Public Sphere, and Internet in Indonesia." In *Asia.com: Asia encounters the Internet*, edited by Kong-Chong Ho, Randy Kluver and Kenneth C. C. Yang, 113–128. London: Routledge, 2003b.

Lim, Merlyna. "Many Clicks but Little Sticks: Social Media Activism in Indonesia." *Journal of Contemporary Asia* Volume 43 Issue 4 (2013): 636–657.

Lim, Merlyna. "The Internet, Social Networks, and Reform in Indonesia." In *Contesting Media Power: Alternative Media in a Networked World*, edited by Nick Couldry and James Curran, 273–88. Maryland: Rowman & Littlefield, 2003a.

Nugroho, Yanuar, and Sofie Shinta Syarief. *Beyond Click-Activism? New Media and Political Processes in Contemporary Indonesia*. Berlin: FES-MediaAsia, 2012.

Nugroho, Yanuar. *Citizens in @ction.* Manchester: Manchester Institute of Innovation Research, 2011.

Nugroho, Yanuar. *Does the Internet Transform Civil Society? The Case pf Civil Society Organizations in Indonesia.* Dissertation. Manchester: The University of Manchester, 2007.

## News and Internet Sources

"Digital Literacy and Citizenship Curriculum proposes eleven basic questions to identify quality information." Accessed January 29, 2017. http://archive.ikeepsafe.org/educators_old/more/google/

Dyah, Indira Prana Ning, and Naomi Theresa. "Warnet Kian Tergerus Internet Ponsel." *Kompas.com.* Accessed on Friday, August 13, 2010. http://tekno.kompas.com/read/2010/08/13/12342240/Warnet.Kian.Tergerus.Internet.Ponsel

Moore, Michael. "5 Things You Can Do Right Now About Donald J. Trump - from Michael Moore." Accessed January 29th, 2016. https://www.facebook.com/mmflint/posts/10154046637756857

# Bibliography

Abdullah, Taufik. *Indonesia: Towards Democracy*. Singapore: Institute of Southeast Asian Studies, 2009.

Afrizal, R., and Prakoso I. "Berbagi Kisah dari Seantero Negeri: Upaya-upaya Penanggulangan Bencana oleh Radio Komunitas." In *Mengudara Menjawab Tantangan*, edited by A. Nasir, P. Wijoyono and A. Tanesia, 19–47. Yogyakarta: Combine Resource Institute, 2009.

Alampay, Erwin. *Living the Information Society in Asia*. Singapore: ISEAS, 2009.

Anderson, Benedict R.O'G. *Imagined Communities: Reflections on the Origin and Spread of Nationalism*. First published in 1983. Revised edition. London: Verso, 1991.

Anderson, Benedict R.O'G. *Mythology and the Tolerance of the Javanese*. Ithaca: Cornell University, 1996.

Anderson, Benedict R.O'G. *Language and Power: Exploring Political Cultures in Indonesia*. Jakarta: Equinox Publishing, 2006a.

Anderson, Benedict R.O'G. *Java in a Time of Revolution: Occupation and Resistance, 1944–1946*. Jakarta: Equinox Publishing, 2006b.

Anderson, Benedict R.O'G. "The Idea of Power in Javanese Culture." In *Culture and Politics in Indonesia*, edited by Claire Holt, 1–70. Singapore: Equinox Publishing, 2007.

Antlöv, Hans. "The Social Construction of Power and Authority in Java." In *The Java That Never Was: Academic Theories and Political Practices*, edited by Hans Antlöv and Jörgen Hellman, 43–66. Münster: Lit Verlag, 2005.

Appadurai, Arjun. *Modernity At Large: Cultural Dimensions of Globalization*. Minneapolis: University of Minnesota, 1996.



A. Seto, *Netizenship, Activism and Online Community Transformation in Indonesia*, DOI 10.1007/978-981-10-5397-9

Balsamo, Anne Marie. *Technologies of the Gendered Body: Reading Cyborg Women*. Durham: Duke University Press, 1996.

Balzac, Honoré de. *My Journey from Paris to Java*. Translated by Barry Winkleman. Paris: Editions Didier Millet, 2010.

Barendregt, Bart. "Sex, Cannibals, and the Language of Cool: Indonesian Tales of the Phone and Modernity". *The Information Society: An International Journal* Volume 24 Issue 3 (May 2008): 160–170.

Barendregt, Bart. "The Ghost in the Phone and Other Tales of Indonesian Modernity." In *Mobile Communication and Asian Modernities*, edited by S. Barnes and S. Huff, 47–70. Hong Kong: Hong Kong University, 2005.

Basso, Ellen B. and Gunter Senft. "Introduction." In *Ritual Communication*, edited by Gunter Senft and Ellen B. Basso, 1–20. Oxford: Berg, 2009.

Bauckhage, Christian and Kristian Kersting. "Strong Regularities in Growth and Decline of Popularity of Social Media Services." *arXiv.org* (2014): 1–11. Retrieved from Cornell University Library, eprint arXiv:1406.6529. Accessed July 30, 2014.

Baudrillard, Jean. *Simulacra and Simulation*. Translated by Sheila Faria Glaser. Ann Arbor: Michigan University Press, 1994.

Bauman, Zygmunt. *Postmodernity and its Discontents*. Cambridge: Polity, 1997.

Bauman, Zygmunt. *Work, Consumerism and the New Poor*. 1st Edition. Buckingham: Open University Press, 1998.

Bauman, Zygmunt. *Community: Seeking Safety in an Insecure World*. Cambridge: Polity, 2001.

Bell, David. *An Introduction to Cybercultures*. London: Routledge, 2001.

Bell, Genevieve. "Satu Keluarga, Satu Komputer [One Home, One Computer]: Cultural Accounts of ICTs in South and Southeast Asia." *Design Issues* Volume 22 Number 2 (2006): 35–55.

Bemmelen, Sita van, and Mies Grijns. "What has Become of the Slendang? Changing Images of Women and Java." In *The Java That Never Was*, edited by Hans Antlöv and Jörgen Hellman. Münster, 97–132. Lit Verlag, 2005.

Benamou, Marc. *Rasa: Affect and Intuition in Javanese Musical Aesthetics: Affect and Intuition in Javanese Musical Aesthetics*. Oxford: Oxford University Press, 2010.

Beniger, James R. "Personalization of Mass Media and the Growth of Pseudo-community." *Communication Research* Vol. 14 No.3 (1987): 352–371, accessed March 1, 2014. DOI: 10.1177/009365087014003005.

Ben-Porat, Amir. "Split Loyalty: Football-cum-Nationality in Israel". In *Fringe Nations in Soccer*, edited by Kausik Bandyopadhyay and Sabyasachi Mallick, 106–121. Oxon: Routledge, 2013.

Birowo, Mario Antonius. "Community Radio and the Empowerment of Local Culture." In *Politics and the Media in Twenty-First Century Indonesia: Decade of Democracy*, edited by Krishna Sen and David Hill, 49–66. Oxon: Routledge, 2011.

Boellstorff, Tom. *Coming of Age in Second Life*. New Jersey: Princeton University Press, 2008.

Bowen, John R. *Islam, Law, and Equality in Indonesia: An Anthropology of Public Reasoning*. Cambridge: Cambridge University Press, 2003.

Brandt, Agnes. *Among Friends?On the Dynamics of Māori-Pākehā Relationships in Aotearoa New Zealand*. Göttingen: V&R Unipress, 2013.

Bräuchler, Birgit. "Cyberidentities at War: Religion, Identity, and the Internet in the Moluccan Conflict." *Indonesia* 75 (April 2003): 123–51.

Bruhn, John G. *The Sociology of Community Connections*. Second Edition. Dordrecht: Springer, 2011.

Bunt, Gary R. *Islam in the Digital Age: E-Jihad, Online Fatwas and Cyber Islamic Environments*. London: Pluto Press, 2003.

Bünte, Marco, Andreas Ufen. "The new order and its legacy: reflections on democratization in Indonesia" in *Democratization in Post-Soeharto Indonesia*, edited by Marco Bünte and Andreas Ufen, 3–29. New York: Routledge, 2009.

Burawoy, Michael. "The Fate of Post-Revolutionary Egypt: An Interview with Mona Abaza." *Global Dialogue*, International Sociology Association Volume 7, Issue 1 (March 2017): 4–8.

Burbules, Nicholas C. and Thomas A. Callister. *Watch It: The Risks and Promises of Information Technologies for Education*. Colorado: Westview Press, 2000.

Cammaerts, Bart, Alice Mattoni, Patrick McCurdy. *Mediation and Protest Movements*. Bristol: Intellect Books, 2013.

Castells, Manuel, Mireia Fernández-Ardèvol, Jack Linchuan Qiu, and Araba Sey. *Mobile Communication and Society: A Global Perspective*. Massachusetts: MIT Press, 2009.

Castells, Manuel. *The Rise of the Network Society*. West Sussex: Wiley-Blackwell, 2000.

Castells, Manuel. *The Power of Identity: The Information Age: Economy, Society and Culture, Volume II of The Information Age*. 2nd Edition with new Preface. West Sussex: Willey-Blackwell, 2010.

Castells, Manuel. *Networks of Outrage and Hope: Social Movements in the Internet Age*. Cambridge: Polity Press, 2012.

Chin, James. "Malaysiakini.com and Its Impact on Journalism and Politics in Malaysia." In *Asia.com. Asia Encounters the Internet*, edited by K.C. Ho, Randolph Kluver and Kenneth C.C. Yang, 129–142. London: Routledge Curzon, 2003.

Cogburn, Derrick L. and Fatima K. Espinoza-Vasquez. "From Networked Nominee to Networked Nation: Examining the Impact of Web 2.0 and Social Media on Political Participation and Civic Engagement in the 2008 Obama Campaign," *Journal of Political Marketing* 10 (1–2) (2011): 189–213. Doi: 10.1080/15377857.2011.540224.

Crouch, Harold A. *Political Reform in Indonesia After Soeharto*. Singapore: Institute of Southeast Asian Studies, 2010.

Danet, Brenda. *Cyberpl@y: Communicating Online*. Oxford: Berg, 2001.

Davidson, Jamie and David Henley. "Introduction: Radical Conservatism – The Protean Politics of Adat". In *The Revival of Tradition in Indonesian Politics: The Deployment of Adat from Colonialism to Indigenism*, edited by Jamie Davidson and David Henley, 1–49. Oxon: Routledge, 2007.

De Graaf, Hermanus Johannes. *Runtuhnya Istana Mataram*. Jakarta: Pustaka Utama Grafiti, 1987.

De Grave, Jean-Marc. "L'initiation Rituelle Javanaise et ses. Modes de Transmission: Opposition Entre Javanisme et Islam." *Techniques & Culture* Volume 1 No.48–49 (2007): 85–124. Accessed March 1, 2014. DOI: 10.4000/tc.3032.

De Grave, Jean-Marc. "The Training of Perception in Javanese Martial Arts." In *Martial Arts As Embodied Knowledge*, edited by D. S. Farrer, 123–144. New York: SUNY Press, 2011.

Donath, Judith S. "Identity and Deception in the Virtual Community." In *Communities in Cyberspace*, edited by Marc A. Smith and Peter Kollock, 27–58. London: Routledge, 1999.

Du Bois, John W. "Interior Dialogues: The Co-Voicing of Ritual in Solitude." In *Ritual Communication*, edited by Gunter Senft and Ellen B. Basso, 317–340. Oxford: Berg, 2009.

Dundes, Alan. *Life is Like a Chicken Coop Ladder: A Study of German National Character through Folklore*. Detroit: Wayne State University Press, 1989.

Eklof, Stefan. *Power and Political Culture in Suharto's Indonesia: The Indonesian Democratic Party (PDI) and Decline of the New Order (1986–98)*. Copenhagen: NIAS Press, 2004

El-Nawawy, Mohammed, and Sahar Khamis. *Egyptian Revolution 2.0: Political Blogging, Civic Engagement, and Citizen Journalism*. New York: Palgrave Macmillan, 2013.

Emmerson, Donald K. *Indonesia Beyond Suharto: Polity, Economy, Society, Transition*. New York: Asia Society and M.E Sharpe, 1999.

Endraswara, Suwardi. *Filsafat Kejawen Dalam Aksara Jawa*. Jakarta/Yogyakarta: Gelombang Pasang, 2006

Evers, Hans-Dieter and Rüdiger Korff. *Southeast Asian Urbanism: The Meaning and Power of Social Space*. 2.Auflage. Münster: LIT Verlag, 2003.

Fearnley-Sander, Mary, and Ella Yulaelawati. "Citizenship Discourse in the Context of Decentralization: The Case of Indonesia". In *Citizenship Curriculum in Asia and the Pacific*, edited by David L. Grossman, Wing On Lee, and Kerry J. Kennedy, 111–126. Hong Kong: Comparative Education Research Center and Springer Media, 2008.

Florida, Nancy. "Writing Traditions in Colonial Java: The Question of Islam." In *Cultures of Scholarship*, edited by Sarah C. Humphreys, 187–217. Ann Arbor: University of Michigan Press, 1997.

Florida, Nancy. *Writing the Past, Inscribing the Future: History as Prophecy in Colonial Java*. Durham: Duke University Press, 1995.

Foulcher, Keith. "The Construction of an Indonesian National Culture: Patterns of Hegemony and Resistance." In *State and Civil Society in Indonesia*, edited by Arif Budiman, 301–320. Clayton: Centre of Southeast Asian Studies, Monash University, 1990.

Fuchs, Christian. *Internet and Society: Social Theory in the Information Age*. New York: Routledge, 2008.

Geertz, Clifford. "Religious Belief and Economic Behavior in A Central Javanese Town: Some Preliminary Remarks," *Economic Development and Cultural Change* Vol. 4 No. 2 (1956), 134–158.

Geertz, Clifford. *The Religion of Java*. Chicago: University of Chicago Press, 1976.

Geertz, Hildred. *The Javanese Family: A study of kinship and socialization*. Michigan: University of Michigan Press, 1961.

Gerbaudo, Paolo. *Tweets and the Streets: Social Media and Contemporary Activism*. London: Pluto Press, 2012.

Ginsburg, Faye. "Culture/Media: A (Mild) Polemic". *Anthropology Today* 10(2) (1994): 5–15.

Ginsburg, Faye. "Rethinking the Digital Age". In *The Media and Social Theory*, edited by David Hesmondhalgh and Joan Toynbee, 127–144. New York: Routledge, 2008.

Goffman, Erving. *The Presentation of Self in Everyday Life*. New York: Anchor, 1959.

Guinness, Patrick. *Kampung, Islam and State in Urban Java*. Singapore: NUS Press, 2009.

Gurak, Laura. "The Promise and Peril of Social Action in Cyberspace." In *Communities in* Cyberspace, edited by Marc A. Smith and Peter Kollock, 241–262. London: Routledge, 1999.

Habermas, Jürgen. *On the Pragmatics of Communication*. Cambridge: MIT Press, 1998.

Habermas, Jürgen. *Postmetaphysical Thinking*. Translated by William Mark Hohengarten. Massachusetts: MIT Press, 1992.

Habermas, Jürgen. *The Structural Transformation of the Public Sphere*. Translated by Thomas Burger. First publication in 1989. Massachusetts: MIT Press, 1991.

Hashemi, Nader. "Religious Disputation and Democratic Constitutionalism: The Enduring Legacy of the Constitutional Revolution on the Struggle for Democracy in Iran." *Constellation* Volume 17 Issue 1 (March 2010): 50–60.

Headley, Stephen Cavanna. *Durga's Mosque: Cosmology, Conversion and Community in Central Javanese Islam*. Singapore: ISEAS, 2004.

Hefner, Robert W. "Introduction: Modernity and the Remaking of Muslim Politics." In *Remaking Muslim Politics: Pluralism, Contestation, & Democratization*, edited by Robert W. Hefner, 1–36. New Jersey: Princeton University Press, 2005.

Hill, David T. and Krishna Sen. *The Internet in Indonesia's New Democracy*. Oxon: Routledge, 2005.

Holden, Todd Joseph Miles. "Theorizing Media in Asia Today." In *Medi@sia: Global Media/tion In and Out of Context*, edited by Holden, Todd Joseph Miles and Timothy J. Scrase, 1–22. Oxon: Routledge, 2006.

Honneth, Axel. *The Struggle for Recognition: The Moral Grammar of Social Conflicts*. Translated by Joel Anderson. Cambridge: MIT Press, 1995.

Howard, Philip N. and Muzammil M. Hussain. *Democracy's Fourth Wave? Digital Media and the Arab Spring*. Oxford: Oxford University Press, 2013

Hughes-Freeland, Felicia. *Embodied Communities: Dance Traditions and Change in Java*. New York: Berghahn Books, 2008.

Humboldt, Wilhelm Freiherr von. *Über die Kawi-Sprache auf der Insel Java: nebst einer Einleitung über die Verschiedenheit des menschlichen Sprachbaues und ihren Einfluss auf die geistige Entwickelung des Menschengeschlechts, Volume 1*. Amsterdam: Druckerei der Königlichen Akademie der Wissenschaften, 1836.

Ingold, Tim and Jo Lee Vergunst. *Ways of Walking*. Surrey: Ashgate, 2008.

Ingold, Tim. *Being Alive Essays on Movement, Knowledge and Description*. Oxon: Routledge, 2011.

Ingold, Tim. *The Perception of the Environment: Essays on Livelihood, Dwelling & Skill*. London: Routledge, 2000.

Ingold, Tim. "Epilogue: Towards a Politics of Dwelling." *Conservation Society* Volume 3 No. 2 (2005): 501–508.

Ingold, Tim. "The Textility of Making." *Cambridge Journal of Economics* 2010/34 (1) (2010): 91–102. Accessed March 1, 2014. doi: 10.1093/cje/bep042.

Ingold, Tim. *Lines: A Brief History*. Oxon: Routledge, 2007.

Irvine, Judith T. "Formality and Informality in Communicative Events." *American Anthropologist* 81 (4) (1979): 773–790. Accessed March 1, 2014. DOI: 10.1525/aa.1979.81.4.02a00020.

Irvine, Judith T. "Ideologies of Honorific Language." *Pragmatics Volume* 2:(3) International Pragmatics Association, (1992): 251 –262.

Iskander, Elizabeth. "Connecting the National And The Virtual: Can Facebook Activism Remain Relevant After Egypt's January 25 Uprising?" *International Journal of Communication* 5 (2011): 13–15.

Jones, Steven G. "The Internet and Its Social Landscape". In *Virtual Culture: Identity and Communication in Cybersociety*, edited by Steven G. Jones, 7–35. First publication in 1997. London: Sage, 2002.

Jones, Steven G. *Cybersociety: Computer-Mediated Communication and Community*. Thousand Oaks: Sage, 1995.

Jurriëns, Edwin. "The Cosmopolitanism of Indonesian Radio Active and Public Sphere". In *Cosmopatriots: On Distant Belongings and Close Encounters*, edited by Edwin Jurrlëns, Jeroen De Kloet, 105–132. Amsterdam: Rodopi, 2007.

Jurriëns, Edwin. "'Radio Active': The creation of media literate audiences in post-Suharto Indonesia". In *Politics and the Media in Twenty-First Century Indonesia: Decade of Democracy*, edited by Krishna Sen and David Hill, 141–158. Oxon: Routledge, 2011.

Kam, Garrett. "Wayang Wong in the Court of Yogyakarta: The Enduring Significance of Javanese Dance Drama," *Asian Theatre Journal* Vol. 4 No. 1 (Spring, 1987), 29–51. DOI: 10.2307/1124435.

Katz, Elihu, and Daniel Dayan. *Media Events.* First publication in 1992. Second edition. Cambridge: Harvard University Press, 1994.

Katz, James E. "Mainstreamed Mobiles in Daily Life: Perspectives and Prospects." *Handbook of Mobile Communication Studies*, edited by James E. Katz, 433–446. Massachusetts: Massachusetts Institute of Technology Press, 2008.

Kobayashi, Tetsuro. "Bridging Social Capital in Online Communities: Heterogeneity and Social. Tolerance of Online Game Players in Japan." In *Human Communication Research* 36 (2010): 546–569.

Laksono, Paschalis Maria. *Tradition in Javanese Social Structure: Kingdom and Countryside: Changes in the Javanese Conceptual Model.* London: Coronet Books, 1986.

Levmore, Saul, and Martha C. Nussbaum. *The Offensive Internet.* Cambridge: Harvard University Press, 2010.

Lewis, Kevin, Kurt Gray, and Jens Meierhenrich. "The Structure of Online Activism". *Sociological Science* Vol.1 (February 2014): 1–9. Accessed March 1, 2014. DOI 10.15195/v1.a1.

Liebes, Tamar, and James Curran. *Media, Ritual and Identity.* London: Routledge, 2002.

Lim, Merlyna. "The Internet, Social Networks, and Reform in Indonesia." In *Contesting Media Power: Alternative Media in a Networked World*, edited by Nick Couldry and James Curran, 273–88. Maryland: Rowman & Littlefield, 2003a.

Lim, Merlyna. "From Real to Virtual (and Back again): Civil Society, Public Sphere, and Internet in Indonesia." In *Asia.com: Asia encounters the Internet*, edited by Kong-Chong Ho, Randy Kluver and Kenneth C. C. Yang, 113–128. London: Routledge, 2003b.

Lim, Merlyna. *Archipelago Online: The Internet and Political Activism in Indonesia.* Dissertation. Twente: Universiteit Twente, 2005.

Lim, Merlyna. "Clicks, Cabs, and Coffee Houses: Social Media and Oppositional Movements in Egypt, 2004–2011". *Journal of Communication* 62 (2012): 231–248.

Lim, Merlyna. "Many Clicks but Little Sticks: Social Media Activism in Indonesia." *Journal of Contemporary Asia* Volume 43 Issue 4 (2013): 636–657.

Magnis-Suseno, Franz. *Etika Jawa: Sebuah Analisa Falsafi Tentang Kebijaksanaan Hidup Jawa.* Jakarta: Gramedia, 1988.

Magnis-Suseno, Franz. *Pijar-pijar filsafat: dari Gatholoco ke filsafat perempuan, dari Adam Müller ke Postmodernisme.* Yogyakarta: Penerbit Kanisius, 2005.

Mead, Herbert. *Mind, Self, and Society.* Chicago: University of Chicago Press, 1934.

Mead, Herbert. *The Philosophy of the Act*. Chicago: University of Chicago Press, 1938.

Merleau-Ponty, Maurice. *Phenomenology of Perception*. London: Routledge, 2002.

Merleau-Ponty, Maurice. *The Primacy of Perception: And Other Essays on Phenomenological Psychology, the Philosophy of Art, History, and Politics*. Evanston: Northwestern University Press, 1964.

Miller, Daniel, and Don Slater. *The Internet: An Ethnographic Approach*. Reprinted edition. Oxford: Berg, 2001.

Moertono, Soemarsaid. *State and Statecraft in Old Java: A Study of the Later Mataram Period, 16th and 19th Century*. Singapore: Equinox Publishing, 2009.

Mrázek, Jan. *Puppet Theater in Contemporary Indonesia: New Approaches to Performance Events*. Michigan: University of Michigan, Centers for South and Southeast Asian Studies, 2002a.

Mrázek, Rudolf. *Engineers of Happy Land: Technology and Nationalism in a Colony*. Princeton: Princeton University Press, 2002b.

Mulder, Niels. *Inside Indonesian Society: Cultural Change in Java*. Third edition. Yogyakarta: Penerbit Kanisius, 2005.

Newberry, Janice C. *Back Door Java: State Formation and the Domestic in Working Class Java*. Toronto: University of Toronto Press, 2006.

Nilan, Pam. "Mediating the Entrepreneurial Self: Romance Texts and Young Indonesian Women." In *Medi@sia: Global media/tion In and Out of Context*, edited by Todd Joseph Miles Holden and Timothy J. Scrase, 62–81. Oxon: Routledge, 2006.

Nordhausen, Frank, und Thomas Schmid. *Die Arabische Revolution: Demokratischer Aufbruch von Tunesien bis zum Golf*. Berlin: Ch. Links Verlag, 2012.

Nugroho, Yanuar, and Sofie Shinta Syarief. *Beyond Click-Activism? New Media and Political Processes in Contemporary Indonesia*. Berlin: FES-MediaAsia, 2012.

Nugroho, Yanuar. *Citizens in @ction*. Manchester: Manchester Institute of Innovation Research, 2011.

Nugroho, Yanuar. *Does the Internet Transform Civil Society? The Case pf Civil Society Organizations in Indonesia*. Dissertation. Manchester: The University of Manchester, 2007.

Nurshodiq, Nurshodiq. "Tradisi Suran Dalam Masyarakat Jawa: Studi Perbandingan Antara Wilayah Surakarta dengan Wonosobo". In *Journal Of Educational Social Studies*, Vol. 1, No. 1, June 2012: 55–59.

O'Rourke, Kevin. *Reformasi: The Struggle for Power in Post-Soeharto Indonesia*. New South Wales: Allen & Unwin, 2002.

Olson, David R. *The World on Paper: The Conceptual and Cognitive Implications of Writing and Reading*. Cambridge: Cambridge University Press, 1994.

Pariser, Eli. *The Filter Bubble: What the Internet Is Hiding From You*. London: Penguin UK, 2011

Pearce, Celia, and Artemesia. *Communities of Play. Emergent Cultures in Multiplayer Games and Virtual Worlds*. Massachusetts: MIT Press, 2009.

Pemberton, John. *On the Subject Of "Java"*. Ithaca: Cornell University Press, 1994.

Perlman, Marc. *Unplayed Melodies: Javanese Gamelan and the Genesis of Music Theory*. Berkley: University of California Press, 2004.

Pickard, Victor. "Media Failures in the Age of Trump" *The Political Economy of Communication* 4(2) 2016: 118–122.

Preece, Jennifer J. and Ghozati, K. "Experiencing Empathy Online". In *The Internet and Health Communication: Experience and Expectations*, edited by R. R. Rice and J. E. Katz, 237–260. Thousand Oaks: Sage Publications, 2001.

Putnam, Robert D. *Bowling alone: The Collapse and Revival of American Community*. New York: Simon and Schuster, 2000.

Quan-Haase, Anabel, Barry Wellman, James C. Witte, and Keith Hampton. "Capitalizing on the Net: Social Contact, Civic Engagement and Sense of Community." In *The Internet in Everyday Life*, edited by Barry Wellman and Caroline Haythornthwaite, 291–324. Malden: Blackwell Publishers, 2002.

Ramshaw, Gregory. "Food, Heritage and Nationalism." In *Heritage Cuisines: Traditions, Identities and Tourism*, edited by Dallen J. Timothy, 53–64. Oxon: Routledge, 2016.

Ras, J. J., and S. Stuart O. Robson. *Variation, Transformation and Meaning: Studies on Indonesian Literatures in Honour of A. Teeuw. Working Papers/ Koninklijk Instituut voor Taal-, Land- en Volkenkunde Leiden Volume 144*. Leiden: KITLV Press, 1991.

Rheingold, Howard. *Virtual Community*. Originally published by Addison Wesley, 1993. Massachusetts: MIT Press, 2000.

Richter, Max M. "Other Worlds in Yogyakarta: From Jatilan to Electronic Music". In *Popular Culture in Indonesia: Fluid Identities in Post-Authoritarian Politics*, edited by Ariel Heryanto, 164–181. Oxon: Routledge, 2008.

Ricklefs, Merle Calvin. *A History of Modern Indonesia Since C. 1200*. Stanford: Stanford University Press, 2001.

Ricklefs, Merle Calvin. *Jogjakarta Under Sultan Mangkubumi, 1749–1792: a History of the Division of Java*. London: Oxford University Press, 1974.

Rogers, Everett M. *Diffusion of innovations* (1st ed.). New York: Free Press of Glencoe, 1962.

Rosenthal, Sandra B. and Patrick L. Bourgeois. *Mead and Merleau-Ponty: Toward a Common Vision*. New York: SUNY Press, 1991.

Rukmana, Deden, and Djarot Purbadi. "Street Vending in Indonesian Cities: Their Characteristics and Activities in Yogyakarta". In *Transforming Asian Cities: Intellectual Impasse, Asianizing Space, and Emerging Translocalities*, edited by Nihal Perera and Wing-shing Tang, 123–136. London: Routledge, 2013.

Sagar, Krishna Chandra. *Foreign Influence on Ancient India*. New Delhi: Northern Book Centre, 1992.

Santoso, Priyo Budi. *Birokrasi Pemerintah Orde Baru: Perspektif Kultural Dan Struktural*. Jakarta: Raja Grafindo Persada, 1993.

Santoso, Soewito, and Kestity Pringgoharjono. *The Centhini Story: The Javanese Journey of Life: Based on the Original Serat Centhini*. Singapore: Marshall Cavendish, 2006.

Sears, Laurie J. "Intellectuals, Theosophy, and Failed Narratives of the Nation in Late Colonial Java". In *A Companion to Postcolonial Studies*, edited by Henry Schwarz and Sangeeta Ray, 333–359. Malden: Blackwell Publishing, 2005.

Sears, Laurie Jo. *Shadows of Empire: Colonial Discourse and Javanese Tales*. Durham: Duke University Press, 1996.

Seaton, Jean. "Brexit and the Media" *The Political Quarterly* Volume 87, Issue 3, 2016: 333–33. DOI: 10.1111/1467-923X.12296.

Seligson, Mitchell. "The Rise of Populism and the Left in Latin America." *Journal of Democracy* Volume 18 Number 3 (July 2007): 81–95.

Sen, Krishna. "Radio Days: Media-Politics in Indonesia." *The Pacific Review* Vol. 16 No.4 (2003): 573–589.

Sen, Krishna, "Introduction: Re-forming media in Indonesia's transition to democracy." In *Politics and the Media in Twenty-First Century Indonesia: Decade of Democracy*, edited by Krishna Sen and David Hill, 1–12. Oxon: Routledge, 2011.

Siegel, James T. *Solo in the New Order: Language and Hierarchy in an Indonesian City*. New Jersey: Princeton University Press, 1993.

Sindhunata. *Putri Cina*. Jakarta: Gramedia Pustaka Utama, 2007.

Siswoyo, Bambang. *Huru Hara Solo Semarang: Suatu Reportase*. Jakarta: Bhakti Pertiwi, 1981.

Slama, Martin. "The Agency of the Heart: Internet Chatting as Youth Culture in Indonesia." *Social Anthropology/Anthropologie Sociale* European Association of Social Anthropologists. Vol.18/3(2010): 316–330. Accessed February 15, 2012. doi: 10.1111/j.1469-8676.2010.00110.x.

Stange, Paul. "The Logic of Rasa in Java". *Indonesia* No. 38 (Oct., 1984): 113–134. DOI: 10.2307/3350848.

Steinbock, Dan. *The Mobile Revolution: The Making of Mobile Services Worldwide*. London: Kogan Page, 2005.

Sumarno. "Upacara Tradisi Wilujengan Negari Mahesa Lawung Kraton Surakarta Di Krendhawahana". In *Jantra* Vol. 8 No. 2 (Desember 2013): 189–200.

Sumarsam. *Javanese Gamelan and the West*. Rochester: University Rochester Press, 2013.

Supanggah, Rahayu. "Campur Sari: A Reflection" *Asian Music* Vol. 34, No. 2, Spring – Summer (2003): 1–20.

Suprapto, Hadi and Fajar Sodiq. "Kisruh Panjang Keraton Solo, Apa Sebabnya?" *VivaNews*, August 27, 2013. Accessed August 27, 2013. http://fokus.news.viva.co.id/news/read/439386-kisruh-panjang-keraton-solo-apa-sebabnya

Suryanis, Afrilia. "Bisnis Internet Mobile Makin Cerah." *Tempo*, March 18, 2012. Accessed November 15, 2012. http://www.tempo.co/read/news/2012/03/19/090391182/Bisnis-Internet-Mobile-Makin-Cerah

Sutardja, M. *Dora-Sembada. Dutch East Indies. Commissie voor de Volkslectuur Serie no. 234.* Amsterdam: Indonesische Drukkerij, 1917.

Sutton, Anderson. *Traditions of Gamelan Music in Java: Musical Pluralism and Regional Identity.* Cambridge: Cambridge University Press, 1991.

Taufiqurrohman. *64 Ritual Syirik Nusantara.* Yogyakarta: Pusat Ilmu, 2015.

Tjakraatmadja, Jann H., A. Wicaksono and L. Martini. "Knowledge Sharing in the Indonesian Context: Institut Teknologi Bandung (ITB) as Potential Knowledge Hub to Create Value from Academia, Business and Government Linkages." In *Beyond the Knowledge Trap: Developing Asia's Knowledge-Based Economies,* edited by Thomas Menkhoff, Hans-Dieter Evers, Yue Wah Chay, Eng Fong Pang, 269–298. Singapore: World Scientific, 2011.

Tomsa Dirk. *Party Politics and Democratization in Indonesia: Golkar in the Post-Suharto* Era. New York: Routledge, 2008.

Tönnies, Ferdinand. *Gemeinschaft und Gesellschaft.* Leipzig: Fues's Verlag, 1887.

Triastuti, Endah and Inaya Rakhmani. "Cyber Taman Mini Indonesia Indah: Ethnicity and Imagi-Nation in Blogging Culture". *Internetworking Indonesia Journal* Vol. 3/No. 2 (2011): 5–11. Jakarta, 2011.

Turkle, Sherry. *Alone Together: Why We Expect More from Technology and Less from Each Other.* Reprinted edition. New York: Basic Books, 2012.

Turkle, Sherry. *The Second Self: Computers and the Human Spirit.* Massachusetts: MIT Press, 2005.

Van Dijk, Jan A.G.M. *The Network Society: Social Aspects of New Media.* First publication in English in 1999. Second edition. London: SAGE Publications, 2006.

Van Klinken, Gerry. *Communal Violence and Democratization in Indonesia.* Oxon: Routledge, 2007.

Van Loon, Joost. *Media Technology Critical Perspective.* Berkshire: Open University Press McGraw-Hill Education, 2008.

Veblen, Thorstein. *The Theory of Leisure Class.* New York: Dover, 1994.

Wallach, Jeremy. *Modern Noise, Fluid Genres: Popular Music in Indonesia, 1997–2001.* Madison: University of Wisconsin Press, 2008.

Wayansari, Agustina. "The Internet and the Public Sphere in Indonesia's New Democracy: a Study of Politikana.com." In *Internetworking Indonesia Journal* Vol. 3/No. 2 (2011): 23–33. Jakarta, 2011.

Webster, Frank. *Theories of the Information Society.* Third Edition. Oxon: Routledge, 2006.

Wellman, Barry and Milena Gulia. "Virtual Communities as Communities: Net Surfers Don't Ride Alone". In *Communities in Cyberspace,* edited by Marc A. Smith and Peter Kollock, 167–194. London: Routledge, 1999.

Wellman, Barry, and Caroline Haythornthwaite. *The Internet in Everyday Life.* Malden: Blackwell Publishers, 2002.

Wellman, Barry. *Networks in the Global Village: Life in Contemporary Communities.* New York: Westview Press, 1999.

Yumarma, Andreas. *Unity in Diversity: A Philosophical and Ethical Study of the Javanese Concept of 'Keselarasan'*. Roma: Editrice Pontificia Universita Gregoriana, 1996.

## Reports

"Ericsson Mobility Report: South East Asia And Oceania". *Ericsson Mobility Report*, November 2014. Accessed December 15, 2014. https://www.ericsson.com/res/docs/2014/emr-november2014-regional-appendices-raso.pdf

Asosiasi Jasa Penyelenggara Internet Indonesia. *Penetrasi dan Perilaku Pengguna Jasa Internet Indonesia 2016*. Jakarta: Asosiasi Jasa Penyelenggara Internet Indonesia, 2016.

Badan Pusat Statistika. *Surakarta dalam Angka 2011*. Surakarta: Badan Pusat Statistika, 2011.

Badan Pusat Statistika. *Ekonomi Kota Surakarta 2014*. Surakarta: Badan Pusat Statistika, 2015a.

Badan Pusat Statistika. *Surakarta Dalam Angka 2014*. Surakarta: Badan Pusat Statistika, 2014.

Badan Pusat Statistika. *Surakarta dalam Angka 2015*. Surakarta: Badan Pusat Statistika, 2015b.

Tim Gabungan Pencari Fakta. *Fact Finder Join Team Report*. Accessed November 1, 2013. http://semanggipeduli.com/tgpf/laporan.html on June 2011.

## Internet Sources

"Digital Literacy and Citizenship Curriculum proposes eleven basic questions to identify quality information." Accessed January 29, 2017. http://archive.ikeepsafe.org/educators_old/more/google/

"Editorial: Goodbye, People Power." *The Jakarta Post*, January 29, 2010. Accessed January 29, 2010. http://www.thejakartapost.com/news/2010/01/29/editorial-goodbye-people-power.html.on

"In Indonesia, a New Digital Class Emerges." In *Emarketer Report*. Accessed March 12, 2013. http://www.emarketer.com/Article/Indonesia-New-Digital-Class-Emerges/1009723#bqTGyZxJGZ8MDkOV.99

Balea, Judith. "The Latest Stats in Web and Mobile in Indonesia". *TechninAsia*, January 28, 2016. Accessed January 28$^{th}$, 2016. https://www.techinasia.com/indonesia-web-mobile-statistics-we-are-social, on January 28$^{th}$, 2016.

Beaumont, Peter. "The Truth About Twitter, Facebook and The Uprisings in the Arab World." *The Guardian*, February 25, 2011. Accessed on February 25, 2011. http://www.theguardian.com/world/2011/feb/25/twitter-facebook-uprisings-arab-libya

Goldman, Lisa. "Social Media Has Been a Mixed Blessing for the Arab Spring." *Techpresident*, February 15, 2013. Accessed February 15, 2013.http://techpresident.com/news/wegov/23510/social-media-harming-arab-uprising

Miller, Daniel. "Facebook's So Uncool, but It's Morphing into a Different Beast." *The Conversation* December 20, 2013. Accessed on December 20, 2013. http://theconversation.com/facebooks-so-uncool-but-its-morphing-into-a-different-beast-21548

Moore, Michael. "5 Things You Can Do Right Now About Donald J. Trump – from Michael Moore." Accessed January 29th, 2016. https://www.facebook.com/mmflint/posts/10154046637756857

# News

"Alasan.Jokowi.Gunakan.Istilah.Aku.Rapopo," *Kompas*, March 25, 2014. Accessed March 25, 2014. http://megapolitan.kompas.com/read/2014/03/25/1704217/Alasan.Jokowi.Gunakan.Istilah.Aku.Rapopo

"Konflik di Solo Bernuansa SARA." *Berita Satu*, May 20, 2012. Accessed May 20, 2012. http://www.beritasatu.com/nasional/46268-konflik-di-solo-bernuansa-sara.html

"Why Do Children in Developing Nations Need Laptops?" In *Frequently Asked Questions Page of Onelaptop.org*, Accessed October 10, 2013. http://one.laptop.org/about/faq

Asril, Sabrina. "Provokasi di Facebook, Perusuh di GBK Diamankan." Kompas, June 1, 2012. Accessed June 6, 2012. http://megapolitan.kompas.com/read/2012/06/01/14523461/Provokasi.di.Facebook..Perusuh.di.GBK.Diamankon June 1st, 2012.

Dyah, Indira Prana Ning, and Naomi Theresa. "Warnet Kian Tergerus Internet Ponsel." *Kompas.com*. Accessed on Friday, August 13, 2010. http://tekno.kompas.com/read/2010/08/13/12342240/Warnet.Kian.Tergerus.Internet.Ponsel

HAW. "Solo Bakal Miliki Jalur Akses Internet Terpanjang di Indonesia." *Solopos*, October 11, 2011. Accessed October 11, 2011. http://www.solopos.com/2011/10/11/solo-bakal-miliki-jalur-akses-internet-terpanjang-di-indonesia-119241

MSH. "Koin Untuk Prita Bisa Diangkut 5 Truk." *Kompas*, December 19, 2009. Accessed March 1, 2012. http://nasional.kompas.com/read/2009/12/19/10215466/koin.untuk.prita.bisa.diangkut.5.truk

Purwanto, Didik. "Ponsel Pintar di Indonesia Cuma untuk SMS dan Media Sosial." *Kompas*, June 6, 2012. Accessed June 6, 2012. http://tekno.kompas.com/read/2012/06/06/18403922/ponsel.pintar.di.indonesia.cuma.untuk.sms.dan.media.sosial

Russell, Jon. "Jakarta Named World's Facebook Capital." *Asian Correspondent*, March 18, 2011. Accessed Nov. 15, 2012. http://asiancorrespondent.com/50592/jakarta-recognised-as-the-worlds-facebook-capital/

Sarifah, Siti Alia and Mitra Angelia. "Kaskus Klaim Punya 8,6 Juta Pengunjung Aktif, Siap meramaikan ulang tahun melalui gerakan sosial." *VivaNews*, November 6, 2015. Accessed November 6, 2015. http://teknologi.news.viva.co.id/news/read/696512-kaskus-klaim-punya-8-6-juta-pengunjung-aktif

Sidner, Sara. "Indonesia: Twitter Nation." *CNN*, November 23, 2010. Accessed November 15, 2012. http://articles.cnn.com/2010-11-23/tech/indonesia.twitter_1_twitter-nation-social-media-social-networking?_s=PM:TECH

Tait, Robert. "Censorship Fears Rise as Iran Blocks Access to Top Websites." *The Guardian*, December 4, 2006. Accessed December 9, 2006. http://www.theguardian.com/technology/2006/dec/04/news.iran

Wahyudi, Reza. "Naik 13 Juta, Pengguna Internet Indonesia 55 Juta Orang." *Kompas*, October 28, 2011. Accessed October 30, 2011. http://tekno.kompas.com/read/2011/10/28/16534635/Naik.13.Juta..Pengguna.Internet.Indonesia.55.Juta.Orang

Yusuf, Oik. "Transaksi FJB Kaskus Rp 575 Miliar Per Bulan." *Kompas*, November 25, 2012. Accessed December 3, 2012. http://tekno.kompas.com/read/2012/11/25/13233388/Transaksi.FJB.Kaskus.Rp.575.Miliar.Per.Bulan

## Links and Online Forums

http://kaskus.co.id

http://archive.ikeepsafe.org/educators_old/more/google/

http://one.laptop.org/about/mission

http://opensource.telkomspeedy.com/wiki/index.php/WARNET

http://www.worthofweb.com/website-value/kaskus.co.id on February 14, 2017.

https://books.google.com/ngrams

https://trends.google.com/trends/

https://www.facebook.com/mmflint/posts/10154046637756857

https://www.socialbakers.com/

https://www.statista.com/statistics/242606/number-of-active-twitter-users-in-selected-countries/

https://www.statista.com/statistics/268136/top-15-countries-based-on-number-of-facebook-users/

# Index[1]


**A**

Arab Spring, 2, 3, 5, 6, 8–10
association, 10, 42, 43, 69, 107, 154, 224, 230, 235

**B**

blogging, 25

**C**

coming of age, 102, 124, 125, 135, 148, 149, 195, 234

**D**

digital citizenship, 2, 171

**E**

elitism, 9, 202, 206
emoticon, 45–7, 59, 61, 62, 72, 74, 105, 166, 169, 213
emotion, 46, 47, 54, 62, 64, 190, 196, 205, 206

**F**

Facebook, vi, vii, 5–10, 16, 17, 21, 27n15, 51, 52, 66, 73, 105, 106, 132, 168, 173, 179, 182n6, 205, 214, 229
freedom, online, 43, 84, 86, 92, 93, 95, 125, 150, 192, 194, 198, 221–3, 233
future, subject of, 17, 60, 67, 121, 124, 134, 143, 148, 152, 187, 188, 192, 193, 195, 214, 220, 221, 223, 224, 235


[1] Note: Page numbers followed by "n" refer to notes.





A. Seto, *Netizenship, Activism and Online Community Transformation in Indonesia*, DOI 10.1007/978-981-10-5397-9

**G**
gathering, annual, 63, 105, 106, 110, 111, 121, 122, 134, 143, 145, 146, 151, 180, 189, 191, 200, 207, 230
gender and media, 21, 24, 80, 92, 93, 95, 101, 205, 223
Google Trends, vi
guilt, 138, 140–2, 145–7, 155, 229, 231, 234

**H**
hoax, viii, 57, 161, 168, 172, 231
Hoax, 56–60
home, subject of, v, 15, 17, 19, 20, 23, 25, 41, 42, 49–51, 68, 72, 74, 80, 88, 92–6, 98, 104, 109, 120, 128n26, 133, 139, 140, 149, 151, 168, 172, 175, 181, 195, 202, 210, 222, 223, 225n8, 232
Hot Thread, 39, 106, 109, 132

**I**
intersubjectivity, 4, 26n6, 26n7, 59, 60, 74, 96, 97, 137
Islam and media, 7, 23, 24, 169, 176

**J**
junker, 56, 58, 76n3, 87, 89, 98, 192

**K**
Kaskus, history of, 11, 12, 85, 87

**M**
militancy
  discipline, viii, ix, 5, 10, 38, 50, 66, 68, 70, 71, 75, 89, 101, 102, 142, 161, 167, 175, 182, 212, 215, 229, 231
  outcasting, 97
  reflexivity, 2, 118, 140, 147, 153–5, 161
  submission, 95, 96, 148, 154, 195
militancy, digital, 56
monitoring
  bully, online, 92, 198, 225n1
  green-badge, 53–6, 217, 233
  red-brick, 53–5

**N**
netizenship, ix, 131, 138, 142, 151, 162, 182, 234

**O**
Occupy Movement, 2
off-screen, xiii, 16, 135, 153, 201, 202
online-offline transformation, vii, 10, 115, 120, 121, 124, 141, 154, 203, 208, 210, 217, 230
organic, community, ix, 1, 188–96, 198, 201, 220, 223, 224, 229, 231, 233–5

**P**
particularity-universality, vii
perception, viii, 14, 59, 64, 71, 72, 74, 118, 121, 140, 149, 169, 177, 188, 189, 197, 198, 206, 209–13, 216–18, 230, 232, 233
  perceptual experience, 15, 140
power, digital, 138–41
Prita Campaign, 3
protest, mediated, 2, 3, 20, 22, 24, 91, 95, 117, 135, 167, 223
prudence, ix, 131–56, 189, 191, 200, 203, 210, 216, 219, 229, 231, 233, 234
  fairness, 136–8, 140, 141, 231

public sphere, 3–7, 20, 23, 28n27, 125, 145, 162, 167, 168, 172

R

radio, 17–19, 22, 23, 81, 110, 196
rasa, 25, 26, 58, 74, 97, 146, 147
reconnection, 2, 109, 131, 132, 140, 149, 151, 230, 231
resource, 5, 7, 12, 18, 60, 70, 102, 149, 155, 191, 195, 220, 221

S

social media, vi, viii, 0–4, 7, 8, 10, 11, 51, 57, 71, 73, 105, 115, 132, 147, 167, 171, 174, 177, 179, 204, 206, 224, 230, 231, 233
Solonese, being, vii, 15, 23–6, 41, 108, 117, 122–4, 127n21, 128n25, 151, 169, 170, 175, 181, 192, 195, 207, 221, 222, 224, 230
speedy response, 45, 46, 138, 145, 176, 180, 197, 215, 217, 233
Suharto, vii, 7, 11, 18–20, 22, 26, 124, 126n8, 155, 156n7, 164, 176, 232

T

texting, 21
touch, cybersense and, 69, 71–5, 197
Twitter, vi, 5–7, 9, 16, 17, 24, 27n14, 51, 52, 66, 73, 99, 105, 106, 171, 205, 214, 235

U

Umbrella Movement, 2, 3

V

visuality, viii, 10, 17, 38, 40, 49, 60, 66, 71, 84, 95, 105, 118, 133, 145–7, 165, 206, 224, 233
vocabulary, normative, 25, 96, 178, 194, 220, 221

W

Warnet, 19–22
wayang, 25, 124, 223
wayfaring, viii, 2, 13, 14, 22, 26, 75, 124, 126, 131, 149, 150, 154, 188, 191–4, 197–200, 217, 221, 222, 230, 233–6
Widodo, Joko, 24, 25, 29n33, 173, 174, 176, 177, 179–82, 222, 233

FSC
www.fsc.org
MIX
Papier | Fördert
gute Waldnutzung
FSC® C083411

Kolibri 360 GmbH
Ferdinand-Jühlke-Straße 7
99095 Erfurt, Deutschland
produktsicherheit@kolibri360.de